Ellen A. Brantlinger

Studies in Inclusive Education

Series Editor

Roger Slee (*University of South Australia, Australia*)

Editorial Board

Mel Ainscow (*University of Manchester, UK*)
Felicity Armstrong (*Institute of Education, University of London, UK*)
Len Barton (*Institute of Education, University of London, UK*)
Suzanne Carrington (*Queensland University of Technology, Australia*)
Joanne Deppeler (*Monash University, Australia*)
Linda Graham (*Queensland University of Technology, Australia*)
Levan Lim (*National Institute of Education, Singapore*)
Missy Morton (*University of Canterbury, New Zealand*)

VOLUME 43

Critical Leaders and the Foundation of Disability Studies in Education

Series Editor

Linda Ware (*Independent Scholar*)

VOLUME 1

The titles published in this series are listed at *brill.com/clfd*

Ellen A. Brantlinger

*When Meaning Falters and Words Fail,
Ideology Matters*

Edited by

Linda Ware and Roger Slee

BRILL
SENSE

LEIDEN | BOSTON

Cover illustration: *Ellen*, drawing by Elizabeth Edinger

The Library of Congress Cataloging-in-Publication Data is available online at http://catalog.loc.gov

Typeface for the Latin, Greek, and Cyrillic scripts: "Brill". See and download: brill.com/brill-typeface.

ISSN 2666-1772
ISBN 978-90-04-40268-3 (paperback)
ISBN 978-90-04-40260-7 (hardback)
ISBN 978-90-04-40269-0 (e-book)

Copyright 2020 by Koninklijke Brill NV, Leiden, The Netherlands, except where stated otherwise.
Koninklijke Brill NV incorporates the imprints Brill, Brill Hes & De Graaf, Brill Nijhoff, Brill Rodopi, Brill Sense, Hotei Publishing, mentis Verlag, Verlag Ferdinand Schöningh and Wilhelm Fink Verlag.
All rights reserved. No part of this publication may be reproduced, translated, stored in a retrieval system, or transmitted in any form or by any means, electronic, mechanical, photocopying, recording or otherwise, without prior written permission from the publisher.
Authorization to photocopy items for internal or personal use is granted by Koninklijke Brill NV provided that the appropriate fees are paid directly to The Copyright Clearance Center, 222 Rosewood Drive, Suite 910, Danvers, MA 01923, USA. Fees are subject to change.

This book is printed on acid-free paper and produced in a sustainable manner.

Contents

Series Introduction   VII
   Linda Ware
Notes on Contributors   XI

Introduction: Honoring of the Research, Scholarship, and Activism of
Ellen A. Brantlinger   1
   Linda Ware and Roger Slee

1   Risk Taker, Role Model, Muse, and "Charlatan": Stories of Ellen, an
    Atypical Giant   11
       David J. Connor

2   Including Ideology   28
       Julie Allan

3   Research, Relationships and Making Understanding: A Look at
    Brantlinger's Darla and the Value of Case Study Research   46
       Janet Story Sauer

4   When the Light Turns Blue: Journeying into Disability Studies Guided by
    the Work of Ellen Brantlinger   62
       Kathleen M. Collins and Alicia A. Broderick

5   Challenging the Ideology of Normal in Schools   80
       Subini A. Annamma, Amy L. Ferrel, Brooke A. Moore and Janette Klingner

6   Vulnerable to Exclusion: The Place for Segregated Education within
    Conceptions of Inclusion   102
       Emily A. Nusbaum

7   The Impact of Standards-Based Reform: Applying Brantlinger's Critique of
    "Hierarchical Ideologies"   125
       Jessica Bacon and Beth Ferri

8   Family Portraits: Past and Present Representations of Parents in Special
    Education Text Books   144
       Dianne L. Ferguson, Philip M. Ferguson, Joanne Kim and Corrine Li

Index   167

Series Introduction

> Change is often unpredictable and indirect. We don't know the future. We've changed the world many times, and remembering that, *that history*, is really a source of power to continue and it doesn't get talked about nearly enough.
>
> REBECCA SOLNIT (2017, emphasis added)

∵

Critical Leaders and the Foundation of Disability Studies in Education aims to formalize the significance of early histories of understanding disability drawn from the scholarship of those who turned away from conventional status quo and pathologized constructs commonly accepted worldwide to explain disability in schools and society. The series begins with recognition of North American scholars including: Ellen Brantlinger, Lous Heshusius, Steve Taylor, Doug Biklen, and Thomas M. Skrtic. We will expand the series to include scholars from several international countries who likewise formed analyses that shaped the terrain for the emergence of critical perspectives that have endured and slowly given rise to the interdisciplinary field of Disability Studies in Education.

Critical Leaders and the Foundation of Disability Studies in Education singles out individuals who began their professional careers in the shadow of traditional special education research and practice. However at an important juncture, each forged a critical turn from status quo beliefs and practices about disability in schools and society. They dared to challenge the inherited orthodoxy of special education and through their individual and collective efforts professional criticism of special education grew in increasing larger circles among like minds. Their scholarship represents a persistent commitment to reconstruct the narrative in schools and society that marginalized children and minimized life opportunities for disabled people. Mapping their efforts over time, these individuals were subsequently distinguished as among the earliest voices of critical special education (Gallagher et al., 2004; Ware, 2001, 2004, 2017).

Each book began as an invited symposia presented at the annual meeting of the American Educational Research Association—beginning in 2012 and continuing to the present. The symposia panelists were invited to consider the influence made by each scholar featured in *Critical Leaders and the Foundation of Disability Studies in Education*.

The series unpacks the insights of these individuals—who initially worked in isolation—unaware of their common interests that would ultimately lead to this collective. Their thinking served as the initial grounding for disability studies in education despite the fact that none such community actually existed until late in the 1990s. Steven J. Taylor offered that many in this circle of critical special educators advanced disability studies in education "before it had a name" (Taylor, 2006, *Vital Questions Facing Disability Studies in Education*). He explained:

> [T]he key themes underlying Disability Studies in Education can be traced back many years before it was identified as an area of inquiry or associated with professional groups, conferences, and scholarly publications. Of course, in earlier times, some of these themes were not fully developed, and their implications not completely explored. Yet, an understanding of the intellectual forbearers of Disability Studies in Education can help us understand more clearly the foundational ideas underlying this area of scholarship. (p. xiii)

Critical Leaders and the Foundation of Disability Studies in Education articulates this history through the remembering, as Solnit suggested, of our history and to intentionally proclaim this history as a "source of power [that] doesn't get talked about nearly enough" (2017). The series weaves across decades to plot the arc of scholarly accomplishment, inviting readers to look back, while also looking forward in an attempt to build a more capacious and generative DSE community marked by its clear divergence from special education. The claim that "DSE is not SPED!" is a familiar rallying cry among our contemporaries, however, few are aware that Thomas M. Skrtic, writing in 1988, suggested that the "alternative paradigm" he outlined would give way to a discernable reorientation that would "produce a community of special education professionals who would think and act in ways substantially different from their contemporary counterparts" (p. 444).

Today, through professional affiliations and publications, Disability Studies in Education authorizes Skrtic's imagined future—a space for professionals who think and act in ways that differ substantially from those who align with special education. We articulate our commitment to:

> [U]nderstand disability from a social model perspective drawing on social, cultural, historical, discursive, philosophical, literary, aesthetic, artistic, and other traditions to challenge medical, scientific, and psychological models of disability as they relate to education. (Disability

Studies in Education Special Interest Group, American Educational Research Association)

Disability Studies in Education makes specific the authority of an agenda to support the development of research, policy, and activism that:
- Contextualises disability within political and social spheres
- Privileges the interest, agendas, and voices of people labeled with disability/disabled people
- Promotes social justice, equitable and inclusive educational opportunities, and full and meaningful access to all aspects of society for people labeled with disability/disabled people
- Assumes competence and reject deficit models of disability.

Informed in a myriad of ways meticulously braided back to those who early on voiced dissent, discontent, and disavowal, Disability Studies in Education scholars have authored a resounding critique of education that pushes our thinking beyond the binary of the social/medical model debate located within the contexts of schooling—and special education in particular. Over two decades following on the "official" launch of the Disability Studies in Education Special Interest Group (SIG) in affiliation with the American Education Research Association, and the subsequent convening of the annual/bi-annual Disability Studies in Education conference co-hosted in partnership with various universities nationally and internationally, we advance a persistent critique of: classification schemes; categorization rituals; hostile behavior/reductionist practice; isolated/segregated/separate placements, and the unreflective and pervasive stigmatization of disabled children and youth embedded in the special education knowledge base. Each volume in this series reminds readers of the enduring influence and leadership of these critical special education scholars. Disability Studies in Education scholars whose work is cast within the shadows of this scholarly legacy are indebted to the bold and unrestrained thinking that remains provocative to this day.

Finally, the series aims to encourage future generations of scholars and educators to find their way "back" to Disability Studies in Education foundational knowledge sooner, rather than later in their careers. We recognize that the most courageous work remains ahead for budding scholars as they declare an explicit "anti-special education" focus in their research, scholarship and teaching. Understanding that individuals considered in this series made a critical turn away from the ideology that shaped special education orthodoxy (Gallagher et al., 2004), and as a consequence many mid-career and senior disability studies in education scholars forged a professional identity challenging status quo thinking about disability common in higher education and teacher preparation programs. Readers will find, we hope, power in knowing that perhaps we need not rage against the machine, yet, roar we must.

Critical Leaders and the Foundation of Disability Studies in Education provides purposeful connections to the wisdom and enduring ideas of these critical thinkers to reveal the depth of their imprint on current research in the field of disability studies in education. However, we caution that this series is not to be read as a compendium of their contributions. What we hope to encourage is that future generations of scholars will mine the original works of these scholars and excavate primary source materials in an effort to reinforce and renew the foundation of disability studies in education. It is a movement that will prosper when informed of its complex and confounding roots.

Linda Ware
Editor of *Critical Leaders and the Foundation of Disability Studies in Education*

Notes on Contributors

Julie Allan

is Professor of Equity and Inclusion and Head of the School of Education at the University of Birmingham, UK. Her research focuses on inclusive education, disability studies and children's rights and she been advisor to the Scottish Parliament, the Welsh Assembly and the Dutch and Queensland Governments and Council of Europe. Her recent books include *Psychopathology at School: Theorising Mental Disorder in Education* (with Valerie Harwood) and the 2017 *Routledge World Yearbook in Education – Assessment Inequalities* (with Alfredo Artiles).

Subini A. Annamma

(Ph.D.) is Associate Professor at the Graduate School of Education, Stanford University. Her research and pedagogy focus on increasing access to equitable education for historically marginalized students and communities, particularly students of color with disabilities. Specifically, she critically examines the social construction of race and ability; how the two are interdependent, how they intersect with other identity markers, and how their mutually constitutive nature impacts education experiences. She centers this research in urban education and juvenile incarceration settings and focuses on how student voice can contribute to dismantling systemic inequities and identifying exemplary educational practices.

Jessica Bacon

is an Assistant Professor at Montclair State University in the Department of Early Childhood, Elementary and Literacy Education. Jessica is the program coordinator for the five-year Bachelor's to Masters program in Early Childhood and Elementary Inclusive Education. With Dr. Susan Baglieri, Jessica is a co-founder of the Increasing Access to College project, which provides opportunities for college-aged students with intellectual and developmental disabilities to partake in academic, social and recreational aspects of college life. Jessica's research draws upon the traditions of disability studies in education, while examining educational policy, inclusion in K-12 and higher education, and disability identity in schooling contexts. Jessica has recently published in journals such as *Disability & Society, Young Exceptional Children,* The *International Journal of Inclusive Education* and *Teachers College Record.*

Alicia A. Broderick

is a Professor of Education in the College of Education and Human Services at Montclair State University, New Jersey, U.S.A. Her work deploys Disability

Studies (DS), in intersection with other critical conceptual frameworks, in critiquing the structural inequities inherent in formal, compulsory education systems, as well as in exploring the potential for more liberatory learning and living outside of those systems. She is additionally engaged in an ongoing critical analysis of the intersections of behaviorism and capitalism underlying what she terms the Autism Industrial Complex.

Kathleen M. Collins

(Ph.D.) is Associate Professor of Language, Culture and Society, and Co-Director of the Center for Disability Studies in the College of Education at the Pennsylvania State University. Her research program investigates the production of educational (in)equity and deficit positioning at the intersections of literac(-ies), dis/ability, and race.

David J. Connor

(Ed.D.) is Professor Emeritus in the Learning Disabilities Master's Program and the Instructional Leadership Doctoral Program at Hunter College, City University New York. His research interests include using Disability Studies in Education as a theoretical lens to support inclusive practices. His most recent books are *Contemplating Dis/Ability in Schools and Society: A Life in Education* (2018, Lexington Books), and the second edition of *Rethinking Disability* (2019, Routledge) co-authored with Jan Valle.

Dianne L. Ferguson

is a retired professor who recently held the position of Director of Program Improvement and Accreditation at Chapman University. Her areas of interest and expertise included school inclusion, family experiences and the relationships between school personnel and families, administrator and teacher support for licensure and professional development and collaboration, use of interpretivist research methods in education, and disability studies. Dr. Ferguson has taught classes and provided consultation for general and special educators in Canada, Iceland (Fulbright Scholar), Finland, Norway, Sweden, Denmark (Fulbright Scholar), New Zealand and India, as well as numerous states in the United States.

Phillip M. Ferguson

is Professor Emeritus at Chapman University in Orange, California. For over three decades he has pursued an interest in the field of disability studies with an emphasis on issues affecting people with intellectual disabilities. His research is focused on family/professional interactions and support policy, social policy and the history of disability, as well as qualitative research methods in disability studies and education.

NOTES ON CONTRIBUTORS

Amy L. Ferrell

(formerly Boelé) is an Assistant Professor of Special Education in the School of Education and Human Development at the University of Colorado Denver, where she studies community, discourse, and literacy for people with disabilities. Her work, which situates disability research in social, cultural, historical, racial, linguistic, and political contexts, has appeared in journals such as *Harvard Educational Review, Reading Research Quarterly, Urban Education, Linguistics and Education*, and *International Journal of Inclusive Education*. She is coauthor of the second edition of *The Ethics of Special Education* (2018, Teachers College Press).

Beth Ferri

(Ph.D.) is a Professor of Inclusive Education and Disability Studies at Syracuse University, where she also coordinates the Doctoral program in Special Education. Professor Ferri has published widely on the intersection of race, gender, and disability. In addition to over 50 articles and chapters, she has also published three books: *Reading Resistance: Discourses of Exclusion in Desegregation and Inclusion Debates* (2006, Peter Lang); *Righting Educational Wrongs: Disability Studies Law and Education* (2013, SU Press); and *DisCrit: Critical Conversations Across Race, Class, & Dis/ability* (2016, Teachers College Press).

Joanne Kim

is a clinical coordinator at ECPHP, an early intervention program for young children suspected of or diagnosed with autism spectrum disorder, located at UCLA. She supervises an interdisciplinary team; works closely with parents and caregivers to ensure their goals and concerns are being addressed; and provides education related to community services. She is also a lecturer for a Disability Studies course at UCLA that focuses on the study of disability versus disability studies, the autism construct, and complex familial perspectives of autism.

Janette Klingner

(deceased) was a respected scholar, colleague and mentor to many of her students, including those who collaborated with her on this chapter. She was a professor of bilingual special education at the University of Colorado, Boulder. She was a K-8 bilingual special education teacher for 10 years before earning a Ph.D. in Reading and Learning Disabilities from the University of Miami. She was committed to mixed methods and the merger of new methodologies as evidenced by this chapter.

Corrine Li

is a pediatric speech-language pathologist practicing in Southern California. Her therapeutic approach emphasizes relationships in natural environments, and her research focuses on family understanding of (dis)ability.

Brooke A. Moore

(Ph.D.) is an Assistant Professor/Department Chair in the Advanced Education Programs Department in the College of Education at Fort Hays State University in Hays, Kansas. Formerly a special educator working primarily with students with learning disabilities, her research focuses on helping educators create equitable and inclusive learning environments for all students. She focuses on supporting rural educators in developing high leverage, evidence-based instructional practices that target the needs of students with high incidence disabilities.

Emily A. Nusbaum

is an Associate Professor at University of San Francisco. She has won awards for her dissertation and early career contributions to disability studies in education and social justice initiatives. Emily teaches graduate courses in DSE and critical, qualitative research.

Janet Story Sauer

is Professor at Lesley University, Cambridge, Massachusetts. She uses ethnography in her research and teaching about the lived experiences of immigrant families of children with disabilities. Sauer's scholarship is informed by scholarly and community partners in the development of policy and practice informed by the value of parent experience and expertise. Her work is recognized as alongside many of the most formidable scholars who advanced the need to legitimize parents and families as authorities and advocates.

Roger Slee

is Professor at the School of Education, University of South Australia. He is Founding Editor of the *International Journal of Inclusive Education* and has published widely over the course of a long and distinguished career.

Linda Ware

(Independent Scholar) survived a lengthy academic career at universities from New Mexico to New York. Her publications appeared in prestigious national and international academic journals. In addition to this series, *Critical Leaders and the Foundation of Disability Studies in Education*, she edited *Ideology and the Politics of (in)Exclusion* (2004, Peter Lang) and most recently *(Dis)Assemblages: An International Critical Disability Studies Reader* (2020, Springer). She is also a Section Editor for *Beginning with Disability A Primer* (2017, Routledge, L. J. Davis, Editor). Ware happily resides near Santa Fe, New Mexico.

INTRODUCTION

Honoring of the Research, Scholarship, and Activism of Ellen A. Brantlinger

Linda Ware and Roger Slee

I am neither a trained historian nor a political scientist, but as with all scholars, I tell about disability, social class, and equality and justice from my own perspective and in my own terms.

ELLEN BRANTLINGER, *Focus on Exceptional Children* (March 2001)

∴

When Meaning Falters and Words Fail, Ideology Matters celebrates the work of and is dedicated to the memory of Ellen A. Brantlinger, a scholar-activist who spent most of her professional career as a professor of special education at Indiana University in Bloomington, Indiana in the United States of America. Ellen was recognized internationally as an educator and critical theorist and celebrated for her incisive and unyielding critique of special education research, policy, and practice that spanned several decades. Brantlinger held that the impoverished nature of special education theory and practice was rooted to conformance with the most rigid constructs of standardization, normalcy, and its resulting inequitable outcomes for children with disabilities. When the push for inclusion gained currency in some quarters in the United States (mid-1980s), Brantlinger was among a handful of scholars who identified special education as the major obstacle to the inclusion of disabled students in the educational system. She was widely published in North American journals well known in special education, teacher education, multicultural education, sociology of education, urban education, school counseling, curriculum theory, qualitative education, and feminist teaching.

One of her most frequently cited works, 'Using Ideology: Cases of non-recognition of the politics of research and practice in special education' (Brantlinger, 1997) was published by the American Educational Research Association in the *Review of Educational Research* (*RER*). Brantlinger challenged the orthodoxy of special education by revealing its own ideological

© KONINKLIJKE BRILL NV, LEIDEN, 2020 | DOI:10.1163/9789004402690_001

underpinnings. This was especially significant given the fervent critique by those she referred to as traditional special educators' rampant proclamations of neutrality and objectivity in orthodox special education research. Brantlinger, like Tomlinson (1982) offered an early dissection of their unchallenged authority and claim to scientific objectivity. On many levels, this article served as a flashpoint in the development of 'critical special education' described by Ware (2001, 2005). For many of the contributors to this book, the article and the debate it generated influenced their turn away from special education towards the then nascent field of disability studies in education.

This book offers an elaboration of the scholarly contributions made by Ellen Brantlinger to research in education, special education, inclusive education, and the early development of Disability Studies in Education (Ware, 2001, 2004, 2010; Connor, 2013). Many of it's contributors move between the paradigmatic locations of special education, inclusive education, and disability studies as they consider Ellen's influence. In order to minimize the conflation of these paradigmatic locations for an international audience, we will provide contextual background borrowing from the 1999 International Colloquium on Inclusive Education (ICIE) that featured Ellen Brantlinger as a keynote speaker and others who wrote in response to her *RER* article.

The ICIE was a small collective of international disability scholars who met annually throughout Europe, Australia, New Zealand and the United States for more than a decade (1990–2002), to debate the meaning of 'inclusion' and 'inclusive education.' Each host country set the agenda for discussion and participants sent their papers in advance of the meeting to ensure robust and relevant critique by the participants. Most years the conference papers were published in edited collections that provided the earliest debate about inclusive education in comparative contexts (see Clark, Dyson, & Millward, 1995; Booth & Ainscow, 1998; Ballard & McDonald, 1999; Allan, 2003; Booth, Nes, & Stromstad, 2003; Ware, 2004). It was during this period that *The International Journal of Inclusive Education* began publication, prompted in part, by the robust debates among those in attendance who recognized inclusion as a complex global phenomenon that was not exclusive to public school settings.

The 1999 ICIE was organized by Linda Ware while on faculty at the University of Rochester and with funding she received from the Chicago-based Spencer Foundation. The tradition of restricting the annual meeting to less than 20 participants was abandoned and several guest speakers were invited who were not then active in the ICIE. They included Sally Tomlinson (United Kingdom), Len Barton (United Kingdom), Lous Heshusius (Canada), Thomas Skrtic (United States), and Ellen Brantlinger (United States). In addition, faculty from North American universities and their graduate students were also invited to attend, with the hope of breathing new life into discussion about disability in schools and society. Although some ICIE members expressed concern that the conference had grown 'too large' in size, Ware pressed on. Included among those who participated in 1999 were: Julie Allan (Scotland), Keith Ballard (New Zealand), Tony Booth (United Kingdom), Marit Stromstad (Norway), Kari Nes (Norway), and Roger Slee (Australia). By all accounts, consensus held that the Rochester meeting was a success, clearly due to the expanded roster of presenters and the graduate students who were supported to attend and or present at the conference.

The call for papers outlined three primary goals informed by Brantlinger's *RER* article:

1 To explore how a very narrow framework for understanding disability has led to inequitable educational policy and practice;
2 To examine the historic relationship between disability, special educational needs/schooling, and general education; and
3 To encourage understanding of the moral consequences of espoused ideology versus lived ideology among academic researchers.

The convening of so many internationally known critical scholars at the 1999 ICIE prompted new conversations about the politics of research and practice in special education at a moment when the micropolitics of disability identification and the macropolitics of failed social structures so clearly intersected and impacted (1) the education of students with disability and (2) the full participation of disabled people in society. The belief that disability demanded more complex analyses than medical research and practice alone could provide would invite increased reliance on the then nascent DS literature. The assumption that special education held exclusive rights to all discussions about disability in schools was unequivocally challenged in light of the fact that educational inclusion could no longer be considered in a vacuum in the absence of understanding historic and research tensions in the field of education and special education, in particular. At the level of practice as well, purposeful attention *away* from simple solutions and recipes for inclusive education in K-12 settings was encouraged throughout the conference to ensure a more complex and richly layered analysis of educational and social exclusion (Ware, 2004).

This moment signaled a critical turn towards broader engagement with critical special education scholarship and international disability issues that would, in very short order, pave the way for the successful launch of Disability Studies in Education (DSE) and considered in various publications (Connor, 2013; Ware, 2004, 2010). One of the contributors to this special issue, Alicia Broderick, attended the ICIE as a graduate student at the time. And in this book, her co-authored chapter with Kathleen Collins they link the ICIE (1999) as a moment of shifting consciousness to the realisation that within a more broadly conceived discursive community, the mandate for debate was assumed and not foreclosed by tradition. Collins & Broderick remark that unlike prior engagement with special educators, those in attendance at the ICIE were *not* intimidated by 'political discussion, debate, and dissent about what inclusive schooling is or could be or should be' (Collins & Broderick, 2013, p. 1270). Entering into debate about the positivist assumptions that ground special education with those who held eminence in the authorship of this same critique came at just the right moment for Broderick who was then a budding scholar and experienced educator. Further, for those in attendance who were new to critical scholarship on special education and inclusion, access to the issues was made more memorable by Ellen's own 'stance of self-critique, and her assertions about the importance of engaging in political and ideological critique (including self-critique).

Throughout Brantlinger's career, she made her 'stance' known *without apology*. She did not come to her politics by popular poll. In her ICIE keynote, 'Ideologies discerned, values determined: Getting past the hierarchies of special education,' Brantlinger stressed the danger of approaching our work in schools—including academe—in the absence knowing what ideology does:

> The stories we tell about ourselves, others, and the way life should be are forms of ideology that have a great impact on daily life in schools and communities. Because of ideology's profound influence, there is a need to discern how it works in order not to be stymied by 'undesireable' ideologies. There also is a need to imagine ideal [inclusive] communities (Anderson, 1983) and develop moral missions likely to capture the imaginations of others (Schudson, 1998) and persuade them to adhere to ideologies that are conducive to inclusion and that provide direction and inspiration for actions. (Brantlinger, 2004a, p. 14)

This preoccupation with transparency surfaced early in Brantlinger's career. In the introduction to 'Sterilization of People with Mental Disabilities: Issues, Perspectives, and Cases' (1995), she noted four relevant observations that served to ground her standpoint in that early research. For our purposes here, two in particular, bear mention. First, she underscored the underlying assumption that the 'idea of disability makes people uncomfortable; consequently, disability concerns are often denied and ignored' (preface). Second, she held firm to the position that sterilization is 'an area of discrimination in that people with disability are treated differently than people without disabilities' (Brantlinger, 1995). That book followed on her earlier publications dating back to 1983 in which Brantlinger exposed the limits of existing service delivery

HONORING OF THE RESEARCH, SCHOLARSHIP, AND ACTIVISM

models, care provision, education, and professional training as each was deeply embedded in ideology that was neither neutral nor value-free. It is no surprise that throughout her career she refined her critique of ideology whether taking aim at the 'big boys' of special education (see Allan); the value of qualitative inquiry in special education research (see especially Bacon and Ferri; Collins and Broderick; Nusbaum; & Sauer here); the need for strong feminist teachers in K-12 education; or in the example of local issues of voter redistricting in her own community in the state of Indiana. Research, scholarship, and community activism were so intertwined for Brantlinger that in an editorial published by the Bloomington Herald Times upon her passing, she was remembered as a long respected 'go-to-source' for local reporters and celebrated as 'a conscience for the community.'

When Meaning Falters and Words Fail, Ideology Matters cannot begin to capture the vastness of the enduring impact that Ellen Brantlinger made on the fields of education, special education, and Disability Studies in Education. Among the multiple strands of research and scholarship she conducted over a lifetime, only a handful is considered here. We hope that this book will encourage readers to return to her work—or discover it for the first time— and to mine from her insights, the demand that we 'unmask' the ideology that shapes educational and social reform. Because Ellen was known to many of the contributors as a mentor, a collaborator, and/or friend, this book is organised with the intention to capture the spirit of these intersecting conversations.

David J. Connor, in 'Risk Taker: Role Model, Muse, and Charlatan: Stories of Ellen—An Atypical Giant,' provides a rich introduction for those who did not know Brantlinger personally while simultaneously recounting her strengths to those who knew her well. Informed by the celebrated narrative researcher, Carolyn Ellis (2009), Connor's 'storying' of his experience is offered in the hope of the 'possibility of turning something chaotic into something intelligible and meaningful' (Ellis, 2009, p. 280). By utilizing the tools of autoethnography and storytelling, Connor extolls the profound influence Brantlinger exerted on his thinking and writing in special education, inclusion, and Disability Studies in Education (DSE). The value of her mentorship and friendship over the first 10 years of his career as a Disability Studies scholar, he maintains have been integral to shaping his personal and professional stake in Disability Studies. Julie Allan follows with 'Including Ideology' providing a theoretical overview of Brantlinger's contribution to the discussion of ideology and its effects in inclusive education. As Allan notes, Brantlinger was 'most interested in what ideological critique enabled her to understand about the position and practices of others' (Chapter 2). And of equal importance in the process, she made her own ideology transparent by 'work[ing] out her positionality' (Chapter 2). Allan draws upon Foucault's 'askesis' whereby 'thought as the work of problematizing, is what opens up the dimension of the possible' (McGushin, 2007, p. 16, cited by Allan, Chapter 2). Allan shows readers how the transgressive effects of Brantlinger's writing served to make her ideological work of enduring relevance to researchers whether novice or experienced—a perspective made evident in the work of several contributors to this book.

Janet Sauer builds on the perspectives presented by both Connor and Allan in, 'Research, Relationships and Making Understanding: A Look at Brantlingers Darla and the Value of Case Study Research.' Sauer revisits the often-cited book, *Fighting for Darla; Challenges for family care and professional responsibility* (Brantlinger, Klein, & Guskin, 1994) in reflection on her position as the mother of a son with 'significant disabilities,' a qualitative researcher, and one who is acutely aware of the collateral issues of consent and participants' agency in the research process. Risk is troubled on many levels for Sauer in this article. In particular, that which is relative to her son, who does not share the same disability 'label' as Darla. However, he is by virtue of his disability, likely to be denied the opportunity for agency and sexual expression, and the voice to claim his place in the world. The related elements of risk that researchers undertake in their efforts to give voice to experience under 'close examination' were complicated by the fact that some voices—those deemed 'unfit to participate'—remain 'edited' out of the typical academic journal (Sauer, Chapter 3). Although 'Darla' was published prior to the development of Disability Studies in Education as an academic field of study, Sauer's problematization of ability, agency, and voice is very much in keeping with the tenets that frame Disability Studies research (Baglieri et al., 2011; Connor & Valle, 2017; Ware, 2010). In this way, Sauer offers a glimpse into the significance of Brantlinger's influence as a critical special education scholar whose legacy shaped the evolution of Disability Studies in Education as a formidable field of study—applicable in ways that are as pragmatic as aesthetic.

Co-authors, Kathleen Collins and Alicia Broderick take up the value of Brantlinger's mentorship in 'When the Light Turns Blue: Journeying into Disability Studies Guided by the Work of Ellen Brantlinger.' Culling from Brantlinger they offer guidance for untenured faculty in higher education who aim to develop a Disability Studies agenda while 'housed' in a special education program. Collins and Broderick are well-respected Disability Studies scholars who hold 'day jobs' as special education program faculty at two different institutions, and who, by virtue of their research methodology, course content, political/ideological orientation, scholarly publications, and professional identities, grapple with the shared goal of advancing collective activism within academe as Disability Studies activist teachers and scholars. Their reflections will resonate with readers who have experienced an uneven path to advancing a Disability Studies identity in academe.

HONORING OF THE RESEARCH, SCHOLARSHIP, AND ACTIVISM

A similar agenda lies at the center of the multi-authored chapter, 'Challenging the Ideology of Normal in Schools' by Annamma et al. This chapter follows on the call by Collins and Broderick for collaboration and collective activism as these authors draw upon Critical Race Theory, Disability Studies, and Cultural/Historical Activity Theory literatures. They outline a conceptual framework that captures the value of research partnerships that broaden the discursive treatment of disability informed by historic tensions as well as those in the present moment. They remind us that: 'throughout history, children have been placed in special educational based on cultural and linguistic differences deemed deviant from the norms of "regular" education' (Chapter 4). It is this history, intersecting with other social locations of institutional exclusion that propels these researchers to deconstruct the historical and cultural foundations of the ideology of normal. Theirs is a robust critique of US education policy including the *No Child Left Behind* (NCLB) legislation and proposed intervention strategies such as Response to Intervention. They contest theories that purport to address the achievement gap in education given that many such theories maintain the segregation of students with disabilities, dismiss the overrepresentation of minority students in special education, eschew the schools-to-prison pipeline, and ignore the historic unequal discipline practices in schools directly tied to race and disability. Annamma et al. demonstrate the potential for alliance with other critical scholars willing to *deconstruct* the current, westernized, static ideology of normal that can increase the likelihood of leveraging lasting change for disabled people.

The two chapters that follow serve as exemplars of Allan's discussion of the impact Brantlinger made on educational researchers and their research projects (see also, Allan, 2010). In 'Vulnerable to Exclusion: The Place for Segregated Education within Conceptions of Inclusion' by Emily Nusbaum and 'The Impact of Standards-Based Reform: Applying Brantlinger's Critique of 'Hierarchical Ideologies' by Jessica Bacon and Beth Ferri these researchers consider the new accountability and standards movement in the USA as it interacts with educational inclusion. The chapters speak in tandem across the East and West coasts of the USA as Nusbaum draws on research she conducted in one California elementary school and Bacon and Ferri report from their research in an elementary school and district in New York state. Together these works denounce the current Standards-Based Reform (SBR) 'reform' agenda as it has proven to be on a collision course with the inclusion 'transformation' agenda that preceded it. These works are nuanced by location and of course, by the researcher(s) framing of the issues under study, however, what is common to both is the total absence of understanding by their research participants relative to how ideology shapes the institution, the practices, and the people who work within these settings. As Annamma et al. demonstrate with reference to Brantlinger (2004b), 'the genius of the accountability and standards movement is in the "ideologies that obfuscate power imbalances"' (Chapter 5). Nusbaum expands on that very point in 'Vulnerable to Exclusion: The Place for Segregated Education within Conceptions of Inclusion' as she traces the malleability of educators within shifting discourses on disability in the absence of ideological grounding among administration, faculty, and staff surrounding school policies. Nusbaum struggles to contain her own astonishment in the face of the refusal of her research participants to collectively engage in ideological and moral conversations about inclusive education. Her positionality figured in to her work, and yet, it was managed, and all but silenced for fear that ideological conversations on inclusion in school settings often 'cause disruption' (Nusbaum, Chapter 6). The moral imperative Brantlinger encouraged as a frame for school-based research became increasingly less important to the participants in Nusbaum's study than she had hoped to discover.

Bacon and Ferri point to similar collateral damage authored by education policy in collision with special education reform. 'The Impact of Standards-Based Reform: Applying Brantlinger's Critique of 'Hierarchical Ideologies"' provides an analysis of the NCLB legislation and the SBR strategies implemented in one school in New York State. Although these researchers hoped to study mandated reform measures intended to raise test scores, they found instead that SBR opened the floodgates for regressive measures that foreclosed any opportunity to shape inclusive transformation in the school they studied. Bacon and Ferri note 'SBR appears to be re-validating the taken-for-granted hierarchical ideologies of special education traditionalists' (Chapter 7). Similar to Nusbaum they were astonished to realize the ease with which administrators and educators in each of these schools and districts return to exclusion and segregated settings in the name of compliance with educational mandates. These researchers were caught in a moment of realising how much undoing would be needed before any redoing of reform might be possible. Ever hopeful, Bacon and Ferri conclude with Brantlinger's call for a 'countermovement to oppose stratifying measures and work to overcome hierarchical and excluding relations in school and society' (2006, p. 224). They maintain that this was nothing short of a 'clarion plea' to the 'inclusion movement and to those of us who attempt to extend her work through disability studies in education. We would do well to heed her call in promoting policies and practices that support the inclusion of all students' (Bacon & Ferri, Chapter 7).

The final chapter 'Family Portraits: Past and Present Representations of Parents in Special Education Textbooks' is multi-authored by Ferguson et al. These authors focus on the treatment of families rendered by textbooks, revisiting one of Brantlinger's enduring critiques of special education

HONORING OF THE RESEARCH, SCHOLARSHIP, AND ACTIVISM 9

practice—its over-reliance upon the 'introductory' textbook. They recover many of the problematic and critical issues endemic to the construction of disability in traditional textbooks as they trace critical incidents over time that provide a status report in the present moment as the role of parents has shifted from the designation of 'problem' to 'partner.' They deploy a Disability Studies perspective to build on the often-cited critique of the 'Big Glossies' authored by Brantlinger in 2006. Noting that Brantlinger raised questions specific to the construction of disability itself in that research, their analysis is focused on the construction of parents. Among the important issues this chapter considers is the belief that although 'discussion of families in these [newer] textbooks has evolved more quickly than the discussion of disability in general' discussion of social and cultural capital remain underexplored. Given that the two lead authors, Dianne and Philip Ferguson were long-time colleagues of Brantlinger, they conjecture that given her longstanding advocacy for 'listening to the voice of the marginalized and devalued in society' she would still hold reservations about the over-reliance on even the most recent textbooks for introductory coursework. The authors contend that textbook publishers would do well to draw upon the burgeoning Disability Studies in Education literature so as to more completely and complexly render contemporary portraits of the family.

In conclusion, we hope that *When Meaning Falters and Words Fail, Ideology Matters* invites conversation among the readers and prompts new explorations into the writing, thinking, and research of Ellen Brantlinger, one of strongest voices for educational and social injustice in all forms. Among the key words that might refine a search of her scholarship all of the following could apply: disability, ability, race, gender, class, mental retardation, adolescence, parenting, special education, in-service and pre-service teacher attitudes, and professional attitudes (in many contexts). These many interests secured the reach of Ellen Brantlinger's critical perspective into a range of publications, casting a wide net for us to sort through and to weigh against her example, our own activist scholarly agendas with equal rigor and *without apology.*

References

Allan, J. (2007). *Rethinking inclusive education: The philosophers of difference in practice.* Dordrecht: Springer.

Baglieri, S., Valle, J. W., Connor, D. J., & Gallagher, D. (2011). Disability studies and special education: The need for plurality of perspectives on disability. *Remedial and Special Education, 32*(4), 267–278.

Brantlinger, E. (1995). *Sterilization of people with mental disabilities: Issues, perspectives, and cases.* Westport, CT: Auburn House.

Brantlinger, E. (1997). Using ideology: Cases of non-recognition of the politics of research and practice in special education. *Review of Educational Research, 67*(4), 425–459.

Brantlinger, E. (2001). Poverty, class, and disability: A historical, social, and political perspective. *Focus on Exceptional Children, 33*(7), 1–49.

Brantlinger, E. (2006). The big glossies: How textbooks structure (special) education. In E. Brantlinger (Ed.), *Who benefits from special education? Remediating (fixing) other people's children*. Mahwah, NJ: Lawrence Erlbaum.

Brantlinger, E. A., Klein, S. M., & Guskin, S. L. (1994). *Fighting for Darla; Challenges for family care and professional responsibility*. New York, NY: Teachers College Press.

Campbell, F. K. (2009). *Contours of ableism: The production of disability and abledness*. London: Palgrave Macmillan.

Eagleton, T. (1994). Ideology and its vicissitudes in Western Marxism. In S. Zizek (Ed.), *Mapping ideology*. London: Verso.

Linneman, R. D. (2001). *Idiots: Stories about mindedness and mental retardation*. New York, NY: Peter Lang.

Rosetti, Z., Ashby, C., Arndt, K., Chadwick, M., & Kasahara, M. (2008). "I like others to not try to fix me": Agency, independence, and autism. *Intellectual and Developmental Disabilities, 46*(5), 364–375. doi:10.1352/2008.46:364–375

Shostak, J. (2002). *Understanding, designing and conducting qualitative research in education*. Buckingham/Philadelphia, PA: Open University Press.

Slee, R. (2011). *The irregular school: Exclusion, schooling, and inclusive education*. New York, NY: Routledge.

Ware, L. (2004). *Ideology and the politics of (in)exclusion*. New York, NY: Peter Lang.

CHAPTER 1

Risk Taker, Role Model, Muse, and "Charlatan": Stories of Ellen, an Atypical Giant

David J. Connor

Abstract

This chapter weaves personal recollections of my encounters with Ellen Brantlinger and a sampling of her works that continue to exert a profound influence on my own thinking and writing within both special education and Disability Studies in Education (DSE). I begin by describing how, as a first-year doctoral student I encountered the scholarly work of Ellen and consequently never saw the world in the same way again. Second, I share how I came to know Ellen as a generous person who took an active interest in my fledgling scholarship and subsequent budding academic career. Third, narrating the decade in which our professional paths crisscrossed, I reveal how coming to know Ellen on a personal level shaped my view of her as—among many other things—a risk-taker, a role model and (although she would modestly eschew this), a muse. Fourth, I discuss the impact Ellen has had on a wide group of scholars through fearless critiques of special education, resulting in her being branded as a "charlatan" by some of the field's most powerful figures. In closing, I offer thoughts on the influence of Ellen as an atypical giant.

Keywords

risk taker – role model – muse – "charlatan"

1 A Note on Framework and Format

This chapter is designed to engage the reader through my own stories about Ellen. In each of the following four sections I share stories that are contextualized against descriptions of selected works by Ellen that engaged my thinking in such powerful ways that they remain with me to this day. The description of each text, therefore, is placed within memories of ways in which the work

© TAYLOR & FRANCIS, 2013 | DOI:10.1163/9789004402690_002

intersected with elements of my own life as I made the transition from doctoral student to fledgling scholar to tenured academic, revealing Ellen's undisputable role in that growth.

2   Ellen as Risk Taker

In fall of 1999 when I entered the doctoral program at Teachers College, Columbia University, like many—if not most—students I felt I had stepped into another world. The yearlong introductory doctoral seminar introduced me to the terrain of educational research. Only it wasn't a sedate, pastoral landscape, but rather a battlefield in which epistemologies, ontologies, methodologies, and ideologies fought for hegemony. Our learning curve was steep. While being exposed to multiple theories, alternative histories, educational movements, governmental policies, and shifting paradigms, we sorted through what made sense to our own (then) worldview. Of course that worldview was inevitably challenged, and ultimately destabilized from the fixity of its foundations (Oh, those were the days!). Of course this disequilibrium served to prompt self-analysis in regard to: How do we know what we know? What is the meaning of knowledge? Where does it come from? How is it constructed? What influences that construction? Why? When? Where? How? And so on.

I'd entered the doctoral program as a career-long educator from New York City's public schools, someone who had always been critical of special education. Throughout years of teaching high school students labeled learning disabled (LD), emotionally disturbed (ED), and mentally retarded (MR, now known as cognitively impaired, or CI), I had always questioned how the school system was structured, and its seemingly obliviousness toward disadvantaging of students with disabilities. In my subsequent district-level role of coordinating in-service professional development in special education for Manhattan high schools, I continued to advocate for inclusive education, despite push back on many fronts. However, by the time I entered my doctoral program, I was so frustrated with the field of special education's resistance to inclusion, I began to doubt its ability to change—and wanted out.

I often think it is with great irony that I have remained in special education. Despite intentions of using the doctoral program to shift my educational focus to curriculum, in my first semester I encountered two forces that changed my mind—one in person, and one in print. The one in person was Dr. D. Kim Reid, who reframed the concept of learning disabilities into a sociocultural historic context (Reid & Valle, 2004), and became my advisor and dissertation sponsor. The one in print was Ellen

RISK TAKER, ROLE MODEL, MUSE, AND "CHARLATAN"

> Brantlinger, who became a valued friend. The first article I read by her was: "Using Ideology: Cases of Nonrecognition of the Politics of Research and Practice in Special Education" (1997) published in the *Review of Educational Research.*

Simply put, in *Using Ideology* Ellen singularly "took on" an alliance of prominent scholars within the field of traditional special education who are vociferously anti-inclusionist. As a supporter of inclusion, she noticed a systematic affront upon educators and researchers like herself, and the disingenuous nature of those attacks within major journals. In her analysis of 13 articles and 5 book chapters, she deftly illuminates the hypocrisy of traditional scholars who refuse to acknowledge their own ideologies, yet openly attack and denigrate those of others. Of this endeavor, she writes:

> If these papers had been written by unknown figures or published in less prominent journals, I would have ignored them. It is precisely because all of the authors are influential people in my field that I feel it is necessary to speak up and talk back to power. In documenting their abuse of scholarly standards and their ways of undermining best educational practices, I risk seeming unscholarly and vindictive myself. That is a risk I take, albeit with trepidation. (p. 426)

Culling from theorists such as Bourdieu (1984), Gramsci (1971), and Habermas (1978), not only did Ellen relentlessly deconstruct the anti-inclusion rhetoric of traditionalist scholars as being ideologically located (regardless of how they tried to ignore or deny it), she illuminated ways in which such rhetoric was self-serving, and damaging to children. Ellen interpreted the acts of traditionalists who claimed positivistic "scientific" rigor (at the expense of neglecting longstanding issues of social class, race, and culture) as "preserving existing social structures and power relations" (p. 437). She confronted traditionalists who believed they best represented the field of special education by debunking their: reification of disability categories as naturalized "services"; belief in meritocratic need; allowance of bias remaining invisible; creation of a shared, homogenized identity; self-appointed status of standard-bearers; touting of a neutral science; recollection of a mythical ideal past; identification of "contaminating" opponents; foretelling an ominous future for the field of special education; claims of personal victimization; and constant attempts to undermine inclusion with cynicism.

Within this work, Ellen sidestepped polite scholarly etiquette and publicly named names, holding widely respected researchers accountable for their words. As she pointed out, "The academic freedom enjoyed by pillars in a field does not include the right to be free from criticism" (p. 446).

By targeting these prominent scholars who had constantly critiqued inclusive education as being non-empirically researched and based in rhetoric, Ellen showed them—to a large extent using their own terms—how their own position papers were untenable. In brief, their own publications were actually ideological assertions without sufficient empirical evidence to prove special education as a functional success. As the saying goes: she blew them out of the water. And, although only a number of "pillars" of special education had been critiqued, it felt as if the entire field had rightfully been called into question. What power in thinking! What power in writing! Who was this woman clearly naming things about which I always had deep doubts? Who rendered visible the lines of power and oppression that had until then, been obscured? Who held a shared disposition toward special education and its refusal to see itself as a deeply flawed system? As it happens, I was soon to find out.

In 2001 I traveled to Chicago to a small inaugural conference hosted by National Louis University for scholars interested in a new academic discipline called Disability Studies in Education (DSE). When I say small, I mean small—perhaps between 30 to 40 people, mainly professors and doctoral students who were dissatisfied with the restrictive ways in which the field of special education conceptualized disability within scientific, medical, and psychological frameworks. I'd come with three fellow doctoral students to present our collective research on teachers with learning disabilities. However, as we prepared to present our panel, we noticed that there were only four people in the audience that consisted of our diehard supporters: two spouses, one significant other, and our professor/mentor Beth Ferri. At that moment, Beth jumped up and went searching to find an audience for us. Within a few minutes she returned with Ellen, who sat down and listened attentively for the duration.

So, there we were, staring at her name tag—doctoral students who had initially come to know Ellen as an abstraction, an authority, an intellectually courageous she-warrior of Amazonian proportions, now unexpectedly presenting our first attempts at research and scholarly writing to her. Only this "giant" took the form of a bespectacled granny wearing Jesus' sandals, nodding attentively as we spoke, taking notes (We were worthy of this?), and when we finished, posed some very thoughtful questions. I had experienced awe before, usually when meeting music idols such as Deborah Harry of Blondie, Siouxsie from the Banshees, or Chrissie Hynde of the Pretenders. I invoke these names as they convey how, to us, Ellen was akin to a highly acclaimed rock star in the world of educational research.

At that conference, Ellen's generosity of spirit was immediately apparent. She willingly supported unknown doctoral students rather than attending a presentation by a "name." She also became instantly accessible, happy to chat in hallways, elevators, restrooms (if female), and subsequent sessions. When I initiated a conversation about how "Using Ideology" had made such an impact upon me, she shared how the initial submission to a special education journal had been rejected outright, prompting her to submit elsewhere, and incidentally, receive a much wider circulation. Little did I know that she was initiating me into the politics of publishing that lay ahead.

3　Ellen as Role Model

Not only did Ellen take an active interest in doctoral students at conferences, she maintained that interest over time, willing to share her accumulated knowledge, optimistic that such students would grow to influence the fields of special education and DSE. We had a number of overlapping interests within education, including race, class, and disability. The more I saw her present and the more I read her work, the more Ellen became transformed from an abstraction into a living role model, someone I aspired to be like as a researcher and teacher educator. Combining the right balance of idealism and realism, Ellen asserted her convictions and sought movement to changing the status quo of education toward being more inclusive of human diversity.

It was only in my doctoral program that I come to know the social construction of disability as a preferable alternative to deficit-driven perspectives. Although this idea "clicked" immediately into place as to how I already viewed the world, until then I didn't have the words to adequately understand it. Through the guidance of both Kim Reid and Beth Ferri, I came to know the important of social, cultural, and historical (as well as other) interpretations of disability. It was while participating in a project with Kim Reid that I gained further access to Ellen's thoughts. Kim had secured a two-part special issue of Learning Disability Quarterly dedicated to "The Discursive Practice of Learning Disability," in which she and Jan Valle contributed a lead article that would be followed by eleven contributions from leading scholars in the field of LD (Reid & Valle, 2004). I was invited to write the final article to synthesize the issues raised by the lead article and the subsequent wide-ranging responses (Connor, 2005). It was with great pleasure that I read Ellen's contribution titled, "Confounding the Needs and Confronting the Norms: An Extension

> of Reid and Valle's Essay" (Brantlinger, 2004). In it, once again, she succinctly summed up why much the current structure of special education can only be seen as problematic on so many fronts.

In Ellen's self-admittedly "wandering course" (p. 497) within *Confounding the Needs*, she troubled "... entrenched customs and accused multiple agents—many in high places—of benefitting from policies, practices, and ways of thinking that harm others, particularly children who do not do well in school" (p. 497). She does so to make the point that, "... we in special education are entangled in complex and sometimes disturbing practices that may not benefit those we claim to serve" (p. 497). Reading Ellen's work is not always easy as she has a knack of exposing ways in which *everyone* is connected to, and responsible for, the education systems in which we work. Her words can seem harsh on first read, but second time around—once we have been able to steel ourselves to criticism—find elements of truth to emerge.

Calling upon sociological studies by Schmidt (2000) and Silberman (1971), Ellen asserts "most professional jobs are not intellectually challenging and allow only the most constrained creativity... professional socialization in disciplines causes stagnation in intellect and originality. It seems that professionals are held back by normative foundational knowledge" (p. 496). Additionally, she notes "... only a handful of professionals ask why they are doing what they are doing; most educators do not think seriously or deeply about the purposes or consequences of education" (p. 496). Here, she alludes to the hidden curriculum subconsciously acquired through professional enculturation, namely, the unquestioned absorption of what constitutes norms and values. In other words, professionalization of educators tends toward *acriticality*, a state in which employees function unquestioningly in a system they believe is beneficial for all children, unable to see its practices.

As usual, Ellen cuts through the obfuscation of what is actually occurring when professionals use language such as "special needs" and "at risk" students based upon a bell curve of assumed normalcy. In doing so, she questions the very notion of ab/normalcy by exposing how these concepts are hierarchical and serve to empower a portion of the population, while disempowering others. Pointing out absurdities of the concept "average," including the inability of everyone to be so by virtue of its definition, Ellen asks us to ponder "... the imperative of average ... [suggesting] we examine why intellectual uniformity is desired ... [when] in fact, diversity is better than homogeneity from a community perspective" (p. 491).

Acknowledging human diversity in relation to social class has always been at the center of Ellen's diverse body of work (see, for example, 1987, 1995, 1996, 1999). This particular article confirmed my own suspicions about the nefarious nature of normalcy, culturally defined, constructed through arbitrary lines build through collective consensus. At the same time, it triggered years of memories in which I had unconsciously participated in school structures and systems that reified disability as abnormality, even when I resisted that pull.

I continued to see Ellen at conferences, always making it a point to attend her presentations. One in particular was called "The Big Glossies: How Textbooks Structure (Special) Education," at the American Education Research Association (AERA) in San Diego 2004. In this research, Ellen carefully analyzed fourteen special education textbooks typically uses in introductory classes. Her findings showed how special education knowledge was fairly uniformly structured and represented in untruthful, non-representative, disembodied ways through disability type organization, stylized classroom photographs, and authoritative-yet-emotionless third person texts. The books often omitted altogether, or paid nominal reference to, important issues such as universal design, ethnic/racial overrepresentation, social class and structural concerns, disability rights, disability studies, and non-staged pictures (Brantlinger, 2006).

Snatched conversations with Ellen in hallways, up elevators, down escalators were always valued. I knew I was conversing with a rare mind, yet her generosity with time was always unfailing. When I presented at AERA, she often attended my sessions as a gesture of support. I remember sitting alone at my roundtable, feeling like a wallflower that no one wanted to dance with, only to see Ellen's smiling face emerge through the bustle and din of the conference ballroom, ready to engage about my latest paper. At one occasion in Chicago, when I presented on researching disability, race, and class as part of a panel about using qualitative methodologies, an audience member asked me a question about resistance to change in schools. My response contained several reasons, but one was to do with older educators. Ellen immediately castigated me in public, calling me to task for sounding ageist. I was mortified and quickly rephrased my response to convey that it wasn't meant to be critical of people of a certain age, but rather professionals with a certain amount of experience who were often worn out by years of attempted reforms. Still, she did give me food for thought, and I filter my responses more carefully lest they be perceived as discriminatory. Ellen also took time to introduce me to

Roger Slee, then editor of the International Journal of Inclusive Education, and urged me to submit work there. I did, and the journal was such a good fit that I also became a reviewer. I am indebted for such unsolicited professional guidance, as well as her general encouragement to pursue my research agenda.

4   Ellen as Muse

The more I spent time with Ellen, the more I considered her a muse and without wishing to sound too fanciful, a guiding spirit of sorts (although, in her modesty, she would most likely reject this notion). I found that almost everything I wrote pertained to some aspect of her own work, and I would always cite her scholarship, often numerous times within each piece. One of my favorite memories of Ellen is at the Disability Studies in Education International Conference held at Teachers College, Columbia University in 2005. Ellen was scheduled to receive the award of Senior Scholar in Disability Studies in Education, and I was to receive the corresponding award for Junior Scholar. It meant I would read a short introductory speech for Ellen before she gave a presentation on the opening night. Two days later on the closing afternoon of the conference, Ellen would introduce me before I spoke.

I can't recall what I said when introducing Ellen, but I remember experiencing a "double high" due to both recently completing my doctoral degree and sharing the honor of being given an award at the same time as her. Ellen's speech was originally titled, "Special Education Myths that Necessitate a Disability Studies Perspective," but she'd changed her mind en route to the conference and instead spoke about her recent experiences in observing education while traveling through Brazil. Afterwards, we all went out to dinner, including my parents visiting from England. I was so glad that they were able to meet and break bread with Ellen.

To celebrate the 5th year of the conference, during the final afternoon the original founders—Valerie Owen, Paula Neville, Terry Smith, and Ron Ferguson—were presented with awards. Then Ellen introduced me in a way that both celebrated some achievements and poked fun at my non-academic life, including a dubious restaurant I frequently enjoyed called "Trailer Park," that could politely be best described as paying homage to rural America. (At home that night, my mother said of this:

"I loved the way she tapped into your dark side"). The title of my presentation was, "Disability Studies in Education—Looking Back, Facing Forward," highlighting ways in which DSE had served as the lynchpin in the development of my thinking over the previous five years, and ways in which I hoped it would continue to grow in the next five years and beyond.

One of the most interesting aspects of Ellen's work for me has always been her sustained attention to social class. Unlike many other American researchers, especially those in special education, Ellen's focus on social class was core to her work—associated with social structures, schooling practices, power, privilege, and the opportunities (or lack thereof) afforded all citizens in a democracy. Around this time I read her book "Dividing Classes: How the Middle Class Negotiates and Rationalizes School Advantage" (2003) and was stunned by her audacity in researching educational advantage and privilege within her own liberal community.

Dividing Classes is a critical ethnography largely focused upon how White, liberal, educated middle-class parents from the town where Ellen lived and worked for 34 years leveraged resources to ensure that their children would be academically and socially advantaged, although this meant disadvantaging others. In her own words, she "... chose participants similar to myself in ethnicity, educational experience, professional careers, gender (in the case of the study of middle-class mothers), and social class" (p. 27). Her findings revealed that such parents believed

> Poor people were a negation of self and a referent in *legitimizing* status: compared to the poor, the middle class was smart, moral, and hardworking, and thus deserving of superior rank, exclusive conditions, and a larger or better share of community resources. (p. 43)

In advocating for higher tracks within schools, for example, the actions of middle-class parents squeeze down low-income children to lower tracks, leaving Ellen to conclude that "stratified school structures and outcomes are intentional products of middle-class desire" (p. 59).

Teachers, in turn, are influenced by social class and tracking systems, referring to middle-class students variously as "people with ambition," "the stars," "super motivated kids," "ones with the better background," and having "superior intellect." In contrast, referents for low-income students include: "kids who break your heart," "the bad boys and girls," "angry, at risk kids," "lower-class students," and "kids who have free lunch" (pp. 89–90). Ellen found that most teachers appeared to accept social class stereotypes, the stratification they were a part of, and the inequities they upheld. In addition, affluent parents believed that the "best" teachers taught the high tracked students, and were "vehement in that this is the way it should be" (p. 103). Few teachers and parents thought heterogeneous grouping would work and were not usually interested in class desegregation.

In fact, Ellen discussed at length the passivity of teachers, a settling for lack of control over job conditions, the absence of activism, the adoption and maintenance of a middle-class demeanor and sensibility, and an apologetic stance for not talking sufficiently about class disparities. She notes "... the pattern of teachers being in the middle (between higher and lower classes) and subsequently powerless in school decision making is likely to hold true nationally" (p. 135). In addition, Ellen was aware that educational advocacy for the poor is amorphous because, "... unlike gender bias, which to some extent has been successfully addressed by litigation, social class is not a minority category; hence, poor people cannot legally be subjected to discrimination" (p. 141). Her insights create discomfort because she realizes that peers, friends, neighbors, "... people who are radical in their scholarly work or about environmental and international peace issues are not as socially minded about their own children's education" (p. 149). Furthermore, Ellen notes that a "truly equitable, integrated, and high-quality comprehensive schooling could never be accomplished in an unregulated capitalist country where adult life circumstances are so discrepant" (p. 191).

Reading this exquisitely crafted book, I was struck by both the eloquence of Ellen's style and, in her own words, the "unrelenting criticism of participants" (p. vii) who she sincerely thanked in the Acknowledgements section. As an insider, Ellen had chronicled the patterns of how power works to ensure that school systems maintain class privilege. For this, she received an award for outstanding book by AREA. Impressed with such a nuanced analysis of social class in action, I shared the book with Chris Hale, a colleague who writes about middle-class privilege and learning disability (Hale, 2011). He knew I had an "in" with Ellen, so I offered him the opportunity to meet her. Soon after, when she and her husband, son, and grandchildren came to visit New York for a week, we arranged to catch up.

After meeting her family in the shoebox-sized apartment on the Upper East Side that they had somehow borrowed, Chris and I took Ellen out for a chat. She said she didn't mind a bar, so there we were in a nearby dive, the three of us perched on high stools sipping pints of beer. For some reason, a huge pair of old-fashioned knickers ("bloomers" where I come from) hung above our heads—as part of the bar's theme. Ellen fit right in, making jokes about their owner, speculating about the story they could tell. Chris wanted to talk about Dividing Classes, in particular, her methods, ideas, analyses, and findings. He was very curious about the participants asking, "Did they feel betrayed? Did you feel you threw your community under a bus?" Ellen appeared genuinely shocked by such questions. She responded by saying it was an obligation, and her participants took the critique in their stride. As the book really went deep under the skin of that community, we wondered if that was indeed the case. Regardless, the relevance of her findings was significant, for while the book had a feel of small town exposure, we realized that its truths likely echoed throughout so many communities across the country.

Later, we joined her family in a Thai restaurant, and enjoyed the conversation. This was a treat that would happen again when at AERA in Chicago, where Ellen met a life-long friend of mine who was adopted, becoming intrigued by her story. I was happy to engage with Ellen in these informal and formal venues. When coming up for tenure, I did not hesitate to include her name on a list of scholars we were allowed to submit as potential reviewers. After tenure was granted, she forwarded a copy of her letter that was crafted with great care. I realized then that she had likely done this for many of us who self-identify as critical special educators and/or DSE scholars, taking pains to ensure that dissenting voices in our chosen field would find a home in academia.

5   Ellen as "Charlatan"

Thankfully, Ellen's fearless critiques of special education did not go unnoticed. They had a two-pronged effect. On one hand, they contributed to the galvanization of scholars who had long been discontented with special education (see, for example: Danforth, 1997; Ferguson, Ferguson, & Taylor, 1991; Gabel, 2001; Gallagher, 1998; Ware, 2004). On the other hand, she truly struck a nerve with traditionalist scholars cited in "Using Ideology." Attacks upon her appeared personal, indignant, more like outraged foot-stamping than a rigorous scholarly response. For example, James Kauffman's (1999) "Commentary: Today's Special Education and Its Messages for Tomorrow," is an embarrassing rant against scholars such as Ellen who dared to challenge the knowledge base of the field. He refers to her as "loathing" (p. 245), a generator of "scurrilous reviews of special education" (p. 245), among "scam artists" (p. 249) and "charlatans" (p. 250). Kauffman charges that Ellen, along with other critical special educators (Danforth & Rhodes, 1997; Lipsky & Gardner, 1996) was responsible for the erosion of special education and its current state of being: apologetic for existing, unrealistic in expectations, mesmerized by postmodern/deconstructivist inanities, and immobilized by anticipation of systemic transformation.

Being on the receiving end of anger by some of the field's most powerful figures did not faze Ellen. While agreeing that their tone was hostile and unprofessional, Ellen shared that she made it a point to be civil and professional, always wishing her critics a "Good morning" at breakfast-time when they all reviewed grants for the federal government. She learned that being maligned as a fraud and a quack appeared to go with the territory for critical special educators (see Kaufmann and Sasso's, 2006, attack on Gallagher's ideas, for another example).

Arguably, such traditionalist outrage can be expected under the circumstances. After all, what Ellen did was to challenge the entire special education system—from the field's foundational knowledge base to its willful ignoring of race and class, from its unquestioned professional practices to the very efficacy of specialized instruction. In her last edited book, Ellen culled from the work of Delpit (1995) and Gramsci (1971) to craft the provocative title of: *Who Benefits from Special Education? Remediating (Fixing) Other People's Children* (2006a).

Featuring a smorgasbord of scholars both seasoned and new, *Who Benefits?* addresses a wide range of interrelated issues, including: the history of special education curriculum, responsible inclusion, textbooks, race and disability, resistance to multiculturalism, personal narratives, and the impact of general school reform on students with disabilities. Ellen contributed three of the chapters herself, one of them being "Winners Need Losers: The Basis for School Competition and Hierarchies." In this piece, she analyzed the purpose and structure of school hierarchies, including the practice of mandatory-exams that serve to sift out students who struggle in school-based forms of learning. Her observation of disturbing trends chronicle the absurdities of certain educational policies such as one in Florida that "bases promotion largely on tests, with the result that five times as many youngsters were forced to repeat third grade than the previous year" (p. 205). Ellen also captures the pain of such policies, citing a former elementary school principal who works in a dropout prevention program: "These children will either become so angry they're going to be aggressive and discipline problems or be so demoralized and heartbroken and depressed. I know that these children are going to drop out" (p. 205). She notes that the system focuses on who passes, rather than on who fails and validates "middle class success to superior student and family characteristics—again to the personal traits rather than the structural distinctions in institutional response to members of each class" (p. 207). Ellen asserts, "It is no coincidence that those found to be inadequate are the least powerful citizens" (p. 219).

So, who does benefit from special education as it is currently conceived, configured, and operationalized? According to Ellen, many people, including: test producers, transglobal capitalists, media moguls, politicians and political pundits, conservatives, advocates of school privatization, enterprising school superintendents, professionals and the professions, and members of the educated middle class. Each one of these groups profits in some shape or form while working-class and poor children, especially those labeled as disabled, do not.

> This was the last of Ellen's books, and so it is fitting that it challenged the entire machinery of special education. When I told her I'd read it, she mentioned in passing that it had disappointing sales and wondered whether it was because of apathy toward taking on such a behemoth or simply ineffective marketing.
>
> I am not sure how disappointed she was. By this time in her career, on the cusp of her retirement, Ellen must have known the degree her work influenced so many of us. A pioneer in the field of DSE before it had a name—along with Biklen, Heshusius, Skrtic, Slee, and Taylor—Ellen helped shape the consciousness of scholars who formally developed DSE, including Danforth, Ferguson & Ferguson, Ferri, Gabel, Gallagher, Peters, P. Smith, R. Smith, and Ware. Subsequently, doctoral students throughout the last decade such as Broderick, Baglieri, Beratan, Connor, Collins, Narian, and Valle gravitated to the pull of DSE. In turn, another wave of DSE scholars including Arndt, Sauer, Hale, Nussbaum, Valente, Wappet, White, and Young continue to utilize the groundbreaking work of Ellen. In sum, all of us have been moved by the power of her words, penetrating insights, and unwavering commitment to issues of social justice.

Indeed, each of us is indebted to Ellen for her paving the way that allows us to continue challenging the status quo of special education's hegemony in all things pertaining to disability and education. By calling attention to the flaws of special education's research base and how it undergirds oppressive systems, structures, and professional practice, Ellen pulled the rug from under the field's feet. In doing so, she single-handedly stood up to a field that tried to silence her ideas.

How, then, should we best remember Ellen? As the mouse who roared? As David in relation to Goliath? A noble heretic who rejected the orthodoxy of her professional institution? As the poster child for "talking back" to power? As an academic Amazon in the form of a bespectacled-granny wearing Jesus' sandals? As all of the above—and more?

6 Ellen as Atypical Giant

To answer the question of how to best remember Ellen, my response is in simple terms: Ellen symbolizes the ultimate critical special educator/DSE scholar. As previously noted, she was an ideal and real mixture of idealism and realism. Her own words speak for themselves: "In holding what I believe are inclusive, progressive, and democratic beliefs, I admit to an orientation toward utopian visions of school and society" (Brantlinger, 1997, p. 449). At the same time, Ellen was a rarity: a true academic activist, a researcher who lived and worked among communities and advocated for change through a variety of means. She stated that, "Activism requires commitment, hard work, and especially the bravery to leave the privileged center of mainstream life and confront it. Social movements are necessarily extra institutional; for durable change, they must disrupt rather than interrupt dominant practice" (Brantlinger, 2006c, p. 223).

In this chapter I have created incarnations of Ellen as risk taker, role model, muse, "charlatan," and atypical giant. I suspect that she would modestly deny these first four descriptions, and likely reject the last one. I can almost hear her ask: *"Atypical? What's typical? Doesn't that create a binaric hierarchy? Who decides what atypical is? Who doesn't? Who benefits? Who places who where?"* and so on ... However, Ellen *was* atypical. She *was* a giant in our field who had a career of socially conscious research spanning decades. Before the term "intersectionality" became popular, Ellen was writing about social class, disability, race, and gender as part of her moral grounding—concerned with inequities throughout American society and the world. Her thinking was, to use an apt cliché, ahead of the curve in so many ways that it made her a natural leader.

When Ellen retired she and her husband Pat began to travel more, including the Middle East, Far East, and Europe. Our email interchanges shifted from academic topics to exploring the world. In January 2012, I returned from traveling to Antarctica and send her some photographs. It was a place where Ellen said she was curious to visit, but did not have the nerve to make the two day crossing over some of the most tempestuous seas in the world. In return, she told me of travel plans to the Dalmatian Coast, rescheduled for May 2012. However, Ellen died a couple of months before that came to be. On discovering her passing, deeply saddened scholars immediately filled professional listservs with beautiful thoughts about Ellen, recollections of her scholarly contributions, kindnesses, generosity, support, and encouragement of others.

If ever there was an academic that was loved by her peers, it was Ellen. This special volume of the *International Journal of Inclusive Education* is a fitting testimony to commemorate her stature in the field of education. As her peers, we will be forever grateful to have known her. Most importantly, we will continue to take heart and draw courage from Ellen's example in how she lived life.

Thank you, Ellen, for showing so many of us the way forward.

Acknowledgement

This chapter originally appeared in *International Journal of Inclusive Education,* 17(12), 2013, 1229–1240. Reprinted here with permission from the publisher.

References

Bourdieu, P. (1984). *Distinction: A social critique of the judgment of taste.* Cambridge, MA: Harvard University Press.

Brantlinger, E. (1987). Making decisions about special education placement: Do low income parents have the information they need? *Journal of Learning Disabilities,* 20(2), 95–101.

Brantlinger, E. (1995). *Sterilization of people with mental disabilities: Issues, perspectives, and cases.* Westport, CT: Auburn House.

Brantlinger, E. (1996). The influence of preservice teachers' beliefs about pupil achievement on attitudes toward inclusion. *Teacher Education and Special Education,* 19(1), 17–33.

Brantlinger, E. (1997). Using ideologies: Cases of non-recognition in the politics if research and practice in special education. *Review of Educational Research, 67*(4), 14–22.

Brantlinger, E. (1999). Inward gaze and activism as moral next steps in inquiry. *Anthropology & Education Quarterly, 30*(4), 413–429.

Brantlinger, E. (2003). *Dividing classes: How the middle class negotiates and rationalizes school advantage.* New York, NY: Routledge Falmer.

Brantlinger, E. (2004). Confounding the needs and confronting the norms: An extension of Reid & Valle's essay. *Journal of Learning Disabilities, 37*(6), 490–499.

Brantlinger, E. (Ed.). (2006a). *Who benefits from special education? Remediating (fixing) other people's children.* Mahwah, NJ: Erlbaum.

Brantlinger, E. (2006b). The big glossies: How textbooks structure (special) education. In E. Brantlinger (Ed.), *Who benefits from special education?: Remediating (fixing) other people's children* (pp. 45–75). Mahwah, NJ: Lawrence Erlbaum.

Brantlinger, E. (2006c). Winners need losers: The basis for school competition and hierarchies. In E. Brantlinger (Ed.), *Who benefits from special education?: Remediating (fixing) other people's children* (pp. 197–231). Mahwah, NJ: Lawrence Erlbaum.

Connor, D. J. (2005). Studying disability and disability studies: Shifting paradigms of LD – A synthesis of responses to Reid and Valle. *Journal of Learning Disabilities, 38*(2), 159–174.

Danforth, S. (1997). On what basis hope? Modern progress and postmodern possibilities. *Mental Retardation, 35*(2), 93–106.

Danforth, S., & Rhodes, W. (1997). Desconstructing disability: A philosophy for inclusion. *Remedial and Special Education, 18*(6), 357–366.

Delpit, L. (1995). *Other people's children: Cultural conflict in the classroom.* New York, NY: New York Press.

Ferguson, P., Ferguson, D., & Taylor, S. (Eds.). (1991). *Interpreting disability: A qualitative reader.* New York, NY: Teachers College Press.

Gabel, S. L. (2001). "I wash my face with dirty water": Narratives of disability and pedagogy. *Journal of Teacher Education, 52*(1), 31–47.

Gallagher, D. J. (1998). The scientific knowledge base of special education: Do we know what we think we know? *Exceptional Children, 64*(4), 493–502.

Gramsci, A. (1971). *Selection from the prison notebooks* (Q. Hoare & G. N. Smith, Trans.). New York, NY: International Publishers. (Original work published in 1929–1935)

Habermas, J. (1978). *Knowledge and human interests* (2nd ed., J. Shapiro, Trans.). London: Heinemann. (Original work published in 1971)

Hale, C. (2011). *From exclusivity to exclusion: The LD experience of privileged parents.* Rotterdam, The Netherlands: Sense Publishers.

Kauffman, J. M. (1999). Commentary: Today's special education and its messages for tomorrow. *Journal of Special Education, 32*(4), 244–254.

Kauffman, J. M., & Sasso, G. M. (2006). Certainty, doubt, and the reduction of uncertainty. *Exceptionality, 14*(2), 109–120.

Lipsky, D. K., & Gartner, A. (1996). Equity requires inclusion. The future for all students with disabilities. In C. Christensen & F. Rizvi (Eds.), *Disability and the dilemmas of education and justice* (pp. 144–155). Philadelphia, PA: Open University Press.

Reid, D. K., & Valle, J. (2004). The discursive practice of learning disability: Implication for instruction and parent school relations. *Journal of Learning Disabilities, 37*(6), 466–481.

Schmidt, J. (2000). *Disciplined minds: A critical look at salaried professionals and the soul-battering system that shapes their lives.* Lanham, MD: Rowman & Littlefield.

Silberman, C. (1971). *Crisis in the classroom.* New York, NY: Vintage.

Ware, L. (Ed.). (2004). *Ideology and the politics of (in)exclusion.* New York, NY: Peter Lang.

CHAPTER 2

Including Ideology

Julie Allan

Abstract

This chapter explores Ellen Brantlinger's seminal work on ideology, *Using ideology: Cases of nonrecognition of the politics of research and practice in special education* (Brantlinger, 1997). The author examines its significance for inclusive education research and practice by drawing attention to the central role of ideology in research. The non-rational nature of the faux paradigm wars, particularly virulent in the United States, is considered, along with Ellen's own reflections on these, offered in an interview undertaken for a book, *Researching the researchers* (Allan & Slee, 2008). A discussion is offered of the impact of research, again accompanied by Ellen's perspective on the particular power of local impact. The paper ends with some tentative propositions about working with ideology. These propositions, drawing on Ellen's scholarship, will seek to elucidate an approach to apprehending not what ideology is, but what it does.

Keywords

inclusive education – disability – special education – ideology

1 Introduction

It is 'dangerous,' advised Ellen Brantlinger, 'to design or engage in inclusive practice without an understanding of its ideological roots' (Brantlinger, 1997, p. 11). This wise counsel has, however, gone unheeded by some researchers who have both failed to recognise ideology at play in their own work in special education and who have used it as a weapon to attack other researchers and denounce their work on inclusive education as *merely ideological*. This paper considers Ellen Brantlinger's seminal work on ideology, *Using ideology: Cases of nonrecognition of the politics of research and practice in special education* (Brantlinger, 1997) and examines its significance for inclusive education research and practice. The non-rational nature of the faux paradigm wars,

© TAYLOR & FRANCIS, 2013 | DOI:10.1163/9789004402690_003

INCLUDING IDEOLOGY 29

particularly virulent in the United States, is considered, along with Ellen's own reflections on these, offered in an interview undertaken for a book, *Researching the researchers* (Allan & Slee, 2008) and a discussion is offered of the impact of research, again accompanied by Ellen's perspective on the particular power of local impact. The paper ends with some tentative propositions about working with ideology. These propositions, drawing on Ellen's scholarship, will seek to elucidate an approach to apprehending not what ideology is, but what it does. In so doing, I hope to enable and encourage further analysis of ideology and its effects in inclusive education, a project that Ellen accorded great significance to.

2   Knowing Ideology

Ellen Brantlinger's article, *Using ideology*, published in 1997, provided a powerful analysis of the centrality of ideology within the fields of inclusive and special education, arguing that those who try to insist their research is ideology free are somewhat misguided: 'Like the poor, ideology is always with us' (Eagleton, 1994, p. 220). Brantlinger understood ideology as systems of representation which unconsciously mediate people's understanding of the world and which are intertwined with other discourses, such as religion and science, in ways that make them seem respectable (Althusser, 1976; Thompson, 1984). It works through its believers to validate particular 'truths' and deny others and Brantlinger cited Boudon's (1994) example of how this works in relation to the 'egalitarian myth' in the US, whereby societal stratification is masked and the interests of the middle classes are protected. She accepted the arguments of Geertz (1973) and Stanley (1992) that ideology 'saturates' (Brantlinger, 1997, p. 16) institutions and becomes part of their lives while actively reproducing itself and understood that this is why institutions such as schooling remain relatively stable, without challenges to the existing order, and why reforms fail. Brantlinger's affirmation of the centrality of ideology has been been endorsed by others (Ballard, 2004; Sikes et al., 2003; Slee, 2004). Indeed Ballard (2004, p. 90) names and claims his own slogan 'only ideology matters' in the hope that he can persuade us to 'identify, analyse, and evaluate the ethical and social implications of the ideologies that guide our research and our actions in policy and practice' (ibid.). Ballard and McDonald (1999, p. 114) also proclaim the importance of working 'with the emotions of engagement necessary for collaborative research,' asserting that research, if it is to be inclusive, requires that the researchers care, even passionately, to know people and things. So it must be ideological.

Ideology, however, by its very nature, is difficult to discern, has a number of 'loose and bewildering connections' (Brantlinger, 1997, p. 19) and is used theoretically in different ways. Furthermore, our efforts to apprehend ideology, which appear to be irresistible, take us further into the 'trap that makes us slide into ideology under the guise of stepping out of it' (Zizek, 1994, p. 17). Eagleton (1994) reminds us of the murky, devious nature of ideology even though, of course, he also guides us away from seeking to know ideology *in its essence*:

> Ideology is a realm of contestation and negotiation, in which there is a constant busy traffic: meaning and values are stolen, transformed, appropriated across the frontiers of different classes and groups, surrendered, repossessed, reinflected. (p. 187)

It is the very act of seeking to know ideology, through unmasking, exposing or other 'hermeneutics of suspicion' (Ricouer, quoted in Eagleton, 1994, p. 194) that takes us further into it (Allan, 2004) and into a dangerous situation in which 'any criticism of another's views as ideological is always susceptible to a swift *tu quoque*. In pulling the rug out from beneath one's intellectual antagonist, one is always in danger of pulling it out from beneath oneself' (Eagleton, 1994, p. 193). Brantlinger's orientation to 'doing' ideology involved the critique of ideological practices which was strongly influenced by Thompson's (1990) modes of ideological operations and strategies of symbolic construction. This enabled her to analyse how the special educationists, or traditionalists as she called them, engaged in:

> (a) reifying disability categories and naturalizing services, (b) believing the meritocratic creed, (c) allowing bias to remain invisible, (d) creating a shared identity, (e) constructing standard-bearer status, (f) touting a neutral science, (g) recalling an ideal past, (h) recognizing contaminating opponents, (i) foretelling an endangered field, (j) portraying personal victimization, and (k) undermining inclusion with cynicism.

In offering this analysis, Brantlinger emphasised that ideological practices were not specific to this group but that ideology was in all of our work and thought.

For researchers entering the field of inclusive or special education, there is little guidance in how to go about understanding ideology. Generic research books deny both the intensely political aspect of educational research and the interwoven nature of theory, philosophy, practices and material realities (Kuhn, 1970; Schostak, 2002; Punch, 2005). The failure to acknowledge and

INCLUDING IDEOLOGY

engage with these interactions mean that students part with their cash in the hope of gaining meaningful advice and instead find themselves unable to cope with the series of 'derailments' (Schostak, 2002, p. 5) that their research presents and enter the 'logical graveyard where sense and nonsense fuse and meanings are loosened from their anchorage in master narratives' (ibid.). As a consequence, research students struggle to orient themselves and to interpret the political context in which inclusive education functions.

Ellen Brantlinger was one of 12 key scholars interviewed for *Researching the researchers,* a study which I undertook with Roger Slee with the aim of 'lifting the lid' on research within this field and of uncovering some of its messiness and incoherence. We identified one text by each scholar which we had determined as influential in the field and asked them to talk through the research associated with it from its initial conceptualisation through to impact. The text we identified in respect of Ellen was *Dividing classes: How the middle class negotiates and justifies school advantage* (Brantlinger, 2003). Some of the quotations below, from the interview with Ellen, have been reproduced in *Researching the researchers* and some are directly from the interview.

We were particularly interested in the question of ideology and asked each of our interviewees: 'Research in inclusive education has been contested on the basis of a perceived ideological purpose. What do you make of such a challenge?' (Allan & Slee, 2008, p. 18). Ellen's response to this question was forthright, stating that her work was inevitably ideological because of its concern with inequality and injustice, a position echoed by many of the respondents, including Mike Oliver, Len Barton, David Gillbourn and Deborah Youdell. Ideology, for Ellen and for each of these scholars was crucial for understanding how 'meaning in the service of power' (Thompson, 1984, p. 7) disadvantages particular individuals and groups while serving the interests of others.

3   Being (in) Ideology: The Faux Paradigm Wars

Ellen Brantlinger, in *Using ideology,* highlighted the way in which ideology has been used as a weapon by special educationists to attack those advocating inclusion and demonstrated that the position adopted by those special educators embroiled in the paradigm wars (e.g. Kavale & Mostert, 2004; Kaufmann & Sasso, 2006a, 2006b), that their research was ideology-neutral or at least that their ideology was benign with regards to children, was ridiculous. She drew attention to the non-rational way in which accusations of being ideological were made by a series of special education researchers, levelled at researchers—at individuals rather than at their work—in the field of inclusive education. As Dave Gillbourn has observed, the accusation of being ideological is deeply pejorative: 'It's only ever an insult. Ideology is only ever an insult' (Allan & Slee, 2008, p. 53). Ellen took on the traditional special educationists on the basis of their accusations about ideology, making the point that all educational research is ideological, but confessed to being puzzled that values are considered problematic (Brantlinger, 2004a) and that people 'scoff at those who stress the need to base practice on clarified values' (Brantlinger, 2004b, p. 14). She also expressed some anxiety, however, that the act of critiquing ideology could 'seem like more left-wing web-spinning in the ivory tower' (Brantlinger, 2004b, p. 11).

Ellen Brantlinger's *Using ideology* paper is particularly helpful for novice and experienced researchers alike as it demonstrates that while levelling the charge at the inclusionists that ideological positioning is a vehicle that barely conceals flawed research methods, the traditional special educationists fall short, in their presentation of data and its analysis, of their own protocols and research requirements. In other words, not only do they not recognize that their position is deeply ideological and that research choices are epistemic; they also fail to meet the standards of rigour they seek from others. She enlists the Australian education researcher Dunkin (1996) to delineate the flaws and then systematically illustrates those errors in the work of prominent traditional special educationists. For researchers in inclusive education, Dunkin's article remains a foundational text and a guide to research conduct as Brantlinger's comment highlights:

> Yet some of these authors go beyond typical position-paper practice and provide prime examples of the flaws delineated in Dunkin's (1996) article *Types of Errors in Synthesizing Research in Education*. These include the exclusion of relevant literature, unexplained selectivity of sources, lack of discrimination between sources, wrongly reporting details, erroneously summarizing positions and suppressing contrary findings, and stating unwarranted conclusions and generalizations. Dunkin warns that because readers cannot be expected to check the validity of claims by going to original sources, the trustworthiness of a synthesis becomes suspect when errors are discovered in it. The potential impact of fallacious renderings seems especially harmful when they are done by authors so prominent in the field. (Brantlinger, 1997, p. 431)

Several scholars have endorsed Brantlinger's critique of the special educationists' fallacious claims of the non-ideological basis of their research and have further highlighted the problematic nature of special education research which takes up the discourse of science (Gallagher, 1998; Reid, 2001; Ware, 2004). Such research, they argue, 'obfuscates more than it enlightens' (Gallagher, 1998, as cited in Dudley-Marling & Gurn, 2012, p. 1028) and what presents as rigour, for example through matched sampling and randomised control, has the effect of removing important variation between individuals relating to factors such as ethnicity and race. The irony that while special education emerged in order to serve individuals, the particular approach to scientific research which dominates, reduces and excludes individual differences, has not been lost (Dudley-Marling & Gurn, 2012).

4　Doing Ideology: Research with Purpose

Ellen Brantlinger was exemplary in having a clear ideological purpose in her research, wanting 'true inclusion' and thinking such a scenario entirely possible:

> Where nobody knows who the Special Ed teacher is. If a kid has a need, everybody understands that they have a need—the kid too—and ask for the help and it's all done in a generous and non-stigmatising way and so—I think we could train people to do it that way. Now unfortunately the textbooks weren't doing that. So everybody had a textbook for all these intro courses. We had categorical courses, which I tried to change and we had to deal with certain state regulations. I always said, you don't have to teach it. It can't work. This is just kids with problems. (Allan & Slee, 2008, p. 60)

Ellen saw the purpose of her research as not to get rid of the special education system entirely, but to challenge the way in which its existence made it so simple to label and exclude children. She advocated change towards inclusive education which recognised the need to support the teacher and not just the student:

> I really love the inclusion model where people co-taught or shared ideas—where everything is, let's think about what a kid needs in a social situation, whether it's someone being bullied or whether it's somebody with autism or whatever. So unlike some people who totally want to get rid of a whole separate teacher-ed program, I thought given the nature

of schools, if we do it right from a disability studies perspective, to say this is the context and these are the needs that are created and these are the—actually these are the ways kids are born and it's hard for certain teachers to deal with the kids that are very very adverse So how can we support that so the kid doesn't need to be shuffled into an institution or segregated setting. (Interview)

One of the significant challenges to achieving inclusive education, as Ellen saw it, came from the dominance of special education and this was particularly evident in the textbooks available to teacher educators—'the big glossies' (Brantlinger, 2006, p. 45). These have an unreflexive ideological orientation towards special education and the labelling of children and function, according to Ellen (Brantlinger, 2006, p. 67), as 'authoritative purveyors of technical knowledge,' reinforcing expectations of beginning teachers that children's difference has to be *managed* (Brantlinger, 2006; Sleeter, 1987). The segmented way of presenting particular 'conditions' within the texts and the absence of any regard for the intersections of disability with class, race, gender, sexuality or any other aspect of diversity inevitably limits student teachers' understanding and sense of capability (Connor, 2006; Lewis & Armstrong, 2011). Furthermore, the realities presented in the special education textbooks bear little resemblance to the children whom the student teachers encounter and the certainty that they command makes them irresponsible (Allan & Slee, 2008; Brantlinger, 2006).

Ellen, as she progressed in her research for *Dividing classes*, the text which was the focus of our interview in *Researching the researchers,* found inequalities increasingly evident and this in turn had strengthened her resolve to examine and bring these to public attention. She found the experience of interviewing low-income parents surprising and the study grew in depth and in detail as a result:

> And so I went door to door in trailer parks, subsidized housing, and residential areas with houses with outdoor plumbing and no foundations and I interviewed 36 low income parents. As I did those interviews, I got very interested in all the pain they recalled when they told about their own school experiences or their children's education. I was interested in how they constructed the high income people as 'snobs' and 'well-to-do' people, how they narrated various praise for affluent people's intelligence and the fact that they could make it in to the high groups and so forth. But they also expressed real resentment about all of the advantages they witnessed these others receiving. And they talked and talked and talked.

INCLUDING IDEOLOGY

> It turned out to be a big study and I published about 5 or 6 articles based on that data. (Interview)

It was Ellen's growing concern about the injustice that she was uncovering that drove her to seek out a better understanding of ideology and she found inspiration from the UK sociologist, John Thompson (1984, 1990):

> I got very interested in ideology ... I was actually just looking up ideology and not really being interested in it and then started to read the Special Ed journals in a whole different light ... nobody else seems to refer to John Thompson's idea of ideology. Everyone turns to Basil Bernstein and Bourdieu and Foucault but I think [Thompson's] notion of how ideology works is fascinating and it worked beautifully in that paper. (Interview)

Ellen's reading of Thompson's work seemed to both open her eyes and affirm the kinds of analyses of class that she had already been undertaking:

> I was really enraptured with John Thompson's stuff. It stuck with me in a way that I didn't want to leave it with using ideology and as I began to do those interviews with high income—I already knew I was going to deconstruct their discourse because I had been sitting at dinner parties doing it with my friends for years. I mean what are they saying about low-income kids? How are they constructing low-income kids as different? You know, what is the eugenics thinking around all of this, you know of superior races and inferior races and so forth. So I've been doing that kind of deconstruction and then the theory match. So as you read it, as you read the theory, you say, oh ahaa! This is what's happening here. (Interview)

John Thompson's 'stuff,' that so enraptured Brantlinger, was, as previously indicated a systematic framework for critiquing the ideological practices and this enabled her to begin to see how meaning is mobilized to establish and sustain relations of domination (Thompson, 1990), how these relations are systematically assymetrical and how the power of the dominant is inaccessible to some. For Brantlinger, the stakes, in bringing ideology into presence in her writing, were high because of the potential damage done within the field of special education through a misrecognition of ideology, that is a failure to apprehend its potency within one's own context, whilst simultaneously claiming its malevolent presence elsewhere:

So I think in terms of when you're trying to look at a field like Special Education and understand the damage it does to people, the field has sort of proliferated, solidified and there's where ideology comes in again … it also changes people's thinking about—yeah, there are people with disabilities and this is—more and more—I mean now that anybody who is too active has got ADHD and you know, so that idea of using that medical deficit model more and more, for more and more kinds of kids and more and more situations. (Interview)

Brantlinger, in the discussion above, was challenging the medical deficit model of disability, particularly in relation to Attention Deficit Hyperactivity Disorder, a category which has captured a new segment of the student population. She was clear that the impact upon parents, often in disadvantaged contexts, who were made to believe that their child had a medicalised condition, was an ideological effect and an exercise of power on the powerless.

Ideological work is often done through writing and Ellen aligned herself with other academics who cherished writing for enabling her to be 'constantly interrogating, questioning and challenging how context and thinking presents real problems for a certain segment of the population that is pretty powerless' (Interview). In his essay, *Why I write,* George Orwell (1946) listed four reasons: sheer egoism, aesthetic enthusiasm, historical impulse and political purpose. In elaborating on the last of these, Orwell described:

> [a] desire to push the world in a certain direction, to alter other peoples' idea of the kind of society that they should strive after. Once again, no book is genuinely free from political bias. The opinion that art should have nothing to do with politics is itself a political attitude.

In *Using Ideology,* Ellen was making a similar point to Orwell in arguing that any claim to be ideologically neutral was itself an ideological position and this argument, together with an affirmation of the importance of declaring this in one's writing, was also made emphatically by Mike Oliver in his interview for the book, *Doing inclusive education research* (Allan & Slee, 2008, p. 58).

> I think if we see, and I want to see, research as an activity that is going to produce useful and meaningful social change, then one of the first things that we do is we state our ideological position up front in that research rather than somehow try to pretend that we don't have an ideological position. Saying that I don't have an ideological position is in fact an

ideological position. Even Marx knew that and even two hundred years later it's bizarre that most people don't recognize that. But they don't and that's the sad thing.

Whilst positionality is a key element in considerations of ideology, and concerns acknowledgement of one's own values, beliefs and even emotions, Ellen was most interested in what ideological critique enabled her to understand about the positions and practices of others. Nevertheless, Ellen expressed a commitment to being transparent about her own positionality and indicated that she worked this out through her writing. She described her writing as being primarily for herself, enabling her to work out her positionality, almost as the kind of experience of *askesis* that Foucault describes:

It does this by inventing the world anew—creating new kinds of relationships, new practices, asigning new meanings to old practices and relations. Thought reimagines the purposes and possibilities the world offers. It is a response but not a solution. Rather, thinking is the activity that opens up a problem and prepares the conditions for many possible solutions to it. Thought as the work of problematizing, is what opens up the dimension of the possible. (McGushin, 2007, p. 16)

The writing process for Ellen was also highly transgessive, in the sense of breaking rules or crossing lines of what is normally expected. This was especially the case in her book *Dividing classes*, and she described with some pleasure how she broke the rules of writing, yet found her way and her voice and produced a book which satisfied the reviewers and the publishers:

It's interesting to me because, maybe it's just the maturity as a scholar that I was able to put the pieces together—even though I thought of it as my least coherent book because the chapters and the end and the beginning are not ... done in a way that I would guide somebody who's doing a dissertation. I usually say something like you go through the chapters then you look back and go through it again to make sure everything is coherent and consistent. I sort of broke those rules and so I was thinking this thought that the book is going to be panned. So, actually when it came back from the reviewers ... when the galleys came back and I didn't have to make changes, I was amazed [laughter]. (Interview)

Ellen relished the transgressive effects of her writing, which provided a poke in the eye to its readers and an uncertainty about how to react to it.

5 Making a Difference

Ellen was clear about the substantial impact of her research, particularly locally:

> My research and writing have had a local impact. In some ways everything is kind of the same, but in many ways but at least the blatant discriminatory policies are not there ... they've changed a lot of things on the basis of the data that I have reported. (Interview)

The examples she gave were of the impact of an unpublished paper which she gave to administrators. It included changes in the policy of teacher transfers, making it impossible for weak teachers to be given involuntary transfers to low income schools, and permanent positions for principals and full time librarians in low income schools. As Ellen pointed out, these were 'major changes.' The paper had also led indirectly to the firing of the district superintendent:

> I gave it to all of the administrators in the district and the reaction to that—well it was very interesting because the superintendent at the time was terrible—that was one who just catered to high-income—he got fired. Now he got fired, not because, I don't think directly because of my paper but I think there were a lot of school board members who were concerned about class issues and the financial situation in the district. He had new schools built in high-income areas, then because of under-enrolment at other schools, they shut many down so many in the community were angry at him about school closings. The real issue that caused him to be fired was financial dealings. They found out there was money changing hands in the bidding process for land purchase and construction. (Allan & Slee, 2008, p. 87)

The local nature of her research had made it impossible to preserve the anonymity of the subjects but she was unapologetic about revealing the identities of the senior administrators in one of her papers:

> I think I cover about five superintendents in there and one of them was way back and he's the one that I had the most friction with about class issues—and I portray him terribly. And he deserved every bit of it (laughter). I didn't care about that—and everybody—you know, the thing is that when you do a study in a town, everybody knows who you are talking about. (Interview)

INCLUDING IDEOLOGY   39

As a result of her research, Ellen had become the individual whom journalists always called whenever there was an issue concerning social class:

> In terms of the results of this activism, I actually got quite a bit done in my time but I had different reactions from all of these local people— some were just hostility. These people conveyed that attitude that it was rude to bring up social class. You know, their reaction was shut the door on that darn lady. Punish her. Don't let her kids get on the bus. They actually put the bus zone on the other side of my alley and the neighbours were mad at me. I told them let's just go to the bus stop on the first day of school and put our kids on. The bus driver never said a thing. So that solved that. (Allan & Slee, 2008, p. 87)

These transgressive acts were, for Ellen, a way of life, something which she had learned from her parents. They had inculcated in her a strong belief in social justice and had modelled behaviour which set out to right wrongs and she said she had watched these same values and practices being adopted by her son, Andy, with extreme pride. As Foucault (1987) suggests, trangressive practices eventually become unconscious and Ellen offered confirmation of this:

> The other thing about my writing is people often say 'can you tone it down?' And I say 'can you be more specific?' [laughter]. I have no idea what's so radical. I don't know where I crossed the line. (Interview)

A key concern of Brantlinger was to try to bring considerations of ideology into the public domain by using accessible language:

> When they put me in the paper, I talk about myths people have. I don't tend to use the word "ideology." I do talk about the American dream and the myth of the American dream or the myth of meritocracy, that actually people with merit will rise to the top, so those will actually be in the paper. ... I try to make it be accessible. If I use the word meritocracy, I will give a short definition. (Interview)

This, for Ellen, meant, not exposing ideology but making the public, parents, and school board members look beneath what was being claimed and, guided by John Thompson's notion of ideology, scrutinising the language used:

> It ... worked beautifully with the high-income parents. How do they use language and rhetoric to put things one way while they're actually

meaning another? You know if you look at school boards, they'll say, we want to serve all children which means—whenever they say that in my town, it means they're going to start putting layers and layers of gifted and talented classes for the high income kids and who cares about those children, they're getting Special Ed. ... I think, not in any sophisticated way or in any theoretical way I have gotten people to think about ideology. (Interview)

She had also achieved this with her own students, insisting that her students understood how 'rhetoric [is] being used to disguise real desires' (Interview).

6 Working with Ideology

You can't believe the things that people will tell me and it may be the way that I am. Somebody said, 'you're like a St. Bernard dog out there to rescue everybody.' You know how it is you come across—I don't know and part of it is I think when I deal with people who have had—who have been oppressed in some way, whether it is on gender grounds, or race or social class. I'm very empathetic and I think it comes across in my face and I found ... with teachers, I got better responses from the interviews myself because I think I was coming across with the right nods and I think it was true that the interviewer makes a difference. I think I would identify with what they were feeling. It was a process that worked very well for me and I've done zillions of interviews and really enjoy the process. ... I think it's that outsider status that makes me curious about what makes other people work. What are they thinking? And why is it when somebody is terribly homophobic, where did that come from? ... I needed to know what went on in their heads. So that's what I really loved. I really loved getting to know people and interviews are about the only way to do it and so it worked for me. It worked because I got things published. (Interview)

This extended extract from the interview with Ellen for *Researching the researchers* underlines the central role of ideology in inclusive education research and shows emphatically how the practice of researching in this field involves a high level of intensity and personal engagement. In short, Ellen understood that her own capacity to convey her recognition of the struggles against inequality and exclusion, or perhaps her refusal to hide this, was instrumental in gaining greater insight into the very nature of these struggles and their consequences.

INCLUDING IDEOLOGY   41

The image of Ellen Brantlinger as a St Bernard Dog is rather charming but is also poignant, given the strength of the 'rescue' she offers those pursuing research in the field of education research. These take the form of recommended orientations to the 'fact' of ideology and its 'vicissitudes' (Eagleton, 1994, p. 179) and are set out below.

6.1 Recognising that Inclusive Education Is Ideological: And Therein Lies Its Potential

As Slee (2004, p. 56) reminds us 'inclusion speaks to a fragmented, unruly, and discontinuous world—a world receptive to remaking and rediscovery.' The explicitly ideological nature of inclusive education research mandates it—or rather the researchers who engage in it—to act upon the inequalities and exclusion that are uncovered. This is particularly necessary in contemporary contexts, in which ideological practices become even more subtle and all the more embedded in 'rational' economic and social thought (Galbraith, 1992; Ballard, 2004). Ideological critique is a fundamental weapon against the 'power of ideas for evil and the danger of letting a certain style of discourse go unchallenged (St. John, 1995, p. 5). Ellen Brantlinger advises, simply, that we do 'transformative work' (2004, p. 25) and in order to achieve this 'identify the political and personal agendas that our research is likely to serve' (p. 25). Her work succeeded in being transformative by exposing the complex and sophisticated ways in which education systems—and the people in them—created and maintained disadvantage and by presenting this in an accessible—and unassailable—way.

6.2 Accepting the Impossibility of Exposing Ideology: And Concentrating Instead on What Ideology Does

Ellen Brantlinger advocates using ideological critique as a tool for discerning both detrimental and beneficial ideologies and examining the consequences of these for individuals and communities. At the same time she urges recognition that ideological critique itself is implicated. Brantlinger calls for scholars to provide leadership in working with communities to articulate the kinds of values that are associated with inclusive lives as well as exposing the values that lead to exclusion of particular individuals and communities. In this regard, Ellen envisaged the notion of ideology as particularly relevant for non-western societies in order to 'untangle the racist and ablest policies of common schools' (Brantlinger, 2006, p. x) and warmly endorsed work of this kind undertaken by Erevelles et al. (2006). Ellen herself set the highest example of such work with the kind of ideological critique that demonstrated what people said and did and tracked the effects of these, and was an exemplary leader within her own community.

6.3 Acknowledging the Importance of Personal Narrative: At Least to Oneself

Ellen advises us to 'direct our gaze inward at ourselves and upward at those in charge, in control, in dominance (i.e., those with power) (Brantlinger, 2004b, p. 25) and in so doing advocates a positional kind of reflexivity. This appears to involve looking at oneself in order to see what has to be done and then looking to whoever can help to do it. Whilst Ellen saw this kind of positionality as secondary to the exercise of ideological critique she was adamant that we should never seek the moral high ground and should always be mindful of our own saturation—that we are always *in ideology*.

6.4 Avoiding the 'Turf Wars': But Realising the Inevitability of Being Caught up in These

Ellen, in taking up the discussion of ideology, provided an important contribution to the field but also intensified the issue for some individuals. The personalised nature of some of the subsequent battles remains perplexing and inevitably detract from considerations of how to optimise the educational experiences of all children. Ellen reminds us, following Thompson (1990, p. 7), that ideology is always concerned with 'meaning in the service of power' and the struggle for inclusive education inevitably involves taking on those exercising power through meaning and upon particular individuals. Ellen, in her *Using ideology* paper, took on the big boys, who might be seen as bullies, on behalf of all of us. It did not stop their behaviour, and indeed they have gone on to denounce other, equally eminent, scholars but Ellen's intervention provided us with a way of reading the accusations levelled at 'inclusionists' as both seeking to deploy power and inept.

Ellen's passion for social justice and inclusion, combined with her remorseless and incisive critique of ideology provides both an inspiration to undertake research in inclusive education and an exemplary model of how to *be* inclusive in one's research.

Acknowledgement

This chapter originally appeared in *International Journal of Inclusive Education, 17*(12), 2013, 1241–1252. Reprinted here with permission from the publisher.

References

Allan, J. (2004). The aesthetics of disability as productive ideology. In L. Ware (Ed.), *Ideology and the politics of in/exclusion*. New York, NY: Peter Lang.

Allan, J., & Slee, R. (2008). *Doing inclusive education research*. Rotterdam, The Netherlands: Sense Publishers.

Althusser, L. (1976). *Essays in self-criticism* (G. Lock, Trans.). London: New Left Books.

Ballard, K. (2004). Ideology and the origins of exclusion: A case study. In *Ideology and the politics of in/exclusion* (L. Ware, Ed.). New York, NY: Peter Lang.

Ballard, K., & McDonald, T. (1999). Disability, inclusion and exclusion: Insider accounts and interpretations. In K. Ballard (Ed.), *Inclusive education: International voices on disability and justice*. London: Falmer.

Boudon, R. (1994). *The art of self-persuasion: The social explanation of false beliefs* (M. Slater, Trans.). Cambridge: Polity Press. (Original work published in 1990)

Brantlinger, E. (1997). Using ideology: Cases of nonrecognition of the politics of research and practice in special education. *Review of Educational Research, 67*(4), 425–459.

Brantlinger, E. (2003). *Dividing classes: How the middle class negotiates and justifies school advantage*. New York, NY: Routledge.

Brantlinger, E. (2004a). Confounding the needs and confronting the norms: An extension of Reid and Valle's essay. *Journal of Learning Disabilities, 37*(6), 490–499.

Brantlinger, E. (2004b). Ideologies discerned, values determined: Getting past the hierarchies of special education. In L. Ware (Ed.), *Ideology and the politics of in/exclusion*. New York, NY: Peter Lang.

Brantlinger, E. (2006). The big glossies: How textbooks structure (special) education. In E. Brantlinger (Ed.), *Who benefits from special education? Remediating (fixing) other people's children*. Mahwah, NJ: Lawrence Erlbaum.

Connor, D. (2006). Not so strange bedfellows: The promise of disability studies and critical race theory. In S. Gabel & S. Danforth (Ed.), *Disability & the politics of education: An international reader*. New York, NY: Peter Lang.

Dudley-Marling, M., & Gurn, A. (2012). Towards a more inclusive approach to intervention research: The case of research in learning disabilities. *International Journal of Inclusive Education, 16*(10), 1019–1032.

Dunkin, M. (1996). Types of errors in synthesizing research in education. *Review of Educational Research, 66*(2), 87.

Eagleton, T. (1994). Ideology and its vicissitudes in Western Marxism. In S. Zizek (Ed.), *Mapping ideology*. London: Verso.

Erevelles, N., Kanga, A., & Middleton, R. (2006). How does it feel to be a problem? Race, disability and exclusion in educational policy. In E. Brantlinger (Ed.), *Who benefits from special education? Remediating (fixing) other people's children.* Mahwah, NJ: Lawrence Erlbaum.

Foucault, M. (1987). *Death and the labrynth: The world of Raymond Roussel* (C. Ruas, Trans.). Berkeley, CA: University of California Press.

Galbraith, J. K. (1992). *The culture of contentment.* Harmondsworth: Penguin Books.

Gallagher, D. (1998). The scientific knowledge base of special education: Do we know what we think we know? *Exceptional Children, 64*(4), 493–502.

Geertz, C. (1973). Ideology as a cultural system. In C. Geertz (Ed.), *The interpretation of cultures* (pp. 197–207). New York, NY: Basic Books.

Kauffman, J., & Sasso, G. (2006a). Toward ending cultural and cognitive relativism in special education. *Exceptionality, 14*(2), 65–90.

Kauffman, J., & Sasso, G. (2006b). Rejoinder: Certainty, doubt and the reduction of uncertainty. *Exceptionality, 14*(2), 109–120.

Kavale, K., & Mostert, M. (2004). *The positive side of special education: Minimizing its fads, fancies and follies.* Lanham, MD: Scarecrow Education.

Kuhn, T. (1970). *The structure of scientific revolutions.* Chicago, IL: Chicago University Press.

Lewis, A., & Armstrong, A. (2011). Editorial: The intersection of gender and disability. *Review of Disability Studies, 7*(1), 3–5.

McGushin, E. (2007). *Foucault's askesis: An introduction to the philosophical life.* Evanston, IL: Northwestern University Press.

Orwell, G. (1946). *Why I write.* Retrieved from http://orwell.ru/library/essays/wiw/english/e_wiw

Punch, K. (2005). *Introduction to social research: Quantitative and qualitative approaches.* London: Sage Publications.

Reid, K. (2001). Mantague and Rinali and Meltzer, Katzir-Cohen, Miller and Roditi: A critical commentary. *Learning Disability Quarterly, 24*(2), 199–205.

Schostak, J. (2002). *Understanding, designing and conducting qualitative research in education.* Buckingham/Philadelphia: Open University Press.

Sikes, P., Nixon, J., & Carr, W. (Eds.). (2003). *The moral foundations of educational research.* Maidenhead: Open University Press.

Slee, R. (2004). Meaning in the service of power. In L. Ware (Ed.), *Ideology and the politics of in/exclusion.* New York, NY: Peter Lang.

Sleeter, C. (1987). Why is there learning disabilities? A critical analysis of the birth of the field in its social context. In T. Popkewitz (Ed.), *The formation of school subjects: The struggle for creating an American institution.* London: Falmer Press.

Stanley, W. (1992). *Curriculum for Utopia: Social reconstructionism and critical pedagogy in the postmodern era.* Albany, NY: State University at New York Press.

St. John, S. (1995). *The future of the poverty industry. Thinking about welfare in the 1990s: Liberal and conservative battle lines.* A paper prepared for the New Zealand Council of Christian Social Sciences.

Thompson, J. (1984). *Studies in the theory of ideology.* Cambridge: Polity; Berkeley, CA: University of California Press.

Thompson, J. (1990). *Ideology and modern culture: Critical social theory in the eve of mass communication.* Stanford, CA: Stanford University Press.

Ware, L. (2004). Introduction. In L. Ware (Ed.), *Ideology and the politics of (in)exclusion.* New York, NY: Peter Lang.

Zizek, S. (1994). *Mapping ideology.* London: Verso.

CHAPTER 3

Research, Relationships and Making Understanding: A Look at Brantlinger's Darla and the Value of Case Study Research

Janet Story Sauer

Abstract

This chapter examines Ellen Brantlinger and her colleague's longitudinal casestudy, *Fighting for Darla; Challenges for family care and professional responsibility* (Brantlinger, Klein, & Guskin, 1994). The author describes how this work resonated with her as the mother of a boy considered to have significant disabilities (trisomy 21) and how it informed her practice as qualitative researcher. The chapter explores the relationship between this form of methodology and the 'subjects' agency referring to her research and others in the humanities. Brantlinger's work here is historical in its documentation of the experience of a teenager Darla, a pregnant teenager with autism. Although decades have passed since the publication of this study, the complexities involved in Darla's story remain important to informing those who value the humanity of people with significant disabilities and respect their sense of agency. Finally, the possible implications for the activist researcher, such as Brantlinger, are discussed.

Keywords

significant disability – agency – sexuality – activist research – qualitative research

1 Introduction

My first encounter with Ellen Brantlinger's work was during a doctoral course in qualitative research taught by Disability Studies scholar Deb Gallagher at the University of Northern Iowa in the USA in which we read *Fighting for Darla; Challenges for family care and professional responsibility* (Brantlinger, Klein, & Guskin, 1994). My experiences as an emerging researcher and mother

© KONINKLIJKE BRILL NV, LEIDEN, 2020 | DOI:10.1163/9789004402690_004

of a child with trisomy 21 resonated with some of the comments made by those in the book detailing the account of Darla, a pregnant teenager with autism. Darla did not have use of a reliable shared form of communication and the assumptions surrounding her competence and abilities towards having a sense of agency were limited. Most of the family and caregivers expressed surprise upon learning Darla was pregnant, admitting to not having thought of her as a sexual being. Reading about the complexities involved in Darla's story forced me to re-examine my own assumptions and limited understandings. As an educator I shared the sentiments of some who felt 'uninformed' since the topic of sexuality had not been part of my own prior teacher preparation but I did not agree with those who expressed 'disgust' or 'shock'. Why wouldn't the teenaged Darla seek physical intimacy? Then again, as a parent I empathised with Darla's protective mother who feared for her daughter's safety and therefore scrutinised those hired to educate and care for Darla.

Darla's story raises important social questions. What is meant by consent for youth with disabilities who historically have been denied their sexuality? How is intentionality or agency recognised? What are reasonable limits for parents or other caregivers to both provide protection and yet offer opportunities for developing intimate relationships? Who makes these decisions? What is the impact of class and cultural capital in these situations?

When I first read about Darla's story I was unprepared to anticipate how these issues of agency, sexual identity, and privilege would play out in my own family. My son, then 15 years of age was a freshman in secondary school. In my research I have questioned the role of consent and participants' agency and related elements of risk researchers might have to take in our work (Sauer, 2012a, 2012b). Risk-taking is also required of publishers, and there are implications for those of us who hope to follow in the footsteps of the activist researcher Ellen Brantlinger.

As Brantlinger and her colleagues concluded in *Fighting for Darla*,

> It is necessary to develop an understanding not just of autism as a condition, not just of individuals with disabilities, not just of family strengths and weaknesses, but of the whole community's responsibility for caring for people in a flexible and resilient way that allows dignity and still provides support. (p. 151)

Therefore, this is not only a topic of interest for those of whom disability has a personal or professional impact – such as educators, community support providers and families, but for us all. Brantlinger et al. continue,

Perhaps to do this, each of us must first acknowledge the ways in which our own limited experiences and prejudices may blind us to realities that do not fit our accepted assumptions. Perhaps Darla's story can shock us into beginning such a quest. (p. 151)

1.1 *Darla's Agency*

In this look at Brantlinger's Darla the unique relationship between case study research methodology and agency (Giroux, 1987) is examined. The techniques of qualitative research, such as those utilised in portraiture research (Lawrence-Lightfoot, 2005), provide an opportunity to re-interpret people considered 'on the fringes of the research arena' (Lewis & Kellet, 2005, p. 198) as active agents of power who 'reconstitute their relationship with the wider society' (Giroux, 1987, p. 7). Without explicit discussion of Darla's agency per se, Brantlinger, Klein, and Guskin (1994) certainly describe the teen's actions as purposeful and, I would suggest, illustrate her sense of agency that quantitative or medically based studies would have unlikely documented. In this sense, I consider the poverty of understanding that might follow from such a narrow analysis and the meanings made of disability experience. Take for instance, the professionals' description of Darla upon visiting her at the hospital:

> Upon our arrival Darla was in bed. She took our hands and hugged us. Then she got up, grabbed our hands and led us on a 'tour' of the hospital, showing us the falls, bathrooms, and the playroom...She was smiling and happy. She glued a collage and wove a new reed/ribbon placemat. She sat on my lap and indicated that she wanted to look through a shopping bag that I had with me.... (Brantlinger et al., 1994, p. 76)

The researchers acknowledge in this description that Darla's voice is the faintest in the book, but their detailed observations and those elicited from her family and caregivers show she is 'an expressive and communicative person.' They explain,

> Her moods are evident...when she is happy she smiles, giggles, and laughs. When she is upset, she snarls, moans loudly, or pinches, scratches, and pulls hair. When Darla hurts others, she sometimes smirks. Some people interpret this as a sadistic side of Darla. Others believe it indicates that she knows more than people generally give her credit for. Still others attribute the smirk to Darla's pleasure at her power to provoke an expressive reaction from others...Darla likes to do things her own way.

RESEARCH, RELATIONSHIPS AND MAKING UNDERSTANDING

> She backs off if someone tries to teach her something new. She will strike out or fall prone to the floor if pressured to conform. Darla learns best by observing. (pp. 2–3)

Darla's interactions with others were carefully monitored and, one could argue, overly supervised. Darla's agency, however, is evident in how she negotiates her position within relationships. In the first excerpt above she took the lead in providing the visitor with a tour of the hospital. The second excerpt makes clear the sophistication of Darla's communication despite its unconventionality for someone her age.

What remains unclear is the extent to which Darla sought out or the nature of her response to what we learn to be her sexual relationship with her younger brother. The researchers did not have access to interview Darla's brother, and Darla was not supported in conventional forms of communication (nor did Brantlinger and her colleagues describe efforts to try to learn about Darla's perspective on the circumstances), so readers are left to speculate about their relationship. We are left with questions, some of which reach beyond Darla's sexuality to consider her efforts and others with significant disabilities to, as Giroux (1987) explains, reconstitute their relationship with the wider society.

How does a person viewed by society as less than fully human and without the ability to provide consent, negotiate intentionality? Who is prepared to acknowledge and support their agency?

Most scholarship about youth with disabilities focus on those considered to have mild disabilities or learning disabilities. The literature concerning youth with significant disabilities tends to focus on transition to employment, though more recently, a few studies examine their sexuality or the possibilities of college life (Couwenhoven, 2007; Stokes & Kaur, 2005; Tissot, 2009). There are a handful of edited collections featuring the contextualized lived experiences of adults with significant disabilities (Biklen, 2005; Ferguson, Ferguson, & Taylor, 1992; Taylor, Bogdan, & Lutfiyya, 1995). Yet, there is a dearth of current detailed ethnographic descriptive books about the daily lives of young people with significant disabilities; Linneman's (2001) study of four children and their caregivers offers a rare exception. These types of studies are most readily found in academic journals and therefore, unfortunately, much of the richness and complexity we find in Brantlinger's *Darla* is edited out. With that in mind, I provide in the following section a brief description of other young people's agency and how qualitative methodology using a longitudinal case study approach similar to that of Brantlinger and her colleagues suggests possibilities for re-interpretations rarely found in today's educational research arena.

1.2   *Agency in Educational Research*

Educational researchers have increasingly studied children's sense of agency and its relationship to status and power (Aitken, 2009; Ayton, 2012; Walters, 2011). The interest in the agency of children and how they position themselves within educational contexts has recently expanded to include students with disabilities. Although Reid and Button's (1995) study of students with learning disabilities did not use the word *agency*, they describe the importance of using Mishler's (1990) narrative inquiry process to understand the youths' experiences being labelled disabled. In an effort 'to give them voice,' the researchers provide readers with several direct quotes from the students who at times, the researchers noted, increased the volume of their expressions of isolation and feelings of oppression. They provide an interesting collaborative essay combining excerpts from their young participants starting off strong and exemplifying agency: "People call us retarded. When people call you names or tell lies about you, it makes you feel bad. We get mad" (Reid & Button, 1995, p. 609). This paper offered one of the early studies where students with disabilities directly challenged the educational structures purported to support these students.

More recently, Rosetti, Ashby, Arndt, Chadwick, and Kasahara (2008) explained the importance of recognising agency as "expressions of control, personality, and self-determination" in order to disrupt communication patterns that lead to misinterpretations of incompetency. In their interpretivist qualitative study of nine individuals with autism, they

> Conceptualize *agency* as describing the opportunity to initiate a topic or agenda, participate in a dialogue, move a conversation in a particular direction, interpret others, affect the person with whom one is in dialogue, make a point, interact as a peer, and be seen as a person with ideas to contribute and a personality to inject into the conversation. (Rosetti et al., 2008, p. 365)

One of the most prevalent ways in which their participants expressed agency was in making choices, but what the researchers noted was that opportunities for choice making must have first been created along with an expectation that the student was capable of making choices. Furthermore, the researchers described how others needed to be active listeners who might have to relinquish traditional positions of power in these negotiations. They explain how a cursory observation might otherwise interpret interactions as the teacher in this case 'being "soft" on discipline or manipulated' (p. 371). Finally, the researchers discuss how the participants' agency 'troubled traditional notions of independence' indicating that one can be dependent upon others for communication while at the same time exercise their agency.

In her qualitative study about the self-determination of four African American women with disabilities from disadvantaged backgrounds, Petersen (2009) utilises poetry to illustrate her participants' experiences. She explains how she found that despite the original intent of self-determination to provide opportunities for choice and self-advocacy, the way it has been enacted in school curricula actually *undermines* its principles. Petersen (2009) describes how 'students with disabilities are rarely provided with opportunities to exert personal agency. She refers to Brewer (2002) who asks, 'How can an educational system that tightly controls curricula and hold teachers and districts to strict accountability guidelines empower and support students in exerting personal agency?' Petersen explains this dilemma for educators, a dilemma I found equally challenging as a researcher, and as I mentioned earlier, as a parent. This tension is born out of conflicting expectations and understandings between a societal emphasis on independence and the natural interdependence often found in reciprocal meaningful relationships.

1.3   *Agency in Portraiture*

Portraiture's (Lawrence-Lightfoot, 2005) underlying 'co-constructive structure' assumes a shared active interpretation of the data, whereby the people who live in the social contexts under study additionally review the data, reflect upon it and offer their own interpretations. In contrast to case studies which tend to objectify the persons of interest, where a person is referred to as a 'case', portrait data is not restricted to the researcher alone. Instead, the data is shared with the participants, who are acknowledged for their active role in negotiating meaning and thus the typical power relationship is disrupted. In this sense, portraiture intentionally provides openings for personal transformation. Personal transformation can co-occur among the various participants, which includes the participant researcher as well. As such, this personal enlightenment of sorts can lead to social transformation. In other words, in order for social transformation to take place it is necessary for 'a critical collective of individuals[to] open their eyes to inequities and recognize that a problem exists' (Blanchett, Brantlinger, & Shealey, 2005, p. 66).

In her introductory article to an issue of *Qualitative Inquiry* dedicated to portraiture, Lawrence-Lightfoot (2005) explains how she developed this method of inquiry to fill a need she saw while studying teenagers in the early 1980's. She sought 'a text that came as close as possible to the realms of painting with words' (p. 6). Rather than objectifying the subjects of study, portraiture seeks understanding. Educational researchers subsume their traditional role as expert and negotiate meaning with the primary participants taking the context into consideration, forcing reflective thought about knowledge ownership. As is common in qualitative research, the relationship between the researcher and the participants changes over the course of time. In these terms, the researcher critically examines the social interactions with the development of her relationship with the study participants. In a critique of Lawrence-Lightfoot and Davis' (1997) text in which they outline the features and steps of portraiture methodology, Vallance (1998) questions their claim to 'have really invented a wholly new methodology', but applauds them for providing educational researchers with a reminder of the alternative and richer 'ways to understand the world than through controlled experiments and 'objective' studies that deny the special character of their subjects' (p. 70).

A few researchers have utilised portraiture in their studies of youth with 'mild' disabilities (Chapman, 2007; Connor, 2006; McNeil, 2005) where intersections with race and social class were examined and agency emerged as an important consideration. My portraiture study (Sauer, 2012b) into the complexities involved in the communication between three young people with significant disabilities and their families, teachers and service providers revealed agency in ways similar to Chapman's (2007) students in that they 'spoke to power'. I describe in detail elsewhere the agency of my three study participants and their families (Sauer, 2012a) where 17-year-old Kari asserted, 'This [study] is about me'. Initially I resisted her efforts to take control of our shared time, but I soon recognised the benefit of relinquishing that control by giving up my digital voice recorder to her. In time I gave recorders to my other participants as well and subsequently gathered unique narratives that contributed valuable understandings of their daily lives.

In part because Kari was much older than the other participants and she was both articulate and literate, she became much more of a co-contributor to the research project. In fact, she later co-presented her portrait with me at a national conference (Sauer & Fordice, 2008) and subsequently wrote the epilogue to my book about the study (Sauer, 2012b). As a participant-observer, I collected official documents, audio- and video-recordings of the participants in multiple settings that were transcribed, as well as drawings, photographs, and writings of the participants. Although Kari was readily conversant and her spoken language became more easily discernible over time, eight-year-old Marie and ten-year-old David hardly spoke. David occasionally used a voice output device but most often he either communicated using pictures or used body movements to indicate his preferences or needs. For instance, David would acknowledge my presence with a barely perceptible slide of his hand over my open palm. He would make sounds those close to him knew as expressing excitement, he hummed when seemingly content, and he jumped up and down and more rapidly and using a higher pitch sound to indicate he was agitated. His mother explained 'he communicates with behavior,' and she interpreted some of his behaviours as 'his way to protest'. Marie also used pictures, movement and tonal differences in her vocalisations to communicate, but she had greater verbal facility and unfamiliar listeners could easily understand her short phrases that were often spoken in ways that commanded attention. In school I observed a number of occasions where Marie raised her hand while saying loudly, 'Look at me!'

All three participants engaged music in interesting ways that seemed to both facilitate verbal expression and provide them with greater access for exerting their agency. In addition to music, I found the arts including drawing, storytelling and theatre as avenues to access the participants' active engagement in negotiating shared meaning. Taken together these young people seemed 'to reconstitute their relationship with the wider society' (Giroux, 1987, p. 7). I found the time spent in the field getting to know my participants, as well as a willingness to relinquish control of the process and use active listening techniques, facilitated a greater understanding of lived experiences of my participants, as well their families and others who were part of their lives that I think would have been inaccessible should I have tried to rely upon large quantifiable data sets.

In the reporting of my primary participants and their families, friends and other people in their lives, I used portraiture (Lawrence-Lightfoot & Davis, 1997). These portraits included a collection of lengthy data vignettes incorporating both spoken words and detailed descriptions (Sauer, 2012b). Admittedly less than *full* co-constructions, the three portraits based on a year-long qualitative study engaged the primary participants in ways that I hoped acknowledged their agency and thus seemed to provide a richer and more complex interpretation of the participants' lives than other methodological approaches would have offered. Portraits are rendered to 'convey the perspectives of the people who are negotiating those experiences', write Lawrence-Lightfoot and Davis (1997); they 'are shaped through dialogue between the portraitist and the subject' (p. 3). The youth's agency seemed to me as a qualitative researcher more accessible than I could imagine had I only visited them a couple of times or in only one context.

Certainly there are limitations to all research approaches and I could never claim to have fully captured the experiences of my primary participants, their families or support personnel. I also was not entering contexts as socially stigmatised as Brantlinger and her colleagues (1994) did when documenting Darla's experiences as a pregnant teenager with autism. However, I hope to have contributed to a greater understanding of the complexities involved in the lives of young people with significant disabilities. Like Brantlinger and her colleagues (1994), I am committed to making the material as accessible as possible (p. 10). As they abruptly pointed out decades ago something that remains relevant today, family members, school teachers, lawyers, doctors, students, policy planners and other people in the community need more information about people with complex support needs and opportunities to reevaluate their/our own assumptions. Although the agency of the young people I studied would not likely shock readers, I hope educators, service providers, families and others will exercise a greater awareness of how meaning and power within communication interactions is negotiated, especially among those with disabilities whose powers have already been compromised in society.

1.4 *Risk and Consent in Educational Research*

Despite the value of their research, comments in both the Forward and Acknowledgements in Brantlinger et al.'s (1994) *Darla* illustrate some of the challenges for educational researchers. The then Editor in Chief of *Exceptional Parent* magazine, Stanley Klein explains that the 'unorthodox' nature of this book made it difficult to publish. He acknowledges that 'the authors took the risk' to document what they observed and recorded from their interviews as well as the particular issues they encountered as they inquired about this socially sensitive topic. It seems even less likely today that researchers and participants – or publishers – would be willing to take the necessary risks involved with sharing stories such as Darla's. The authors note the family's willingness to forego their privacy and allow this book to disclose their very personal experiences. The researchers write,

> We are particularly grateful because we recognise that Darla's situation posed potential legal ramifications beyond their control, and, in fact, several of the professionals felt personally threatened and vulnerable in expressing their feelings or in sharing information with the authors. (Brantlinger, Klein, & Guskin, 1994, p. ix)

The process of making public the lived experiences resulting from systemic oppressive structures is risky business. Similarly, participating in self-examination as Brantlinger and her colleagues call their readers to do requires admitting to one's own limited assumptions and responsibilities as researchers, professionals, parents or community members.

In a subsequent piece, Brantlinger, Klingner, and Richardson (2005) argue for the importance of what they call 'experimental' qualitative research.

In their article that appeared in Mental Retardation, they provide several reasons for the unique ways in which these alternative forms of inquiry can contribute to a greater understanding of the needs of children and adults with disabilities. They make the case that 'empirical qualitative designs can meet the criterion of producing science- or evidence-based knowledge to inform policy and practice' (Brantlinger et al., 2005, p. 93) and offer detailed appendices for qualitative researchers to follow in order to meet the rigorous standards of quality work. While acknowledging, 'qualitative researchers still may have to work harder to get research into print' (p. 93), they explain how Glaser and Strauss' (1967) early work served the research community with an important alternative way to develop theories inductively based on the analysis of field-based data. They provide a number of qualitative studies published throughout the 1960s and 1970s that contributed to our understanding of disability where techniques included autobiographies and interviews (Edgerton, 1967; Goffman, 1963; Mattinson, 1971; Mercer, 1973), visual rhetoric (Blatt & Kaplan, 1966) and historical sources (Wolfensberger, 1972). They explain how these studies influenced policy changes, such as the deinstitutionalisation movement, that directly impacted the daily lives of people with disabilities and their families. However, in the current discourses exemplified by phrases such as 'race to the top' and *International Journal of Inclusive Education* 'non-responders to intervention', where calls for papers and funding sources emphasise quantifiable research, it seems we are neglecting the significance of qualitative research. More recently, in what they call 'the research gap', Klingner and Boardman (2011) question randomised controlled trials as 'the gold standard' and make the case for the valuable contributions of qualitative research techniques, particularly in journals whose readership is primarily those of us working with students with disabilities.

The issue of gaining consent from young participants as well as those considered significantly disabled is also challenging. The Institutional Research Boards rightfully hold researchers to strict guidelines in an effort to protect vulnerable populations from harm, but there is an interesting component to this type of work among academics where again differences of philosophy reveal fundamentally different understandings and assumptions. In other words, colleagues within my field of special education might not believe my participants have the capacity to express themselves, much less make a choice of whether or not to participate. For example, during a presentation about my study described above where I focused on the then 17-year-old Kari's agency, her consent was questioned even after I explained the process which involved her family and the fact that she had since turned 18, the age of majority, and co-presented with me at a national conference (Sauer & Fordice, 2008).

I would have understood someone questioning whether I was professionally benefitting from the presentation, but what I found distressing was that the one posing the question argued since the young woman had Down syndrome she wasn't capable of providing consent.

Snelgrove (2005) took up this issue of consent in her article *Bad, mad and sad: Developing a methodology of inclusion and a pedagogy for researching students with intellectual disabilities* where she argued for the value of repositioning the subjects as participants. She describes the process of developing 'an ethics of consent', which began with teaching the meaning of research to the participants, and how it challenged traditional consensual procedures that might have foregone direct involvement of the primary participants and instead relied solely on the parents or guardians. Snelgrove developed a 'plain language' consent form with picture symbols that met the Australian ethical requirements. However, she went beyond 'protecting the other' and implemented a series of lessons to teach vocabulary including 'research university', 'pseudonym' and 'interview'. To address concerns of coercion, Snelgrove purposefully developed lessons to encourage the students to become 'critical respondents' and therefore comfortable with choosing to decline participation. Snelgrove rightly points out how the process of gaining consent from her participants with intellectual disabilities could provide them with useful skills well beyond the study itself. Her detailed presentation of the process of informed consent serves as an exemplar for those of us interested in studying the lives of people considered to have significant disabilities.

Increasingly researchers are interested in interviewing participants considered to have intellectual disabilities (Caldwell, 2011; Nonnemacher & Bambara, 2011) where consent plays an important role in the research process. Caldwell (2011) adopted a 'life story approach' when he video- and audio–recorded 'guided conversations' with 13 elected leaders of self-advocacy groups. The video provided valuable supplemental information to the audio, which was sometimes difficult to transcribe otherwise due to the nuanced verbal expression of the participants. Caldwell met with the participants in locations of their choice, often in their homes, and provided them with copies of his prepared questions in advance in order to provide them with additional time to prepare their responses. Nonnemacher and Bambara (2011) similarly interviewed 10 adult members of self-advocacy groups to examine their perceptions of support staff efforts to facilitate their self-determination. They purposefully selected participants who were deemed to have adequate conversational skills and who had 'expressed a willingness to participate' (p. 329).

Other researchers have moved into co-authorship with people considered to have significant disabilities. Scholar Doug Biklen, for instance, co-authored

RESEARCH, RELATIONSHIPS AND MAKING UNDERSTANDING

the oft-cited piece titled *Presuming Competence* with then high-school student Jamie Burke (Biklen & Burke, 2006). Burke, 16 years old at the time and labelled autistic, echoes the sense of agency I describe in this article when he wrote, "In the ideal school I would be able to tell my thoughts and troubles when I chose, not when others desire" (p. 168). Biklen (2005) has since edited a collection of autobiographical works and produced powerful documentaries to reach a broader audience and to capitalize on the visual intricacies of communication for people with autism. One of the more notable new techniques is Paiewonsky's (2012) participatory action research where she uses digital storytelling and photovoice to co-construct the college experiences of young adults with intellectual disabilities. This interactive and accessible project is in its infancy but seems to offer intriguing possibilities that would certainly encourage Brantlinger and other researchers seeking the perspectives of youth with significant disabilities.

In the process of pursuing participants' consent, negotiations of power are undoubtedly involved and thus are not without influence. That said, we can uphold best practices within educational research when we refer to ethical guidelines, fully disclose our procedures and acknowledge the participants' competency and agency. In his article, *The participant as ally and essentialist portraiture*, Witz (2006) does not address participants with disabilities in particular, but his analysis of a more active role of participants in research methodology serves my purpose here for re-conceptualising the researcher-participant relationship. Witz's (2006) approach, "that is especially sensitive to deeper aspects in the individual" (p. 246), supports my argument for the value of portraiture, or other kinds of qualitative in-depth research like that of Brantlinger et al.'s (1994) *Darla*. An examination of the researcher–participant relationship is expanding among qualitative researchers, but certainly further study is needed particularly as it relates to those considered disabled and therefore often assumed unable to express their opinions. It is useful to keep in mind the idea Cazden (2001) put forth about the speaking rights of young people and heed her words of caution that "Teachers and researchers need to be careful not to interpret silence or one-word answers as lack of knowledge" (p. 86). As researchers, teachers, parents and support providers we have what Cazden (2001) refers to as 'listening responsibilities' that include a way of listening that encompasses careful observation and risk-taking that might disrupt traditional notions of competency.

1.5   *Discussion*

In this article I have tried to show how Brantlinger's work has provided a unique and important contribution to a body of knowledge that tackles challenging questions about consent, sexuality and agency in the lives of young people with significant disabilities. Her legacy is in part how her work supports researchers who grapple with these issues. "It is always possible for there to be different, equally valid accounts from different perspectives" asserts Maxwell (1992, p. 283). Brantlinger's *Darla* artfully illustrates the value of hearing from different perspectives and 'seeing' how disability is experienced in daily life. It is through prolonged engagement and persistent observation that qualitative methods of research contribute to our understanding of our complex social world (Glesne, 1999; Lincoln & Guba, 1985). The detailed descriptions and direct quotes Brantlinger and her colleagues (1994) used in *Darla* provided empirical data to help explain the interrelationships between disability, gender, and class.

The impact of conducting this kind of study on scholars themselves, and thus on the community at large who read their work, is unclear, but a look at some of Brantlinger's subsequent writing illustrates the depth of understanding and the level of risk she was prepared to take in her challenge of educational and service structures. For instance, in her piece published in a mainstream special education journal where she questioned the normative practices of schooling she wrote, "I have troubled entrenched customs and accused multiple agents – some in high places – of benefitting from policies, practices, and ways of thinking that harm others, particularly children who do not do well in school" (Brantlinger, 2004, p. 497). Undoubtedly there were professional consequences for what some would have viewed as threatening the very group in which she was a member.

The implications for respecting the agency of youth considered significantly disabled are messy. Questions of sexuality, intention or consent, abuse, limited 'training' of service providers and teachers, family finances and custody issues are all raised in Brantlinger, Klein, and Guskin's (1994) Darla and they are not easy or comfortable questions to ask. As noted, these studies seem to require some risk-taking on behalf of the participants and the researchers, as well as the publishers. Such important practical questions lead us to the broad social impact of limited knowledge and understanding. Brantlinger, Klein, and Guskin's (1994) *Darla* joins other historically significant studies like Goffman's (1963) *Stigma* and Edgerton's (1967) *Cloak of Competence*, which led to greater understanding and in many instances to policy changes directly influencing the material lives of people with significant disabilities in positive ways.

These historical detailed accounts of the complex interdisciplinary nature of lived experiences influenced subsequent researchers that as a whole provide empirical data that facilitates greater understanding of the impact of class, race and cultural capital on the disability experience. Two decades have passed since Brantlinger, Klein, and Guskin's (1994) study was published and yet the methodology and lessons learned remain important to informing those of us who value the humanity of people with significant disabilities and respect their sense of agency.

References

Aitken, V. (2009). Conversations with status and power: How "everyday theatre" offers "spaces of agency" to participants. *Research in Drama Education: The Journal of Applied Theatre and Performance, 14*(4), 503–27. doi:10.1080/13569780903286022

Ayton, K. (2012). Differing pupil agency in the face of adult positioning. *Ethnography and Education, 7*(1), 127–41. doi:10.1080/17457823.2012.661592

Biklen, D. (2005). *Autism and the myth of the person alone.* New York, NY: New York University Press.

Biklen, D., & Burke, J. (2006). Presuming competence. *Equity & Excellence in Education, 39*, 166–75. doi:10.1080/10665680500540376

Blanchett, W., Brantlinger, E., & Shealey, M. W. (2005). Brown 50 years later – Exclusion, segregation, and inclusion. Guest Editors' Introduction. *Remedial and Special Education, 26*(2), 66–69.

Blatt, B., & Kaplan, F. (1966). *Christmas in purgatory: A photographic essay on mental retardation.* Boston, MA: Allyn & Bacon.

Brantlinger, E. A. (2004). Confounding the needs and confronting the norms: An extension of Reid and Valle's essay. *Journal of Learning Disabilities, 37*(6), 490–499. doi:10.1177/00222194040370060301

Brantlinger, E. A., Klein, S. M., & Guskin, S. L. (1994). *Fighting for Darla; Challenges for family care and professional responsibility.* New York, NY: Teachers College Press.

Brantlinger, E. A., Klingner, J., Richardson, V., & Taylor, S. (2005). Importance of experimental as well as empirical qualitative studies in special education. *Mental Retardation, 43*(2), 92–119. http://dx.doi.org/10.1352/0047 6765(2005)43,92:IOEAWA.2.0.CO;2

Caldwell, J. (2011). Disability identity of leaders in the self-advocacy movement. *Intellectual and Developmental Disabilities, 49*(5), 315–26. doi:10.1352/1934-9556-49.5.315

Cazden, C. B. (2001). *Classroom discourse: The language of teaching and learning* (2nd ed.). Portsmouth, NH: Heinemann.

Chapman, T. (2007). Interrogating classroom relationships and events: Using portraiture and critical race theory in education research. *Educational Researcher, 36*(3), 156–162. doi:10.3102/0013189X07301437

Connor, D. (2006). *Breaking containment: The power of narrative knowing – Countering silences within traditional special education research.* Paper presented at the American Educational Research Association Annual Meeting, San Francisco, CA.

Couwenhoven, T. (2007). *Teaching children with down syndrome about their bodies, boundaries, and sexuality: A guide for parents and professionals.* Bethesda, MD: Woodbine House.

Edgerton, R. B. (1967). *The cloak of competence: Stigma in the lives of the mentally retarded.* Berkeley, CA: University of California Press.

Ferguson, P. M., Ferguson, D. L., & Taylor, S. J. (Eds.). (1992). *Interpreting disability: A qualitative reader.* New York, NY: Teachers College Press.

Giroux, H. (1987). Literacy and the pedagogy of political empowerment. In *Literacy: Reading the word and the world* (pp. 1–28, P. Freire & D. Macedo, Eds.). New York, NY: Bergin & Garvey.

Glesne, C. (1999). *Becoming qualitative researchers: An introduction.* New York, NY: Longman.

Goffman, E. G. (1963). *Stigma: Notes on the management of spoiled identity.* Englewood Cliffs, NJ: Prentice-Hall.

Lawrence-Lightfoot, S. (2005). Reflections on portraiture: A dialogue between art and science. *Qualitative Inquiry, 11*(1), 3–15.

Lawrence-Lightfoot, S., & Davis, J. H. (1997). *The art and science of portraiture.* San Francisco, CA: Jossey-Bass.

Lewis, V., & Kellet, M. (2005). Disability. In S. Fraser, V. Lewis, S. Ding, M. Kellet, & C. Robinson (Eds.), *Doing research with children and young people* (pp. 191–205). London: Sage.

Lincoln, Y. S., & Guba, E. G. (1985). *Naturalistic inquiry.* Beverly Hills, CA: Wadsworth.

Linneman, R. D. (2001). *Idiots: Stories about mindedness and mental retardation.* New York, NY: Peter Lang.

Mattinson, J. (1971). *Marriage and mental handicap.* Pittsburgh, PA: University of Pittsburgh Press.

Maxwell, J. A. (1992). Understanding and validity in qualitative research. *Harvard Educational Review, 62*(3), 279–299.

Nonnemacher, S. L., & Bambara, L. M. (2011). "I'm supposed to be in charge": Self-advocates' perspectives on their self-determination. *Intellectual and Developmental Disabilities, 49*(5), 327–40. doi:10.1352/1934-9556-49.5.327

Paiewonsky, M. (2012, November 30). *Participatory action research: The ins and outs of research partnerships with students labeled with intellectual disabilities.* Presentation at the TASH Annual Conference, Long Beach, CA.

Petersen, A. (2009). Shana's story: The struggles, quandaries and pitfalls surrounding self-determination. *Disability Studies Quarterly, 29*(2).

Reid, D. K., & Button, L. J. (1995). Anna's story: Narratives of personal experience about being labeled learning disabled. *Journal of Learning Disabilities, 28*(10), 602–614.

Rossetti, Z., Ashby, C., Arndt, K., Chadwick, M., & Kasahara, M. (2008). "I like others to not try to fix me": Agency, independence, and autism. *Intellectual and Developmental Disabilities, 46*(5), 364–375. doi:10.1352/2008.46:364–375

Sauer, J. (2012a). "Look at me": Portraiture and agency. *Disability Studies Quarterly, 32*(4). Retrieved from http://dsq-sds.org/article/view/1736/3180 AQ7

Sauer, J. (2012b). *Negotiating the social borderlands: Portraits of three young people with disabilities and their struggle for positive relationships.* Washington, DC: American Association on Intellectual and Developmental Disabilities (AAIDD).

Sauer, J., & Fordice, K. (2008, December). *Kari's story: A portrait of agency.* Paper presented at the Annual TASH Conference, Nashville, TN.

Snelgrove, S. (2005). Bad, mad and sad: Developing a methodology of inclusion and a pedagogy for researching students with intellectual disabilities. *International Journal of Inclusive Education, 9*(3), 313–329. doi:doi.org/10.1080/13603110500082236

Stokes, M. A., & Kaur, A. (2005). High-functioning autism and sexuality: A parental perspective. *Autism, 9*(3), 266–289. doi:10.1177/1362361305053258

Tissot, C. (2009). Establishing a sexual identity: Case studies of learners with autism and learning difficulties. *Autism, 13*(6), 551–566. doi:10.1177/1362361309338183

Vallance, E. (1998). The art and science of portraiture by Sara Lawrence-Lightfoot and Jessica Davis [Book review]. *American Journal of Education, 107*(1), 66–71.

Walters, S. (2011). Masking, mediators and agency: Bilingual children and learning to read. *Journal of Research in Reading, 34*(4), 384–401. doi:10.1111/j.1467-9817.2010.01440.x

Witz, K. G. (2006). The participant as ally and essentialist portraiture. *Qualitative Inquiry, 12*, 246–268. doi:10.1177/1077800405284365

Wolfensberger, W. (1972). *The principle of normalization in human services.* Toronto: National Institute on Mental Retardation.

CHAPTER 4

When the Light Turns Blue: Journeying into Disability Studies Guided by the Work of Ellen Brantlinger

Kathleen M. Collins and Alicia A. Broderick

Abstract

In this essay the authors reflect on the contributions of Ellen Brantlinger to the work of two scholars who view their work as inclusive by design, but informed by disability studies. The authors identify three key *signposts*—lessons from Ellen's work that guided their own journeys and shaped inquiry in Disability Studies in Education writ large and conceptualizations of *inclusivity* in particular. These signposts include the assertions that (1) qualitative research is essential to understanding the contextual factors that shape the identification, location and response to difference as social phenomena, (2) *inclusion* and *exclusion* are political and ideological processes shaped by discursive practices, and (3) research and teaching are forms of (in)activism.

Keywords

activism – advocacy – disability studies – equity – inclusion

> When the light is green you go.
> When the light is red you stop.
> But what do you do
> When the light turns blue
> With orange and lavender spots?
> SHEL SILVERSTEIN, "Signals" (1981/2002)[1]

∴

© KONINKLIJKE BRILL NV, LEIDEN, 2020 | DOI:10.1163/9789004402690_005

For many of us who identify as researchers, scholars, teachers and activists, our working days are filled with Silverstein's "blue light" moments, times when once-familiar and useful signs and directions—the traditional and accepted theories and paradigms of our field—no longer move us forward in helpful ways. This is perhaps most true for those of us in fields like inclusive education which position us as always working between and across the different worlds of children, families, schools, communities, academia and government. We strive to create both real and concrete changes for children and teachers even as we work to develop theoretical and conceptual lenses and design studies that will allow us to see and understand *differently.* Where are the signals to guide such a journey? Where can we turn for directions?

The late Dr. Ellen Brantlinger's scholarship, we argue, provides the type of guidance needed for navigating these challenges. For each of us, the signals we read in Ellen's scholarship served to guide us in those moments in our professional life when the lights of dominant academic theories and accepted "best practices" turned blue with orange and lavender spots. When we sought professional paths that would help us integrate our concerns regarding educational equity, inclusion and advocacy with our responsibilities as researchers and teacher educators, Ellen's research and activism in these areas created opportunities for us to integrate the personal, professional, and political aspects of our work. In doing so, Ellen's professional work, spanning over thirty years, also helped create the new and still-developing field of Disability Studies in Education (DSE) and continues to provide direction as we move forward.

In this essay we reflect on Ellen's contributions by identifying three key *signposts*—lessons from Ellen's work that guided our own journeys and shaped inquiry in Disability Studies in Education writ large and conceptualizations of *inclusivity* in particular. These signposts include the assertions that (1) qualitative research is essential to understanding the contextual factors that shape the identification, location and response to difference as social phenomena, (2) *inclusion* and *exclusion* are political and ideological processes shaped by discursive practices, and (3) research and teaching are forms of (in)activism.

We begin with brief summaries of our own journeys into DSE to contextualize and ground our discussion of Ellen's scholarship. We then discuss each of the signposts identified above in relation to how they have steered our work. In this section we use the first-person singular voice as appropriate and identify the speaker as necessary (e.g., "I, Kathleen Collins, ..."). Finally, we conclude the essay with a consideration of where Ellen's signposts have directed us, the questions that her work positions us to ask, and the direction we need to go as we move forward.

1 Our Journeys into Disability Studies

Each of us has been a recipient of the DSE Junior Scholar Award. Alicia Broderick was the first recipient in 2002 and Kathleen Collins was recognized a decade later in 2012, when the award was renamed in Ellen's honor. Our work in the field that Ellen helped shape thus "bookends" a decade of change and growth, particularly around issues of inclusion, access and equity. In sharing our personal stories here, our hope is that this essay will serve as inspiration for those new to DSE and who may be grappling with the same challenges we encountered. We each found courage and direction through Ellen's work, and we invite others to do the same. In addition, I, Alicia Broderick, had the privilege of knowing Ellen and through her mentorship and friendship am able to share insights gained from those personal encounters.

I, Kathleen Collins, first "discovered" Ellen's work shortly after completing my doctoral work and beginning my first academic position. I had recently completed a multi-sited ethnographic study of one child's participation in the various contexts of his life, both in and out of school. "Jay," a Black boy who lived and attended fifth grade in a predominantly white, rural community, was labeled as "learning disabled or emotionally impaired," in school but participated quite competently and successfully in the other contexts of his life.

Having worked as a high school English teacher and a k-12 literacy specialist, I came to my work with Jay from the perspective of sociocultural studies of language and literacy. I began by exploring the roles of situated literacies and discourses in shaping Jay's social identity as "competent" or "disabled." However, it became clear that educational and social exclusion, social stereotyping, and deficit discourses were all operating to position Jay (along with the other children identified as "different" within this predominately white, rural, middle class school) in categories of deficiency.

After this work was published (Collins, 2003), I searched for ways to continue to explore and investigate the situated and socially constructed nature of dis/ability and its relationship to students' access and full participation in school learning and activity contexts. Literacy studies in general, and studies of multimodal and situated literacy practices in particular, were certainly a part of this. However, I also needed a way to incorporate my passionate interest in disrupting the racialized nature of dis/ability identification and educational inequities. I didn't want to just document the process by which over representation and deficit positionings occurred. I wanted to design a research program that would allow me to actively interrupt the discourses and disrupt the practices that resulted in such positionings.

WHEN THE LIGHT TURNS BLUE

However, when I thought about doing work that was even more explicitly grounded in meshing my personal and political interests and beliefs than my first project had been, I felt stymied and silenced by the voices of critics who dismiss or undermine this form of research. For example, when my dissertation was under review for a prestigious prize at the University of Michigan, I was awarded runner up, not first prize, because one reviewer noted the overtly political and emotional aspects of my narrative study. He noted that I was too emotionally invested, that I *cared* too much, and that this undermined the "validity" of my study. Similarly, once the research was published as a book (Collins, 2003), one reviewer asserted that I had simply gotten it wrong: "Collins's failure to appreciate Jay's limitations is probably due to her stepping out of the role of a scientist and into that of an advocate for Jay" (Goldberg, 2005, p. 172). The same reviewer went on to argue that prescription drugs would be more useful than my examination of the social and cultural aspects of Jay's deficit positionings, writing, "I would venture the hunch that Jay might have benefited more from Ritalin than from the author's attempts to persuade his teacher to adopt a social-constructivist perspective" (Goldberg, 2005, p. 173).

This, then, was a "blue light" moment, a time when I had to turn away from some of the dominant perspectives informing our understanding of students who struggle with school literacies and look for other paths. In turning away from voices such as these, I actively sought individuals and intellectual communities that would embrace my inquiry into the socially constructed nature of dis/ability and my desire to do design experiment, change-oriented work with (not on) teachers and children. Ellen's writings on ideology (Brantlinger, 1997, 2004a) and on the integration of research with activism (Brantlinger, 1999) helped me to identify the critiques of my book as "traditionalist" and to locate them (along with my own emerging program of research) within the larger conversations around special education, inclusion, and the emergent field of DSE. This awareness enabled me to move forward with a series of qualitative studies that followed a design experiment approach to integrating research, professional development, and advocacy (Collins, 2011a, 2011b).

I, Alicia Broderick, first encountered Ellen's work, quite by fortuitous accident, in the summer of 1994, just a couple of months before I began my own full-time graduate work. I had spent the years from 1990–1994 trying to make sense of the experience of autism, and trying to grow into a role as an educator of and ally to autistic children and adults. It was a long, circuitous journey that included initiation into "professional," primarily behaviorist, discourses on autism in a variety of occupational roles and sites (including working in a segregated residential school, an ICF-MR institutional facility, a range of group homes and supported living arrangements, and a segregated classroom in a public school). I encountered my own first blue light with orange and lavender spots in 1991, when I came upon the work of Douglas Biklen through his professional work supporting communication access for nonspeaking autistic people. I was stunned by the apparent implications of this work upon our understandings of autism and notions of mental retardation or cognitive impairment. I could not reconcile what I was learning about autism through Biklen's work with the professional roles I occupied in relation to autistic people. I realized that I simply could not be the ally I wanted to be when I operated as a cog in the institutional bureaucracies that employed me and systematically subjugated autistic people. I had already made the decision to move to Syracuse, NY, to begin my graduate work in the fall of 1994. But, living as I did at the time in Indiana, I wanted to take full advantage, before leaving, of the work of the faculty at Indiana University, Bloomington, who ran a research center on autism. I decided then to drive down to Bloomington to take a summer course on autism before beginning my new life as a full-time graduate student in Syracuse in September. It was there that I first encountered Ellen's work, and thus her work set the stage for the academic career I was about to launch upon my arrival in Syracuse a few short months later.

2 The Importance of Qualitative Research

The first signpost, or beacon, that Ellen's work has provided us is the conviction that (1) qualitative research is essential to understanding the contextual factors that shape the identification, location and response to difference as social phenomena. Ellen defined qualitative research as, "a systematic approach to understanding qualities, or the essential nature, of a phenomenon within a particular context" (Brantlinger, 2005, p. 195) and brought considerable analytic talents to bear on uncovering and disrupting the social practices that shape disability and educational inequity. In doing so she employed a range of qualitative research approaches that allowed her to braid inquiry with advocacy, the personal and the political. Ellen argued that, in order to have "... a transformative effect on society, data collection and analysis should always be integrated with values, theory and activism" (Brantlinger, 1999, p. 413). Brantlinger pressed us to ask ourselves, *"why do research at all, if not to have a transformative effect on some aspect of society?"*

I, Kathleen Collins, found Ellen's explanation of her approaches empowering for my own work, which has been almost exclusively qualitative. In particular Ellen's writing in response to the push for "scientific methods" is instructive for those of us whose strengths lie in working with teachers and students in local contexts. Ellen and her coauthors (Odam et al., 2005) wrote that "education science might be more appropriately seen as a continuum than a fixed point" (p. 145) and argued for the importance of recognizing that different methodologies are more or less suitable for specific research questions.

I, Alicia Broderick, encountered this signpost in my very first exposure to Ellen's work, in 1994. Steeped as I still was, at the time, in "expert," "professional," behaviorist discourses on autism, I believe I expected to learn something very definitive about autism in that summer course, grounded in the expertise of university-based research (conducted at a top research university, no less). And while I did not actually meet Ellen that summer, the course was very much structured around Ellen's newly published, collaboratively written text, *Fighting for Darla: The Case Study of a Pregnant Adolescent with Autism* (Brantlinger, Klein, & Guskin, 1994). I was somewhat flummoxed at the time, and while I found the text interesting, I was not at all clear why we were spending such a large portion of the course delving into such great depth and detail around the experience of a single autistic adolescent. I remember thinking that this was all very interesting, but how many times in my future life am I likely to encounter a situation like Darla's—dealing with the unplanned pregnancy of a nonverbal autistic adolescent? I would later realize how imprinted I was by prior coursework that demanded the pursuit of "generalizable knowledge" that I could "apply" to future circumstances.

I eventually came to understand that the point is not to understand the particularities of Darla's situation simply for its own sake; nor to understand Darla's situation in intimate detail so as to contain others' experiences with autism within the same prescribed parameters of meaning. Rather, the detail of this study illuminated the *context* within which others (parents, care providers, researchers, physicians, social workers, etc.) identified, located, and responded to difference (in this case, to Darla and her experience). Qualitative research became, in that moment, the metaphoric microscope or magnifying glass through which we intimately scrutinize the details of a particular situation for its reflective properties. I realized through this work, in particular, that it is not what we see through the glass that most illuminates our understanding, but rather the image of ourselves we see reflected back in the glass.

Ellen's commitment to qualitative research deeply valued those embedded reflective properties, and for that reason, we can see the nature of her work (and therefore, of her own growth as a researcher and activist) shift over time. For example, it is somewhat jarring, in reading this text today, to realize the extent to which Ellen and her co-researchers accepted as a premise that Darla, as a nonspeaking autistic adolescent with no system of expressive communication, was in fact "mentally retarded." This is a clear example of an ideological assumption that underlay Ellen's work as a researcher at that point in her career (even as the work explicitly undermined other dominant professional assumptions of the time, such as the "asexuality" of a significantly disabled adolescent). It is precisely the sort of assumption that Ellen spent the remainder of her career asserting the need to acknowledge, dispute, and disrupt. She later remarked upon the import of directing that scholarly gaze not only inward, but also upward:

> Because of the phenomenon of burgeoning care-providing bureaucracies, my read on progress (i.e., reducing disparities and increasing equity) is that the scholarly gaze must be turned inward to learn how educated classes benefit from stratified social arrangements and upward at powerful, elite classes who gain from the low wages and poverty of "others" and who influence the media, politics, and public and private institutions. (Brantlinger, 2004b, p. 14)

Our second "signpost" in our journeys into DSE scholarship addresses this commitment not merely to qualitative forms of inquiry, but also to political and ideological forms of inquiry (the absence of which Ellen argued was "dangerous" [2004, p. 11]).

3 The Political and Ideological Nature of (In)Exclusion[2]

A second signpost that Ellen's work has offered us on our own journeys into DSE is the conviction that (2) *inclusion* and *exclusion* are political and ideological processes shaped by discursive practices. Key to finding this particular signpost shining through the misty haze of academia was Ellen's (Brantlinger, 1997) publication of her *Review of Educational Research* (RER) article, "Using Ideology: Cases of Non-recognition of the Politics of Research and Practice in Special Education."

While I, Alicia Broderick, had already read this piece in the course of my graduate education, it was not until 1999 when Linda Ware (co-guest editor of this special edition) organized and hosted a research conference at the University of Rochester sponsored by the Spencer Foundation, titled "Ideology and the Politics of Inclusion," that I had the opportunity to meet Ellen and to engage deeply with her work and that of many international critical DSE scholars. Ellen's RER article served as the conference theme and the call for papers invited an international response to the manuscript, offering in contradistinction "cases of recognition" (Ware, 2004, p. 4).

The 1999 Rochester Conference was a defining moment for me, professionally, as it was the moment wherein I realized that I had an opportunity to join other individuals doing similar critical, activist work around inclusivity in education. It was also at this time that I recognized that even among this group of relatively like-minded individuals, there was nothing even approaching consensus or agreement. Political discussion, debate, and dissent about what inclusive schooling is or could be or should be were alive and well and circulating throughout this intimate and very democratic forum. Each paper was presented in ongoing dialogue with the papers and discussions that had gone before. Witnessing the integrity with which Ellen welcomed and participated in democratic ideological critique of her own position within a community of peers impressed upon me my own desire to become an active participant in such a community of activist-scholars. Indeed, Ellen's own stance of self-critique, and her own assertions about the import of engaging in political and ideological critique (including self-critique), enabled me to engage and participate fully and critically in a discussion of the relative strength of unexamined positivist assumptions among the American scholars compared with many of the international scholars in attendance.

With only 50–60 participants present, we all slept in dormitory housing and took our meals collectively, so that what emerged was a week-long, sustained, cumulative conversation across international contexts on inclusion and disability studies. I vividly recall the interest and investment with which Ellen asked probing questions of my own presentation (Broderick, 1999), treating my work as that of a peer, and not a mere doctoral student, inferior in both status and in scholarly acumen. Continuing that conversation at the dinner table that evening, and even further late into the evening as we brushed our teeth in our pajamas in the dormitory lavatory gave me the confidence to engage critically as a peer later in the conference.

4   Research and Teaching as Forms of (In)Activism

In her 2006 edited volume, *Who Benefits from Special Education? Remediating [Fixing] Other People's Children,* Ellen and the authors of other chapters in the volume confront Gramsci's central question of "who benefits?" from the discourse and practices of special education. In closing the volume, Ellen argues that she has "shown how we, as members of the educated class, are complicit in hierarchies. I ask readers to join a countermovement to oppose stratifying measures and work to overcome hierarchical and excluding relations in school and society" (p. 224). Throughout her lifetime of scholarly work, Ellen argued that the privilege that we enjoy as members of the educated class comes with responsibilities, and that among those responsibilities are that our scholarship and teaching must be lived as forms of activism. Failure to do so constitutes "inactivism," and hence, tacit complicity with the status quo, which systematically marginalizes other people's children. Brantlinger's call to activism in our work as scholars and as teachers has been one that we both have tried to take up, in our own ways, as we continue to develop into activist-scholars and activist-teachers.

Ellen's recognition of the emotional toll that activism and change-oriented research can take helped me, Kathleen Collins, understand the importance of investing myself in my academic work and confirmed that I was not alone in feeling "despondent about struggles that are lost" (Brantlinger, 1999, p. 414). While writing the chapters of my first book (Collins, 2003) that dealt with the focal teacher's lack of change, I was deeply despondent. Despite stepping into an advocacy role, I had not persuaded the teacher to think any differently about the social construction of dis/ability, and these feelings of despondency and failure resurfaced nine years later when I re-immersed myself in the data while compiling the second edition (Collins, 2013). Ellen (1999) noted that activist oriented research has both benefits and risks, that one of the risks is getting hurt, and that "pain is integral to hard fights, especially unsuccessful ones" (p. 414). Yet she also emphasized the pain that comes from witnessing oppression: "It is emotionally wrenching for me to hear influential people state elitist ideas, dismissing opposing arguments, and make decisions that privilege their groups" (p. 414).

What I learned from this despondency and from studying Ellen's work (1999, 2003) was not to avoid "the pain that comes with hard fights," in favor of the pain that comes with bearing witness to oppression and not acting. Rather, I learned to pick both my allies and my goals for change more carefully. In my next large research project, the teacher participants specifically volunteered to engage in change-oriented research. Several were willing to examine their practice reflexively and to participate as co-researchers (Collins, 2011a, 2011b).

Ellen's body of work has been a crucial resource in supporting the ways in which I, Alicia Broderick, have endeavored to engage in activism in my role as a teacher educator. Drawing on the curriculum theorist William Pinar (2002) she reminded that:

> Pinar (2002) similarly accused education schools of having an anti-intellectual climate. Rather than stimulating creative and original thinking, the expectation in teacher education is that teachers and professors should apply what is already known and packaged in available professional resources. (Brantlinger, 2006a, p. 240)

WHEN THE LIGHT TURNS BLUE 71

Key to my own attempts to politicize teacher education students in my coursework has been her chapters from her (2006) text, *Who Benefits from Special Education?* In an introductory course focused on the sociocultural construction of disability in schools and in society, students read her chapters titled "Winners Need Losers: The Basis for School Competition and Hierarchies" and "The Big Glossies: How Textbooks Structure (Special) Education." Taken together, these two chapters critically examine and lay bare the political economies upon which stratified schooling practices in general, and the exercise of special educational practices as an extreme form of stratification in particular, are based. Many students report in class that they had never before regarded schooling in general, nor special education in particular, as industries having foundations in political economy.

After a month of reading texts that position disability, ableism, and disability oppression as sociopolitical relations of power with concrete economic and material manifestations, students read Ellen's work and then engage in a textbook review of a mainstream, introductory special education textbook (what Ellen refers to as a "big glossy"). Had I required one of these textbooks as the central organizing text (in keeping with the tradition in special education teacher education introductory courses), students would likely have accepted the major premises of the text as neutral and objective. They would further construe its contents as valid and their mastery of its contents shaping their own expertise. However, given the backdrop of Ellen's work and the work of other disability rights activists that frame the course, the students come to clearly "recognize" the discursive, ideological, and economic foundations of claims to special education knowledge that are presented. I do not want my students to merely apply what is handed to them (from me or anyone else) about what disability "is" or "means" or "does"; rather, I want them to become critically cognizant of and "recognize" the relations of power inherent in all knowledge production. In this way, I hope that my teaching becomes a form of activism that may develop in my students the critical habits of mind that will enable them to be activist teachers as well.

A second key piece of Ellen's scholarship that has enabled me to conceptualize my own research and teaching as forms of activism, as well as enabling me to support my students in developing a sense of their teaching and research as activism, has been her (2003) text, *Dividing Classes: How the Middle Class Negotiates and Rationalizes School Advantage*. I am a qualitative researcher and I occasionally teach introductory coursework in qualitative research aimed at both masters and doctoral students. Because this text so clearly embeds activist dilemmas within considerations of methodological design, it has helped me to reconfirm my own interpretivist and *criticalist* orientation to research and to bolster my teaching of this approach.

A dilemma that I faced upon initial conceptualization of my own qualitative dissertation research was how one is to be critical of one's own participants. Recognizing their willingness to participate, it was troubling to then unpack, with them, the ways that their own experiences might be better understood. I initially felt limited by the somewhat relativist posture of a social constructionist theoretical framework, and I struggled with the ethical decisions of how *criticalist*, interpretivist methodologies could be applied. Although I did not rely on this particular work, exposure to prior work supported the shifting of my attention from the locus of the parents' individual experiences as they narrated them to me, to the locus of the *discourses* that they drew upon and enacted in the process of that narration (Broderick, 2004). Learning to do *"criticalist,"* and hence potentially activist, research, is a dilemma not merely of one's theoretical or ideological stance or positioning; it is also deeply embedded in questions of inquiry design and method.

In addition, this text figures into my introductory qualitative research course, in response to the fact that many students enter the course with a desire to study the experiences of a particular group or population of people—more often than not, people who have directly experienced marginalization, disenfranchisement, or oppression of some sort. To be sure, qualitative research is extremely well-suited to understanding the particularities and depths and complexities of these individual experiences; yet, I further ask students to consider the import of what Ellen (2003) calls "learning to turn the scholarly gaze inward and upward" (p. 26):

> In this book I do not follow the tradition of studying historically marginalized groups to explain social class reproduction but look upward and inward at segments of the middle class who have high levels of educational attainment as well as high levels of influence on schools .... [B]ecause of the power of middle-class adults to shape education through their professional positions and actions as influential parents, I decided that an understanding of their thoughts about schooling was especially important. (pp. 26–27)

Many students have not yet considered the value and potential power of conducting qualitative research that aims to look inward and upward in the service of disrupting unequal relations of power, and while they may not conduct such work in an introductory course, they nevertheless may add it to their methodological inquiry toolbox for future use.

Finally, a key facet of this work that is instructive for novice researchers seeking to do activist research is Ellen's explicit commitment to the import not only of studying narrative in a qualitative manner, but also coupling that with her commitment to simultaneous ideological critique. Ellen reminds us in this text that "ideologies that mystify class relations take various forms including storytelling" (p. 7), and further,

> I do not always take participants' narratives at face value but rather scrutinize them for deeper, tacit meanings that might explain relations of domination and subordination .... I do an ideological critique of participants' thinking and the tacit sociocultural knowledge embedded in their discourses. (pp. 28–29)

Translating this stance directly into her research design, Ellen utilizes a three-stage interview protocol. The first stage solicits participants' general feelings and beliefs about education, the second solicits those responses in the context of specific, local issues, and the third actually forces a choice on specific issues (e.g., redistricting and tracking) (p. 34). According to Ellen,

> Stage 1 was designed to partly gauge whether participants would bring up social class on their own as well as explore their own ideas about schooling. Stage 2 directed them to talk about class issues. Stage 3 required participants to commit to specific positions about social class relations. (p. 34)

Thus, the design of this study enables Ellen to illuminate the spaces between the narratives that privileged people tell about their commitments to social class equity and the decisions that they actually make in practice, which often belie the narratives they tell. The fact that Ellen was not only willing, but also successfully able to conduct a critical study of this sort in the town and district in which she and her own family lived is testament to her commitment to "walk the walk" herself as an activist researcher. Her work is designed not only to document and study, but also to make an impact in the interest of materially lessening inequities through activist ideological critique.

5   Where Do We Go Next?

Although Ellen left us far too soon, and her absence is deeply felt, she did nevertheless leave us with clear signposts that offer the guidance that many of us have taken up in developing our own identities as DSE activist-scholars. She was explicit on the recommendation that

... scholars do transformative work in which we: (1) are explicit about the values that undergird our research and practice; (2) identify the political and personal agendas our research is likely to serve; (3) direct our gaze inward at ourselves and upward at those in charge, in control, in dominance (i.e., those with power); (4) integrate private and professional lives (engage in praxis); (5) exercise agency when and where activism can have an impact; and (6) act to eliminate oppression. (Brantlinger, 2004b, p. 25)

5.1 How to Be an Activist-Scholar?

As activist-scholars journeying into DSE over the past decade, we can each look upon Ellen's recommendations for conducting transformative DSE work as "touchstones" that we have sought to approximate and enact in various ways over the course of our early careers.

I, Alicia Broderick, understand the first five of these six tenets outlined by Brantlinger (2004b) to work in service of the sixth—to "act to eliminate oppression" (p. 25). (I may be more cynical than Ellen, or perhaps I am merely less ambitious or suffer from a dearth of imaginative powers, but I confess I have not the imagination to envision *elimination* of oppression; I seek rather active disruption, mitigation, lessening of its impact, and I cannot imagine an end to work of this nature.) The first two of Ellen's signposts we've discussed in this manuscript—the assertions that (1) qualitative research is essential to understanding the contextual factors that shape the identification, location and response to difference as social phenomena, and that (2) *inclusion* and *exclusion* are political and ideological processes shaped by discursive practices—have jointly enabled me to pursue lines of scholarship not only as a qualitative researcher, but as a qualitative researcher who engages in "*criticalist*" work that seeks to identify ideological bases of oppression so as to actively disrupt it. I find increasingly, however, that it is the third signpost identified—that research and teaching are forms of (in)activism—that guides me most urgently at this point in my journey. I continue to seek ways to engage in activism (rather than inactivism) in both my individual scholarship and my work as an individual teacher educator.

5.2 How Can We Act Collectively, not Just Individually, as a Critical Collective of Activist DSE Scholars?

Even as we grapple with ways of becoming individual activist-scholars, and even with the benefit of Ellen's signposts and other guidance, we are also critically cognizant of a larger issue percolating in the broader field of DSE—which is not only how do we each individually develop as activist-scholars, but rather, and much more complexly—how do we as a field engage in collective action

WHEN THE LIGHT TURNS BLUE

as activist-scholars? As long as we each continue to act as individual activist-scholars, our impact will be felt but it will be limited. Scholars in general are socialized and prepared for individual, not collective, activity.

5.3 *How to Nurture, Protect, and Strategically Support Early Career Activist-Scholars as Well as DSE-Oriented Teachers?*

Tenure committees decide the value of our imperative to position our work as "activism." Too often, our claims are met with suspicion and surveillance because educational activism and advocacy are derided and denigrated as not "real scholarship."

The last conversation that I, Alicia Broderick, had with Ellen was centered on this very question: *How do we, as DSE scholars, both individually and collectively, engage in work that is activist in nature?* Ellen was outraged at the outcomes of three different recent tenure decisions in which DSE scholars who positioned themselves as activist in their work were denied tenure (at three different universities). She was outraged at how blatantly the decisions appeared to be grounded in ideological differences, and yet how vociferously the various institutions stuck to their stance of "non-recognition" of the ideological basis of their actions, and to their narratives that activist work either was not scholarship at all or was poor scholarship. Ellen shared deep misgivings about her growing sense that the climate of academia was changing in this regard and that the risks to individual scholars of doing such work were increasing. She underscored the need to support and mentor junior activist-scholars to prepare them for the potential professional risks of conducting their early career work.

Nevertheless, Ellen was nothing if not strategic and pragmatic. I shared with her in this conversation a conceptualization I have been using for some years with my own students, in preparing them to be DSE-oriented activist teachers nevertheless employed within the special education bureaucracy (Broderick et al., 2012): Though perhaps slightly hyperbolic, I have talked with my own students about acting as "DSE Maquis," a conceptualization founded on the cellular organizational structure, tactics, and strategies of the French Resistance operating during WWII. In so doing, I stress with them the import of developing strong, trusting alliances with like-minded colleagues in order to act collectively, all the while recognizing the necessity for much of this work to be done "underground." She was very supportive of this conceptualization of political action, and urged me to continue acting against the forces of oppression, while also striving to secure and solidify a base from which to act more effectively and strategically.

We believe that at the center of Ellen's legacy—and one we feel the need for DSE to take up as we move forward—is her deep commitment to engaging with and supporting doctoral students, junior faculty, and classroom teachers. As we transition from early- to mid-career DSE activist-scholars, we are increasingly assuming responsibility for mentoring and protecting the teachers and colleagues with whom we engage in this dangerous and sometimes painful work. How might we act more formally as a DSE community to nurture, protect, and strategically support early career activist-scholars as well as DSE-oriented teachers?

5.4   *How Do We Embrace One Set of Dangers over Another?*

In expressing to me, Alicia Broderick, her concerns about how potentially risky and dangerous activist-scholarship is, never once did Ellen intimate that the work should be shrunk away from, nor would she ever abide the narrative that *not* doing activist-scholarship was somehow safe or without danger. As cognizant as she was of the dangers of doing this work, she was equally if not more cognizant of the dangers of *not* doing the work because "it is dangerous to design or engage in inclusive practice without an understanding of its ideological roots" (Brantlinger, 2004b, p. 11).

Ellen thus occupied the sometimes uncomfortable position of sharing the point argued by Foucault (1983):

> My point is not that everything is bad, but that everything is dangerous, which is not exactly the same as bad. If everything is dangerous, then we always have something to do. So my position leads not to apathy but to hyper- and pessimistic activism. I think that the ethico-political choice we have to make every day is to determine which is the main danger. (pp. 231–232)

It is in this Foucauldian spirit of "hyper- and pessimistic activism" that Ellen's work proceeded, and it is in this Foucauldian space that those of us endeavoring to continue her lifework exist.

What would Ellen have us do? First, we believe that she would have us continue to resist the conceptualization that there are "teaching" and "scholarship," and then there are "activist teaching" and "activist scholarship" (the latter of which are commonly regarded within academia as either not "real" or as of inferior quality to the former). We believe that Ellen would have us embrace, encourage, and assert the "recognition" that our teaching and scholarship are either forms of activism or they are forms of inactivism. Both, as Foucault reminds us, are dangerous. We therefore do not have the luxury of believing that our choice is between the danger of activist teaching and scholarship and the safety of non-activist teaching and scholarship. Non-activism is inactivism,

WHEN THE LIGHT TURNS BLUE   77

and it is dangerous as well. Our Foucauldian ethical and political choice thus becomes to decide, daily, which is the greater danger: the potential danger to self of engaging in activist teaching and scholarship, or the potential danger to the broader society, culture, and other people's children, of engaging in inactivist teaching and scholarship? Which would Ellen have us choose?

We believe that Ellen would clearly have us choose the former: the dangers associated with activist teaching and scholarship. However, she would not have us present ourselves, activist-scholar after activist-scholar, as sacrificial lambs bearing the entire brunt of the danger of this work as isolated individuals. We believe that this is the second, and more radical, action that Ellen would have us take. Ellen's (2004b) six recommendations for scholars to engage in transformative work could be read as her recommendations to individual scholars making individual decisions to engage in teaching and scholarship as individual forms of political action. We believe, rather, that if Ellen were with us today, she would hold those same recommendations before us as maxims for collectivist action. That is, how do we *collectively* explicate our values, identify the political agendas of our work, direct our scholarly gaze not only inwardly at ourselves but also upward at those in power, integrate our private and professional lives, and exercise collective agency where our activism can make an impact, all in the service of acting collectively toward the elimination of oppression (Brantlinger, 2004b, p. 25)? The bright side, we suppose, if Foucault is to be believed, is that we will always, and forever, have something to do. And, a final source of optimism, if we read correctly the signposts that Ellen left us, is that we will never be acting alone.

Notes

1 "Signals" from *A Light in the Attic* by Shel Silverstein, copyright 1981, renewed 2002 Evil Eye LLC. By permission of the Edite Kroll Literary Agency Inc.
2 Ware (2004).

References

Blanchett, W., Brantlinger, E., & Shealy, M. W. (2005). Brown 50 years later—Exclusion, segregation, and inclusion. *Remedial and Special Education, 26*(2), 66–69.

Brantlinger, E. (1997). Using ideology: Cases of nonrecognition of the politics of research and practice in special education. *Review of Educational Research, 67*, 425–459.

Brantlinger, E. (1999). Inward gaze and activism as moral steps in inquiry. *Anthropology & Education Quarterly, 30*(4), 413–429.

Brantlinger, E. (2003). *Dividing classes: How the middle class negotiates and rationalizes school advantage.* New York, NY: Routledge Falmer.

Brantlinger, E. (2004a). Confounding the needs and confronting the norms: An extension of Reid and Valle's essay. *Journal of Learning Disabilities, 37*(6), 490–499.

Brantlinger, E. (2004b). Ideologies discerned, values determined: Getting past the hierarchies of special education. In L. Ware (Ed.), *Ideology and the politics of (in)exclusion* (pp. 11–31). New York, NY: Peter Lang.

Brantlinger, E. (Ed.). (2006a). *Who benefits from special education? Remediating [fixing] other people's children.* Mahwah, NJ: Lawrence Erlbaum Associates.

Brantlinger, E. (2006b). The big glossies: How textbooks structure (special) education. In E. Brantlinger (Ed.), *Who benefits from special education? Remediating [fixing] other people's children* (pp. 45–75). Mahwah, NJ: Lawrence Erlbaum Associates.

Brantlinger, E. (2006c). Winners need losers: The basis for school competition and hierarchies. In E. Brantlinger (Ed.), *Who benefits from special education? Remediating [fixing] other people's children* (pp. 197–224). Mahwah, NJ: Lawrence Erlbaum Associates.

Brantlinger, E., Jimenez, R., Klinger, J., Pugach, M., & Richardson, V. (2005). Qualitative studies in special education. *Exceptional Children, 71*(2), 195–207.

Brantlinger, E., Klein, S., & Guskin, S. (1994). *Fighting for Darla: The case study of a pregnant adolescent with autism: Challenges for family care and professional responsibility.* New York, NY: Teachers College Press.

Broderick, A. (1999). *Beyond "best practice": Deconstructing the political and moral dimensions of educational decision-making for young children labeled with autism.* Paper presented at The Politics of Inclusion: International Research Colloquium on Inclusive Education, University of Rochester, Rochester, NY.

Broderick, A. (2004). *"Recovery," "science," and the politics of hope: A critical discourse analysis of applied behavior analysis for young children labeled with autism.* Ann Arbor, MI: ProQuest.

Broderick, A., with Hawkins, G., Henze, A. S., Mirasol-Spath, C., Pollack-Berkovits, R., Prozzo Clune, H., Skovera, E., & Steel, C. (2012). Teacher counternarratives: Transgressing and "restorying" disability in education. *International Journal of Inclusive Education, 16*(8), 825–842.

Collins, K. M. (2003). *Ability profiling and school failure: One child's struggle to be seen as competent.* Mahwah, NJ: Lawrence Erlbaum Associates.

Collins, K. M. (2011a). "My mom says I'm really creative!": Dis/Ability, positioning and resistance in multimodal instructional contexts. *Language Arts, 88*(6), 409–418.

Collins, K. M. (2011b). Discursive positioning in a fifth grade writing lesson: The making of a bad, bad boy. *Urban Education, 46*(4), 741–785.

Foucault, M. (1983). On the genealogy of ethics: An overview of work in progress. In H. Dreyfus & P. Rabinow (Eds.), *Michel Foucault: Beyond structuralism and hermeneutics, Second edition with an afterword by and an interview with Michel Foucault.* Chicago, IL: The University of Chicago Press.

Goldberg, J. (2005). Book review of ability profiling and school failure: One child's struggle to be seen as competent. *Science Education, 89*(1), 171–173.

Odom, S., Brantlinger, E., Gersten, R., Horner, R., Thompson, B., & Harris, K. (2005). Research in special education: Scientific methods and evidence-based practices. *Exceptional Children, 71*(2), 137–148.

Silverstein, S. (1981). *A light in the attic.* New York, NY: Harper Collins Children's Books.

Ware, L. (Ed.). (2004). *Ideology and the politics of (in)exclusion.* New York, NY: Peter Lang.

CHAPTER 5

Challenging the Ideology of Normal in Schools

Subini A. Annamma, Amy L. Ferrel, Brooke A. Moore and
Janette Klingner

Abstract

The authors build on Brantlinger's work to critique the binary of normal and abnormal applied in US schools that create inequities in education. Operating from a critical perspective, they draw from Critical Race Theory, Disability Studies in Education, and Cultural/Historical Activity Theory to build a conceptual framework for examining the prevailing ideology of normal found in US schools. Their conceptual framework is utilized to *deconstruct* the current, westernized, static ideology of normal in schools. Finally, the authors suggest using the conceptual framework as a tool to *reconstruct* the ideology of normal as something more dynamic and inclusive.

Keywords

critical race theory – cultural historical activity theory – disability studies – normal

1 Introduction

The idea of normal most often ascribed to in schools in the US is based on the Gaussian, normal distribution, bell-shaped curve that has been used to characterize the measurement of achievement (Glass & Smith, 1979) and ability (Shaywitz et al., 1992). Although the Gaussian curve as a statistical measurement tool is reliable and valid for measuring the distribution of random events, its application to humans is erroneous as human behaviors and experiences are far from random (Dudley-Marling & Gurn, 2010). This problematic yet common sense belief about the normal distribution curve promotes the notion that some students will excel, most will be average, and some will fail (Fendler & Muzaffar, 2008).

© TAYLOR & FRANCIS, 2013 | DOI:10.1163/9789004402690_006

The concept of normal pushes humanity towards the average as ideal (Davis, 2006). The word normal continues to imply good across multiple social disciplines, such as psychology, medicine, economics, history and education. Yet, conceptualizing normal as a phenomenon desired by these powerful disciplines maintains that difference is conceived as deviance, an analogy that is fundamentally problematic. In US schools, concepts of normal create boundaries in which some students fit and others are marginalized based solely on issues of race, language, and perceived ability (Prichard et al., 2010). Furthermore, it creates a hierarchy of characteristics commonly assumed to fall along the bell curve (e.g., intelligence, ability, achievement, behavior).

Normal is steeped in unexamined, westernized[1] ideological assumptions. As Brantlinger (1997) stated, "Ideologies are systems of representations (images, myths, ideas) that in profoundly unconscious ways, mediate one's understanding of the world" (p. 438). Additionally, ideology "is determining of people and is determined by people; ideology both structures and is structured by social practices" (Leonardo, 2003, p. 210) and ideology is constructed and perpetuated through language. When the ideology of normal exists as unexamined common sense, it creates the inherent binary of abnormal. Brantlinger (2006) notes,

> Individuals and groups who fail to achieve dominant standards are identified (marked, labeled, branded) with stigmatizing names (e.g., failure, disabled, at-risk) and sent to separated locations (special education rooms, low tracks, vocational schools). These distinction-making processes create a binary of (dominant) insiders and (subordinate) outsiders. (p. 200)

Instead of this limiting binary in which all students are expected to fit into one of two categories, there is diversity in human capabilities and therefore there is a need to reconstruct the ideology of normal into a more expansive understanding of human variability. As Baglieri and Knopf (2004) note, "The question is not whether we perceive differences among people, but, rather, *what meaning is brought to bear on those perceived differences*" (p. 525, italics added for emphasis). An ongoing problem is that many educators subscribe to the often utilized yet rarely examined concept of normal which contributes to educational inequities that are based on race, cultural practices, language, and perceived ability.

Many scholars engage in critical examinations of educational inequities; however, we offer a new contribution to such critiques by combining

Critical Race Theory (CRT), Disability Studies in Education (DSE) and Cultural/ Historical Activity Theory (C/HAT) to create a conceptual framework for examining the ideology of normal. CRT is useful in deconstructing normal because as a theory, one of its main tenets is to challenge Whiteness as the unmarked norm (Gillborn, 2005; Ladson-Billings, 1998). Teachers often define students in relation to racial dimensions of normality, so that students who are not White are often constructed in the mind of educators, consciously or not, as abnormal. Statistically, the majority of the teaching population in the US is White (Hodgkinson, 2002). Yet, even teachers of color typically are trained through teacher education programs that often construct students of color from a deficit perspective (Escamilla, 2006), thus marking White students as the cultural standard. CRT exposes how this limited definition of normal operates in US schools and also provides tools to expand normal to include those who have been traditionally seen as deviant due to the color of their skin. By recognizing intersectionality and utilizing counter-narratives, this narrow ideology of normal can be redefined and difference can be valued by including the voices and experiences of people of color (Matsuda, 1987).

DSE serves as a useful lens to examine the concept of normal because it considers how 'able' is taken for granted as being normal. 'Ableism' is a set of beliefs that guide cultural and institutional practices ascribing negative values to individuals with disabilities[2] while deeming able-bodied and able-minded individuals as normal, therefore superior to their disabled counterparts (Gabel, 2005). In US schools, ableism promotes the idea that students with disabilities are unable to attend to their own needs and learning. This leads to paternalistic notions that students with disabilities should be segregated, managed and monitored by adults for the good of all (Ware, 2002). Education within a DSE framework should be "about critiquing social, economic, and political structures that have constructed the concept of normal, average, equal, and standard" (Nocella, 2008, p. 89) while also valuing and promoting the role of diversity within schools (Slee, 2001). DSE urges society to recognize the ways in which such hegemonic ideas and practices reify the ideology of normal. As Kudlick (2003) states, until a less paternalistic view of disability is adopted, it "will lead to stigma and isolation as long as our culture consciously or subconsciously equates dis-ability with in-ability" (p. 769).

From a C/HAT perspective, cultural artifacts and practices mediate interactions with the social world, and those interactions should be understood in both cultural and historical terms (Cole & Engeström, 1993). For example, Brantlinger (2009) referred to individualized instruction and developmentally appropriate practice, both common cultural practices occurring in schools for students considered 'at-risk', as the 'slippery shibboleths' of special education because they perpetuate segregation and marginalization and can lead to differentiated expectations of students. Differentiated instruction, as a research-based pedagogical practice, is designed to help teachers understand the diverse ways in which students learn and to provide differentiated supports across students so that all reach the same high expectations. However, as Peterson and Hittie (2010) noted, differentiation practices in US schools can inadvertently be misused by teachers in ways that lock students into rigid ability levels. Assumptions about what students can or cannot do, enhanced through the creation of differentiated activities that are assigned to particular groups of students, can lead to differentiated expectations, and the segregation and marginalization of students.

Cultural and historical practices inform teachers' conceptions of what it is to be considered normal, and through reflective analysis, teachers working within the activity system of school can "violate existing practices" (Cole & Engeström, 1993, p. 40) by externalizing new ones that are more inclusive and welcoming of diversity A primary focus of C/HAT is to understand both homogeneity and heterogeneity within the practice of schools, rather than characterizing students through static traits. Additionally, diversity is considered to be the primary source for development and learning (Gutiérrez, Baquedano-Lopez, & Tejeda, 1999). Therefore, C/HAT seeks to challenge monolithic views of normalcy by valuing students who differ from the norm, including consideration of race, ability, language and cultural practices.

In the following sections, we critically deconstruct the ideology of normal through our conceptual framework, considering: (1) the underlying, historically driven conceptions of normal, and (2) how normal is manifested in society in schools. Working together as critical theories, CRT and DSE expose the structural inequities in schools supported by racism and ableism. Weaving in C/HAT allows the consideration of the mediating role of ideology among individuals, while critically examining contradictions within the activity system, which undergirds the sorting of students in schools.

2 Critical Examinations of Normal: Deconstructing Normal

In order to "lift the veil of common sense to arrive at underlying interests and agendas" (Leonardo, 2003, p. 208) surrounding normal, we must first deconstruct the meaning of the word. Deconstruction is "an aggressive, political mode of critical analysis that strips conventional and assumed truths down to the logically insubstantial bare bones" (Danforth & Rhodes, 1997, p. 358). Derrida (1974) argued through deconstruction that one could break through the assumed attached meanings to words that have accrued historically. A word is a symbolic representation of an object, which contains meaning and becomes ideational (Vygotsky, 1986). Behind the meanings lie the socially developed methods of thinking and actions that shape society (Leont'ev, 1978). This bond between a word and its meaning is created over time (Vygotsky, 1986), but is situated within the moment of discourse (Derrida, 1974). A critical examination of a word cannot "wrench the concept" (Derrida, 1974, p. 66) attached to the word itself, but must work to expose the contradictions within the meaning of the word as it has evolved over time.

By unveiling current notions of common sense, we can deconstruct ideologies of normal in which systems of power prevail in their various forms of reification. Yet, problematizing what is readily accepted as common sense is not popular or easy. The concept of the word itself becomes so large as to seem "unpeopled" (Danforth & Rhodes, 1997, p. 359) and seemingly unchangeable by the influence of single individuals. Leonardo (2003) stated, "It is at the reification state where ideology is everywhere yet seemingly nowhere because reality appears as natural or pre-ordained" (p. 205). Deconstruction of the word alleviates the seeming power of the 'unpeopled' ideology behind the word, granting us the ability to reveal, examine and potentially change the meaning of the word. We critically examine and deconstruct normal by first contextualizing it, both culturally and historically.

3   Historical Contextualization of Normal

The US educational system's narrow notion of what constitutes ability has evolved through culture, which is the reproduction of historical practice that is perpetuated in institutions such as schools. Culture is "social inheritance" (Cole & Levitin, 2000, p. 69), the way that human beings develop meaning as the accumulation of the prior generations' practices and beliefs. Specifically addressing power, race, and ability within C/HAT, Trent et al. (2002) explain how historical practices "may result in the perpetuation of hierarchical relationships where power is amassed and maintained by some and denied to others based on characteristics that have historically relegated individuals and groups to dominant or subordinate status" (p. 15). Through cultural practices that have become second nature (Cole & Levitin, 2000) in education, ability has become a perceived neutral means of placing value judgments on individuals in order to justify the existence of dominant or subordinate groups, even though conceptions of ability are biased (Harry & Klingner, 2006). Artiles (2009) suggests that researchers must "adopt an emic perspective; that is, to

CHALLENGING THE IDEOLOGY OF NORMAL IN SCHOOLS

understand school and everyday events as mediated by cultural assumptions and artifacts/tools, and as situated in cultural contexts" (p. 26). In other words, the culture of schools—like all cultures—is not a static, monolithic entity but instead manifests itself in everyday practices that reveal themselves in common sense discussions of normal.

DSE illuminates the historical justification for the positioning of those who did not fit this narrow concept of normal by exposing how the difference/deviance of a person allegedly originates inside of that person and not in the society that labels them. In contrast, Disability Studies scholars view society as obsessed with disabling practices that ultimately are inscribed upon individuals who do not or cannot conform to culturally established standards of normalcy (Baynton, 2001). As Nocella (2008) writes, "Ability is the foundation of the justification of the term and philosophy of disability, while disability has been the justification to kill, test on, segregate, abort, and abandon" (p. 77). This discourse around disability was supported by the Eugenics movement during the mid-1800s which, along with the birth of the statistical bell curve model that followed, suggested ability and intelligence fell along a normally distributed, bell-shaped continuum (Davis, 1999). Those individuals falling at the edges of the bell curve were seen to deviate from the norm, which promulgated the idea of a 'deviant' body compared to an 'ideal' or 'normal' body (Davis, 2006). Consequently, individuals with disabilities were seen as a menace to society and in need of institutionalization for their own protection and benefit (Atkinson & Walmsley, 1999). The average oddly became the ideal. Baynton (2001) wrote:

> Although normality ostensibly denoted the average, the usual, and the ordinary, in actual usage it functioned as an ideal and excluded only those defined as below average. 'Is the child normal?' was never a question that expressed fear about whether a child had above average intelligence, motor skills, or beauty. Abnormal signified the subnormal. (p. 36)

On one hand, special education in the US was founded on principles of inclusion and a right to free and appropriate public education (FAPE). Special education and civil rights for people with disabilities were hard fought rights won through rallies, sit-ins and other protests common of the Civil Rights Movement by people with disabilities (Cone, 1997). Yet on the other, special education enacted and institutionalized paternalistic notions of separating and rehabilitating individuals who are not able to conform to desired standards by those who did (Erevelles, 2000). In other words, it was people without disabilities that began to use special education as a route to segregate and cure those with disabilities. In studying American special education, Milofsky (1986) highlighted ways in which different groups have historically been marginalized and segregated based on differences. In the early 1900s, children of Eastern European immigrants whose language and customs differed vastly from most Americans were labeled 'morons' and 'idiots' and placed into special education (Milofsky, 1986). Following desegregation into the 1960s, White teachers faced with African-American children for the first time found them to be "unacceptable and threatening" (Milofsky, 1986, p. 318). Many were labeled mentally retarded and placed into isolated special education settings. Currently, special education is seeing a growth trend in the Hispanic population throughout the US, often based on speaking a language other than the unmarked norm of English (Sullivan, 2011). Throughout history, children have been placed in special education based on cultural and linguistic differences deemed deviant from the norms of 'regular' education.

CRT and other social justice-oriented scholars expose how people of color have been seen as different (and therefore deviant) throughout American history (Gotanda, 1991). From the systematic extermination of Native Americans as the country was being conquered, to the abhorrent practice of slavery, to the constitution which declared African-Americans as three-fifths of a person, Americans have consistently declared their beliefs that people of color were abnormal (Bell, 1980). Americans have utilized God in Manifest Destiny and Jim Crow Laws (Zinn, 1980), science in Craniology (Menchaca, 1997), Eugenics (Valencia, 1997), culture in The Culture of Poverty (Gorski, 2008) and The Moynihan Report (Moynihan, 1965; Tyack, 1974) in order to prove the inferiority of people of color. McDermott, Goldman, and Varenne (2006) state:

> For 150 years, the West has been rife with rumors about intelligence, primitive minds, and inherited genius, all differentially distributed across kinds of people by race, class, gender and national character. The rumors have encouraged oppression by explanation: Some can, some cannot, and this is why some have and some have not. (p. 13)

History offers evidence of attempts throughout the years to characterize people of color as inferior and therefore abnormal (Gould, 1996). This trend continues, reflected in current educational inequities that negatively impact students of color (Ferri & Connor, 2005). Yet, race simply represents ordinary human variance and dividing people along racial lines is "at best imprecise and at worst completely arbitrary" (Omi & Winant, 1994, p. 55). Any number of markers could have been chosen to categorize people, such as eye color, shape of nose or blood type, but once skin color became a social marker, it became a significant way of separating, identifying and punishing social/ethnic groups for differing from the norm in ways that have, and still have, life impacting consequences (Bell, 1987).

Viewing difference as deviance has both historical and cultural foundations, and these underlying beliefs continue to inform the discourse surrounding the current ideology of normal. Below we examine the ways in which an ideology of normal permeates thinking and actions in westernized society, which currently manifests itself in schools.

4 Current Ideology of Normal in Westernized Society

Unfortunately, despite incremental societal advances away from the demons of our past,[3] the ideology of normal still prevails in schools and society and this reinforces power structures. "To gain a monopoly of winning positions, dominant groups must set, get consensus for, and enforce normative standards that are used to designate themselves as competent and Others as inadequate" (Brantlinger, 2006, p. 200). However, efforts to reinforce these power structures are not explicit. Instead, the ideology of normal is "embedded in cultural milieus and connects local actions to larger historical processes" (Artiles, 2009, p. 26). The macro-discursive structures surrounding the ideology of normal have become inscribed upon the micro, localized practices and beliefs that often are left unquestioned. The outcome is the unconscious division of the total population into those who are normal and those who are not (Davis, 2006). When normal is held as the standard, our systems and structures impose oppressive practices on deviance from the norm (Connor, 2008). Furthermore, the richness of diversity is detrimentally lost.

5 Current Ideology of Normal as Reified in Schools

The current ideology of normal contradicts ideas of equitable education. These prevalent conceptions of normalcy influence where students are socially positioned in a school and how they are treated. McDermott, Goldman, and Varenne (2006) argue that because of the competitive nature of US schooling, students are subjected to hierarchical patterns of those who can, and those who cannot achieve, "Hence American education is well organized to make hierarchy out of any differences that can be claimed, however falsely, to be natural, inherent, and potentially consequential in school" (p. 12). The following section contains examples of ways that the ideology of normal has led to marked educational inequities.

5.1   *Education Policy*

Since 2001, No Child Left Behind (NCLB) has had a profound impact on the ways children are being educated in the US. NCLB has been shown to limit the curriculum, including reducing exposure to subjects that are not tested and limiting instructional strategies through a narrow definition of research-based instruction (Fusarelli, 2004).

Additionally, NCLB has the potential to increase dropout rates and decrease graduation rates (Voltz & Fore III, 2006) and these practices driven by NCLB are most likely to disproportionately affect students of color in urban schools (Goodrich Ratcliffe & Willard, 2006). For all of the intentions that informed NCLB (positive or not), NCLB perpetuates an ideology of normal through its narrow definition of success: achievement on a standardized test. Cole (2006) noted, "The tendency to force a single academic curricular focus and devalue other types of learning may limit the opportunities for students with disabilities to excel" (p. 4). These negative effects also disproportionately impact students of color, students who speak a language other than English and others positioned as abnormal.

As Response to Intervention (RtI) becomes more prevalent in the identification of students with disabilities, so does the concern for lack of attention towards culturally and linguistically diverse learners. Evidence-based interventions are typically evidenced based only for students who fall in the norm, and the implementation of such interventions is done without consideration of what works with whom, by whom and in what contexts (Klingner & Edwards, 2006; Moore & Klingner, 2014). Despite being a framework that attempts to contextualize a learning problem by promoting a change in environmental factors (i.e., instruction), RtI still does not include practices that consider the full cultural-historical contexts that shape learning. A learning problem is characterized as either inadequate instruction or a disability, and broader contextual factors (e.g., classroom learning environments, funding distributions and professional development) are not systematically examined (Artiles, Ball, & King Thorius, 2010). Even though RtI purports to privilege the instructional context, typical RtI practices still locate the deficit within the child through its attempts at treating difficulties through increasing practices of removal, along with overconfidence in unquestioned research-based contexts (Ferri, 2011).

5.2   *English-Only Initiatives*

Monolingual English speakers are the unmarked norm in America (Gutiérrez et al., 2002). Crawford (2004) points out that "[B]ilingualism has proved jarring to many Americans ... Hearing other languages spoken freely in public has fostered the perception that English is losing ground, that newcomers no longer

CHALLENGING THE IDEOLOGY OF NORMAL IN SCHOOLS   89

care to learn the national tongue" (p. 14). Additionally, language can be seen as a proxy for race, and English-only movements often have a racial undertone as they have mostly occurred in states with largely Spanish-speaking populations (Revilla & Asato, 2002). When students speak a language other than English, it is easier for educators to think of them as different, even deficient. In considering stages of language acquisition, for example, the silent period and linguistic errors can be mistaken for a lack of intelligence (Baca & Cervantes, 2004; Hakuta, 1990). Additionally, limited assessment measures that inadequately gauge or even ignore the skills of emerging bilingual students contribute to seeing these students narrowly as limited in English and therefore encourage deficit thinking (Escamilla, 2006).

5.3   *The Achievement Gap*

While the achievement gap seemed to be closing in the 1970s and 1980s in the US, that movement began to slow during the 1990s, causing alarm (Lee, 2002). Some deficit-oriented theories attribute the gap to racial issues, while others point to issues of poverty and conditions in the home. Scholars such as Ladson-Billings (2006) and Noguera and Yonemura Wing (2006) suggest that this hierarchical rating of students remains persistent over time because of ways in which students who fall outside the realm of 'normal' are tracked into remedial classes or special education and given less academically challenging coursework than their more privileged peers.

However, "hierarchies are not purposeless, passive rankings, but represent important interdependent relations among people of different ranks" (Brantlinger, 2006, p. 201). Instead, the achievement gap serves a purpose as superiority needs inferiority to reinforce its goodness.

5.4   *The Segregation of Students with Disabilities*

The special education system has classrooms segregated from general education in order to house individuals deemed to have 'impairments' in environments ostensibly more suitable for meeting their 'needs' (Reid & Knight, 2006). Despite the fact that the Individuals with Disabilities Education Act (IDEA) explicitly stipulates that students with special needs be given access to the general education curriculum, placement into special education often excludes students from the general education curriculum, particularly if the instruction provided to students is only from a prescriptive, basic skills mastery approach (Gallagher, 2005). When students are denied access to grade level, enriched curriculum provided in an environment with their general education peers, it can lead to economic hardships when students who have been tracked through special education struggle to find jobs in a competitive market

(Barton, 1993). Statistics from the World Summit on Social Development in 1995 noted that individuals with disabilities are the largest minority group facing poverty, unemployment and social and cultural isolation. Individuals with disabilities earn only 60% of the income of individuals without disabilities (Erevelles, 2000). Once given a label of disability, students are subject to material consequences from being viewed as abnormal to having limited access to all aspects of society.

5.5 Disproportionate Representation in Special Education

The disproportionate representation of students of color in special education has been studied and identified as a cause of concern for years (Donovan & Cross, 2002; Heller, Holtzman, & Messick, 1982; National Education Association of the United States and National Association of School Psychologists, 2007; Patton, 1998). Disproportionate representation refers to whether the percentage of a group in special education is larger or smaller than the percentage of that group within the educational system as a whole (Harry, 1994). Students of color are over-represented in high-incidence disability categories (i.e., learning disability, emotional–behavioral disability and mild intellectual disability), yet are proportionately represented in low-incidence disability categories (e.g., traumatic brain injury, deafness and blindness) (Albrecht et al., 2012; Harry & Klingner, 2006). Even when students of color have the same disability label as their White peers, research has found that they are more likely to be segregated, thereby limiting their exposure to the general education curriculum (Gandara & Bial, 2001; Losen & Orfield, 2002; Sullivan, 2011). Though the federal government mandates special education funding, there continues to be a lack of resources for those in special education in high minority schools, which leads to a lack of access to equitable education. In other words, special education placement often excludes students, particularly students from high poverty, high minority schools, from the general education curriculum, which results in economic hardships when students struggle to find jobs in the marketplace (Oswald, Coutinho, & Best, 2002). The disproportionate representation of students of color is a clear illustration of how once seen as abnormal, students of color who utilize diverse cultural practices or may speak a language other than English are more likely to be seen as less capable than their White counterparts due to additive stigma. That is, these students would have not only the stigma of having a disability, but also the perceived problematic identities of minority racial status or linguistic practices that contribute to the ways others construct them as abnormal (Kertzner et al., 2009; Mostade, 2004).

CHALLENGING THE IDEOLOGY OF NORMAL IN SCHOOLS 91

5.6 *Unequal Discipline Practices*

Another educational outcome directly tied to race and disability is disparate discipline practices in schools (Mendez & Knopf, 2003). Statistics show that even when controlling for socioeconomic status, students in special education and students of color are over-represented in all disciplinary actions (Skiba et al., 2000). This is important since discipline rates are directly tied to incarceration rates (Arcia, 2006) and evoke the spectre of a school-to-prison pipeline. For example, Wald and Losen (2003) state, "The 'single largest predictor' of later arrest among adolescent females is having been suspended, expelled or held back during the middle school years" (p. 4). Quinn et al. (2005) found that the "number of youth identified and receiving special education services in juvenile corrections is almost four times higher than in public school programs during the same time period" (p. 4). Once seen as abnormal by color, language or ability, students are more likely to be constructed as deviant and even dangerous in behavior (Annamma, Connor, & Ferri, 2013).

Each of these examples of inequities stem, at least partially, from society's binaric conceptions of normal. By positioning students of color, second language learners, those with diverse cultural practices and those with disabilities as abnormal, people are more likely to construct these students as having internal, individual deficits. Consumed with standardization, educators are overly attentive to students who are not 'adequately developed'. Although all students possess differences, some differences are related to larger social, economic or academic disparities of opportunity that result from accumulative practices of oppression (Bruna, 2009). Consequently, this leads to localized interactions that expect students to lose/change/remold part of themselves. The criteria for normal, and thus the accompanying deviations, are clear: the White, middle-class, monolingual English-speaking and average ability criteria for school success contributes to the reproduction of classism, ableism and racism in education.

6 "Who Benefits" under the Ideology of Normal?

Up to this point, we explored 'the how' of the ideology of normal and the ways this ideology is practiced in US schools and society. However, to finish the deconstruction of normal, we must move beyond 'the how' to 'the why'. Why maintain the ideology of normal? There are economic benefits for labelling others as abnormal, such as maintaining the status quo by keeping power nested in the hands of the few. When labeled disabled, individuals tend to experience limited access to equal education and jobs due to societal barriers, leaving more room for those considered normal at the top (Brantlinger, 2006).

Drawing from Gramsci's call to ask, "Who benefits?" when examining social actions, Brantlinger (2004) challenges her readers to ponder the question, who benefits from high-stakes testing? As these tests rank, and categorize, all under the auspices of accountability, these sorting systems work to target those in need of treatment, or intervention, based on their 'Other' status. What is more, the tests remain attractive to all parties involved because, in Gramsci's terms, the dominant group strategically works to persuade the Others that the practice is in their best interest, to help them, all the while working to maintain evidence of their subordinates' inferiority. Of course, testing companies, politicians and school administrators are among the constituents who benefit. However, the genius of the accountability and standards movement is in the "ideologies that obfuscate power imbalances" (Brantlinger, 2004, p. 3). In other words, the ideology of normal lures public education to embrace a system that contributes to its demise out of the fear of dwindling resources and the potential loss of professional legitimacy (Taubman, 2009).

Brantlinger, Majd-Jabbari, and Guskin (1996) further explored this obfuscation of ideology in a study with middle-class mothers when they showed how these mothers were able to tout themselves as caring, compassionate and liberal, all the while using ideology to maintain a propensity towards the status quo, one that allowed them to preserve their power and privilege. The ideology of normal worked to create binaries of "ordinary people and others" (Brantlinger, Majd-Jabbari, & Guskin, 1996, p. 579) and although human variance was recognized, any associated hierarchies were claimed to be naturalized, even deserving.

It is clear that when we enact the ideology of normal, particular populations are subject to oppression and that is not accidental. "The historical debt was not merely imposed by ignorant masses that were xenophobic and virulently racist. The major leaders of the nation endorsed ideas about the inferiority of Black, Latina/o, and Native peoples" (Ladson-Billings, 2006, p. 6). Controlling those who were different became the task of the experts in the jurisprudence and medical fields. The rise of hospitals, mental asylums and penitentiaries is no simple coincidence of historic time periods; these institutions served the purpose of separating the masses into those who belonged and those who did not (Foucault, 1995). Historic inequities that formed around differences from the norm in race, class, language, gender and perceived ability continue to persist today. Due to this belief in inferiority, traditionally those in power—male, able-bodied, monolingual, English speaking, Whites—have had little interest in investing in the education of those who are different. Even today we see funding inequities, which correlate with racial, ethnic and socioeconomic differences. School funding has been shown to rise with an increase in White populations. Though correlation is not causation, these inequities imply a refusal to fund education for those who fall outside of normal (Ladson-Billings, 2006).

In an arena in which test-measured ability is the highest commodity (Brantlinger, 2006), rich and true learning becomes cheap and scarce. Students will do what they can to avoid getting "caught not knowing something and/or getting caught knowing something at just the right time" (McDermott & Raley, 2011, p. 381). Yet still, the ideology of normal continues to persuade others of its rationality, when truly "the requirement of all children to be average is illogical" (Brantlinger, 2006, p. 237), and by definition, impossible. Certainly, removing the high-stakes tests will not eliminate the ideology of normal in schools, for it is far too pervasive. As we have seen through CRT, DSE and C/HAT, ideologies are powerful mediators that are always imbued with power. And paradoxically, those in power (e.g., stakeholders in education) work to fix the powerless (Brantlinger, 2006) or to make the abnormal normal, which in actuality preserves existing power structures, along with the ideology of normal.

Yet in the spirit of deconstruction, we draw inspiration from Brantlinger (2006) as she seeks to upend existing hierarchies: "Rather than insisting on normal, routine, and homogenous academic outcomes, it seems that a realistic problem-solving curriculum focused on actual social, medical, and environmental issues would be far better" (p. 241). To overturn the binary of normal and abnormal requires a demarcation of power structures, with the help of CRT and DSE, as well as an examination of contradictions that keep the hierarchies in place, as C/HAT strives to do. The normal practices of creating winners and losers (Brantlinger, 2006) should be replaced with more abnormal practices of egalitarianism, interdependence and community. Instead of a single narrative by which to aspire and thus assimilate (Slee, 1997), heterogeneous narratives, especially counter-narratives, are privileged.

7 Challenging the Ideology of Normal: Reconstructing Normal as Variability

A critical deconstruction of the ideology of normal, driven by historical and cultural discourse and definitions, makes visible the problematic nature of the current ideology of normal in its binaric construction and in the limited ways it works to position students. Variability exists, which creates contradictions; consider the goal of NCLB to have all third-grade students proficient in reading by 2013–2014 (Department of Education, Federal Register, 2002). As Ball and

Harry (2010) suggest, "We would ask whether the educational establishment in the US could stand to have the level of success reach 100% if the belief in a normal distribution so permeates our beliefs about achievement and other human traits" (p. 115)? If anything is to be considered normal in schools, it should be the existence of variability.

7.1 *Valuing Diversity*

Through statistics that show people of color lagging behind in virtually all facets of life in the US (Bonilla-Silva, 2006), we see evidence that diversity is not truly valued in our society because of the perpetuation of the ideology of normal. Since our societal institutions reflect our cultural values and practices, we see our current education system as one that rewards conformity to cultural standards and punishes and segregates difference from those norms. Incremental steps like African-American History Month can encourage a slow growth approach, allowing US society to avoid making more substantial changes that could truly affect the life outcomes of those who do not fit the cultural norm (Bell, 1987). Ignoring diversity is akin to colorblind racism to us and so we reject it as well (Bonilla-Silva, 2006). Instead, we argue that valuing and accepting diversity is a complex cultural process of change. Not only do we need to think differently (interpersonal), but also our politicians and our institutions (e.g., schools, medical industry and jails) need to change by rejecting the ideology of normal. In order to promote a substantial process of change, the interpersonal and institutional must inform each other. When we argue that we need to accept and value diversity, we are suggesting a fundamental societal shift, and there is nothing trite about changing the way we speak, think and act as people and as a society. Using our conceptual framework of CRT, DSE and C/HAT, we are provided with tools to authentically value diversity which we hope to explore in the future.

Brantlinger has heavily influenced our thinking on the ideology of normal that is pervasive in schools and society. Since we read Brantlinger's (1997) "Using ideology: Cases of nonrecognition of the politics of research and practice in special education," we have journeyed, and continue still, on a multi-year exploration of what the ideology of normal is, who it affects and how we can uncover the way it works to maintain power relations. It is Brantlinger we have in mind as we consider the future work we want to do with this new theoretical framework. Combining CRT, DSE and C/HAT provides us with tools not only to deconstruct the ideology of normal but also to reconstruct it in the future. This constant dialectic between larger, macro, societal discourses and beliefs about what is normal and what is deviant and smaller, micro, localized practices and actions provides fertile ground for us to critique, challenge and reconstruct our ideology of normal. Drawing on the work of Barrett, Brantlinger argues that "organic ideologies" (Barrett, 1994, as cited in Brantlinger, 1997, p. 448) are more useful in dismantling oppressive social forces than polemic ideologies that rely on rhetoric to reify existing social structures. She states, "Arriving at organic ideologies means struggling to intervene in the terrain of common sense by taking steps to counteract familiar, taken-for-granted practices ... and treating the regularities of everyday life as problematic" (Brantlinger, 1997, p. 448). By reconstructing common sense perceptions about what is normal, we stand to create more equitable learning environments for students who have been marginalized and segregated based on perceived differences in cultural practices, race, language use and ability.

Acknowledgements

We dedicate this chapter to the memory of our esteemed colleague, mentor, friend, and fellow author, Dr. Janette Klinger, who passed away in the spring of 2014. Without Janette, we would not have come to know the work of Ellen Brantlinger. As scholars, teachers, and mothers, we passionately carry on the work of both Janette and Ellen in all that we do.

This chapter originally appeared in *International Journal of Inclusive Education, 17*(12), 2013, 1278–1294. Reprinted here with permission from the publisher.

Notes

1 Although our discussion of normal is grounded in westernized ideology, particularly as enacted in the US education system, we recognize how normal can be conceptualized in other cultures. For example, Serpell, Mariga, and Harvey (1993) noted that intelligence in a Zambian community is often characterized by moral abilities rather than cognitive abilities. Congenital hip deformities among the Navajo are not always seen as a disability because they are accommodating for the individual in riding a horse (Locust, 1988). And, at times, epilepsy in a Hmong community is not viewed as a disease or a handicap (Fadiman, 1997). However, in each example a concept of normal continues to exist, though defined by different parameters.

2 Despite the negative assumptions embedded within the term 'disability', many disability rights activists have adopted the term, continuing its usage as a way to push society to recognize the stigma and implications associated with the term and to consider how those with disabilities are treated in society (Nocella, 2008).

3 We have moved past some of this historical, overt discrimination through legislation such as the Civil Rights Act (1964), the Americans with Disabilities Act (1990), and court cases such as Diana vs. State Board of Education (1970) in which the court

ruled that schools could not place a student in special education without testing in their native language. Yet inequities in society based on race still exist.

References

Albrecht, S. F., Skiba, R. J. Losen, D. J., Chung, C., & Middelber, L. (2012). Federal policy on disproportionality in special education: Is it moving us forward? *Journal of Disability Policy Studies, 23*(1), 14–25.

Annamma, S. A., Connor, D., & Ferri, B. (2013). Dis/Ability critical race studies (DisCrit): Theorizing at the intersections of race and dis/ability. *Race Ethnicity and Education, 16*(1), 1–31.

Arcia, E. (2006). Achievement and enrollment status of suspended students: Outcomes in a large, multicultural school district. *Education and Urban Society, 38*(3), 359–369.

Artiles, A. J. (2009). Re-framing disproportionality research: Outline of a cultural-historical paradigm. *Multiple Voices for Ethnically Diverse Exceptional Learners, 11*(2), 24–37.

Artiles, A. J., Ball, A., & King Thorius, K. A. (2010). Back to the future: A critique of response to intervention views. *Theory into Practice, 49*(4), 250–257.

Atkinson, D., & Walmsley, J. (1999). Using autobiographical approaches with people with learning difficulties. *Disability & Society, 14*(2), 203–216.

Baca, L., & Cervantes, H. (2004). *The bilingual special education interface.* Upper Saddle River, NJ: Pearson Education.

Baglieri, S., & Knopf, J. H. (2004). Normalizing difference in inclusive teaching. *Journal of Learning Disabilities, 37*(6), 525–529.

Ball, E. W., & Harry, B. (2010). Assessment and the policing of the norm. In C. Dudley-Marling & A. Gurn (Eds.), *The myth of the normal curve* (pp. 105–122). New York, NY: Peter Lang.

Barton, L. (1993). The struggle for citizenship: The case of disabled people. *Disability, Handicap, & Society, 8*(3), 235–248.

Baynton, D. C. (2001). Disability and the justification for inequality in American history. In P. S. Rothenberg (Ed.), *Race, class and gender in the United States* (6th ed., pp. 93–102). New York, NY: New York University Press.

Bell, D. A. (1980). Brown v. Board of education and the interest convergence dilemma. *Harvard Law Review, 93*, 518–533.

Bell, D. (1987). *And we are not saved: The elusive quest for racial justice.* New York, NY: Basic Books.

Bonilla-Silva, E. (2006). *Racism without racists: Color-blind racism and the persistence of racial inequality in America* (3rd ed.). Lanham, MD: Rowman & Littlefield Publishers.

Brantlinger, E. (1997). Using ideology: Cases of nonrecognition of the politics of research and practice in special education. *Review of Educational Research, 67*(4), 425–459.

CHALLENGING THE IDEOLOGY OF NORMAL IN SCHOOLS 97

Brantlinger, E. A. (2004). An application of Gramsci's "who benefits?" To high-stakes testing. *Workplace, 6.1*. Retrieved February 23, 2005, from http://www.cust.educ.ubc.ca/workplace/issue6p1/brantlinger.html

Brantlinger, E. A. (Ed.). (2006). *Who benefits from special education?: Remediating (fixing) other people's children*. Mahwah, NJ: Lawrence Erlbaum Associates.

Brantlinger, E. (2009). Slippery shibboleths: The shady side of truisms in special education. In S. L. Gabel (Ed.), *Disability studies in education: Readings in theory and method* (Vol. 3, pp. 125–138). New York, NY: Peter Lang Publishing.

Brantlinger, E., Majd-Jabbari, M., & Guskin, S. L. (1996). Self-interest and liberal educational discourse: How ideology works for middle-class mothers. *American Educational Research Journal, 33*(3), 571–597.

Bruna, K. R. (2009). Materializing multiculturalism: Deconstruction and cumulation in teaching language, culture, and (non) identity reflections on Roth and Kellogg. *Mind, Culture, and Activity, 16*(2), 183–190.

Cole, C. (2006). Closing the achievement gap series: Part III – What is the impact of NCLB on the inclusion of students with disabilities? *Education Policy Brief, 4*(11), 1–12.

Cole, M., & Engeström, Y. (1993). A cultural-historical approach to distributed cognition. In G. (Ed.), *Distributed cognition: Psychological and educational considerations*. New York, NY: Cambridge University Press.

Cole, M., & Levitin, K. (2000). *Being humans: Anthropological Universality and particularity in trans-disciplinary perspectives*. Berlin: Walter de Gruyter.

Cone, K. (1997). *Short history of the 504 Sit In*. Retrieved October 3, 2011, from http://www.dredf.org/504site/histover.html

Connor, D. J. (2008). *Urban narratives: Portraits in progress: Life at the intersections of learning disability, race, & social class*. New York, NY: Peter Lang Publishing.

Crawford, J. (2004). *Educating English learners: Language diversity in the classroom*. Los Angeles, CA: Bilingual Education Services.

Danforth, S., & Rhodes, W. C. (1997). Deconstructing disability: A philosophy for inclusion. *Remedial and Special Education, 18*(6), 357–366.

Davis, L. J. (1999). Crips strike back: The rise of disability studies. *American Literary History, 11*(3), 500–512.

Davis, L. J. (2006). Constructing normalcy: The bell curve, the novel, and the invention of the disabled body in the nineteenth century. In L. Davis (Ed.), *The disability studies reader* (2nd ed., pp. 3–19). New York, NY: Routledge.

Derrida, J. (1974). *Of grammatology* (G. C. Spivak, Trans.). Baltimore, MD & London: Johns Hopkins University Press.

Donovan, S., & Cross, C. T. (2002). *Minority students in special and gifted education*. Washington, DC: National Academy Press.

Dudley-Marling, C., & Gurn, A. (2010). Troubling the foundations of special education: Examining the myth of the normal curve. In C. Dudley-Marling & A. Gurn (Eds.), *The myth of the normal curve* (pp. 9–24). New York, NY: Peter Lang.

Erevelles, N. (2000). Educating unruly bodies: Critical pedagogy, disability studies, and the politics of schooling. *Educational Theory, 50*(1), 25–47.

Escamilla, K. (2006). Semilingualism applied to the literacy behaviors of Spanish speaking emerging bilinguals: Emerging biliteracy or biliteracy? *Teacher's College Record, 108*(11), 2329–2353.

Fadiman, A. (1997). *The spirit catches you and you fall down: A Hmong child, her American doctors, and the collision of two cultures.* New York, NY: Farrar, Straus and Giroux.

Fendler, L., & Muzaffar, I. (2008). The history of the bell curve: Sorting and the idea of normal. *Educational Theory, 58*(1), 63–82.

Ferri, B. A. (2011). Undermining inclusion? A critical reading of Response to Intervention (RtI). *International Journal of Inclusive Education, 16*(8), 1–18.

Ferri, B. A., & Connor, D. J. (2005). In the shadow of Brown: Special education and over-representation of students of color. *Remedial and Special Education, 26*(2), 93–100.

Foucault, M. (1995). *The archeology of knowledge and the discourse on language.* New York, NY: Pantheon Books.

Fusarelli, L. D. (2004). The potential impact of the no child left behind act on equity and diversity in American education. *Educational Policy, 18*(1), 71–94.

Gabel, S. (2005). *Disability studies in education.* New York, NY: Peter Lang.

Gallagher, D. J. (2009). Searching for something outside of ourselves: The contradiction between technical rationality and the achievement of inclusive pedagogy. In S. L. Gabel (Ed.), *Disability studies in education: Readings in theory and method.* New York, NY: Peter Lang.

Gandara, P., & Bial, D. (2001). *Paving the way to postsecondary education: K-12 intervention programs for underrepresented youth.* Washington, DC: National Center for Education Statistics, Office of Educational Research and Improvement, U. S. Department of Education.

Gillborn, D. (2005). Education policy as an act of white supremacy: Whiteness, critical race theory and education reform. *Journal of Education Policy, 20*(4), 485–505.

Glass, G. V., & Smith, M. L. (1979). Meta-analysis of research on class size and achievement. *Educational Evaluation and Policy Analysis, 1*(1), 2–16.

Goodrich Ratcliffe, K., & Willard, D. T. (2006). NCLB and IDEA: Perspectives from the field. *Focus on Exceptional Children, 39*(3), 1–14.

Gorski, P. (2008). The myth of the "culture of poverty." *Educational Leadership, 65*(7), 32–37.

Gotanda, N. (1991). A critique of "our constitution is color-blind." *Stanford Law Review, 44*(1), 1–68.

Gould, S. J. (1996). *The mismeasure of man.* New York, NY: W. W. Norton & Co.

Gutiérrez, K. D., Asato, J., Santos, M., & Gotanda, N. (2002). Backlash pedagogy: Language and culture and the politics of reform. *The Review of Education, Pedagogy, and Cultural Studies, 24*(4), 335–351.

CHALLENGING THE IDEOLOGY OF NORMAL IN SCHOOLS 99

Gutiérrez, K. D., Baquedano-Lopez, P., & Tejada, C. (1999). Rethinking diversity: Hybridity and hybrid language practices in the third space. *Mind, Culture, and Activity, 6*(4), 286–303.

Hakuta, K. (1990). *Bilingualism and bilingual education: A research perspective.* Washington, DC: George Washington University, Center for Applied Linguistics.

Harry, B. (1994). *The disproportionate representation of minority students in special education: Theories and recommendations.* Washington, DC: National Association of State Directors of Special Education, U. S. Department of Education, Office of Educational Research and Improvement, Educational Resources Information Center.

Harry, B., & Klingner, J. (2006). *Why are so many minority students in special education?* New York, NY: Teachers College.

Heller, K. A., Holtzman, W. H., & Messick, S. (1982). *Placing children in special education.* Washington, DC: National Academy Press.

Hodgkinson, H. (2002). Demographics and teacher education: An overview. *Journal of Teacher Education, 53*(2), 102–105.

Kertzner, R. M., Meyer, I. H., Frost, D. M., & Stirratt, M. J. (2009). Social and psychological well-being in lesbians, gay men, and bisexuals: The effects of race, gender, age, and sexual identity. *American Journal of Orthopsychiatry, 79*(4), 500–510.

Klingner, J. K., & Edwards, P. (2006). Cultural considerations with response to intervention models. *Reading Research Quarterly, 41*(1), 108–117.

Kudlick, C. J. (2003). Disability history: Why we need another 'other'. *The American History Review, 108*(3), 763–793.

Ladson-Billings, G. (1998). Just what is critical race theory and what's it doing in a nice field like education? *International Journal of Qualitative Studies in Education, 11*(1), 7–24.

Ladson-Billings, G. (2006). From the achievement gap to the education debt: Understanding achievement in U. S. schools. *Educational Researcher, 35*(7), 3–12.

Lee, C. D. (2002). Interrogating race and ethnicity as constructs in the examination of cultural processes in developmental research. *Human Development, 45*(4), 282–290.

Leonardo, Z. (2003). Discourse and critique: Outlines of a post-structural theory of ideology. *Journal of Education Policy, 18*(2), 203–214.

Leont'ev, A. N. (1978). *Activity, consciousness, and personality.* Englewood Cliffs, NJ: Prentice-Hall.

Locust, C. (1988). Wounding the spirit: Discrimination and traditional American Indian belief systems. *Harvard Educational Review, 58*(3), 315–30.

Losen, D. J., & Orfield, G. (2002). *Racial inequity in special education.* Cambridge, MA: Harvard Education Press.

Matsuda, M. J. (1987). Looking to the bottom: Critical legal studies and reparations. *Harvard Civil Rights-Civil Liberties Law Review, 22,* 323.

McDermott, R., Goldman, S., & Varenne, H. (2006). The cultural work of learning disabilities. *Educational Researcher, 35*(6), 12–17.

McDermott, R., & Raley, J. (2011). Toward a natural history of human ingenuity. In E. Margolis & L. Pauwels (Eds.), *The Sage handbook of visual research methods*. Thousand Oaks, CA: Sage Publications.

Menchaca, M. (1997). Early racist discourses: Roots of deficit thinking. In R. Valencia (Ed.), *The evolution of deficit thinking: Educational thought and practice* (pp. 113–131). London: Routledge Falmer.

Mendez, L. M. R., & Knoff, H. M. (2003). Who gets suspended from school and why: A demographic analysis of schools and disciplinary infractions in a large school district. *Education and Treatment of Children, 26*(1), 30–51.

Milofsky, C. (1986). Is the growth of special education evolutionary or cyclic? A response to Carrier. *American Journal of Education, 94*(3), 313–321.

Moore, B. A., & Klingner, J. K. (2014). Considering the needs of English language learners: An examination of the population validity of reading intervention research. *Journal of Learning Disabilities, 47*(5), 391–408.

Mostade, S. J. (2004). *Components of internalized homophobia, self-disclosure of sexual orientation to physician, and durable power of attorney for health care completion in older gay men* (Dissertation). Retrieved from OhioLINK ETD Center

Moynihan, D. P. (1965). *The Negro family: The case for national action*. Washington, DC: U.S. Government Printing Office.

National Education Association. (2007). *Truth in labeling: Disproportionality in special education*. Washington, DC: National Education Association.

Nocella, A. (2008). Emergence of disability pedagogy. *Journal of Critical Education Policy Studies, 6*(2), 77–94.

Noguera, P. A., & Yonemura Wing, J. (2006). *Unfinished business: Closing the racial achievement gap in our Nation's Schools*. San Francisco, CA: Jossey-Bass.

Omi, M., & Winant, H. (1994). *Racial formation in the United States: From the 1960's to the 1990's*. New York, NY: Routledge.

Oswald, D. P., Coutinho, M. J., & Best, A. M. (2002). Community and school predictors of overrepresentation of minority children in special education. In D. Losen & G. Orfield (Eds.), *Racial inequality in special education* (pp. 1–13). Cambridge, MA: Harvard Education Press.

Patton, J. M. (1998). The disproportionate representation of African Americans in special education. *Journal of Special Education, 32*(1), 25–31.

Peterson, J. M., & Hittie, M. M. (2010). *Inclusive teaching: The journey toward effective schools for all learners*. Upper Saddle River, NJ: Pearson Education.

Prichard, B., Annamma, S., Boelé, A., & Klingner, J. (2010, June 22). Race, language, and ability: Deconstructing, reconstructing, and transcending borders of normal. *Teachers College Record*. Retrieved from http://www.tcrecord.org (ID Number: 16028).

Quinn, M. M., Rutherford, R. B., Leone, P. E., Osher, D. M., & Poirier, J. M. (2005). Youth with disabilities in juvenile corrections: A national survey. *Exceptional Children, 71*(3), 339–345.

Reid, D. K., & Knight, M. G. (2006). Disability justifies exclusion of minority students: A critical history grounded in disability studies. *Educational Researcher, 35*(6), 18–23.

Revilla, A. T., & Asato, J. (2002). The implementation of proposition 227 in California schools: A critical analysis of the effect of teacher beliefs and classroom practices. *Equity & Excellence in Education, 35*(2), 108–118.

Serpell, R., Mariga, L., & Harvey, K. (1993). Mental retardation in African countries: Conceptualization, services, and research. *International Review of Research in Mental Retardation, 19*, 1–39.

Shaywitz, S. E., Escobar, M. D., Shaywitz, B. A., Fletcher, J. M., & Makuch, R. (1992). Evidence that dyslexia may represent the lower tail of a normal distribution of reading ability. *New England Journal of Medicine, 326*(6), 145–150.

Skiba, R. J., Michael, R. S., Nardo, A. C., & Peterson, R. (2000). *The color of discipline: Sources of racial and gender disproportionality in school punishment* (Policy Research Report). Bloomington, IN: Education Policy Center, Indiana University.

Slee, R. (1997). Inclusion or assimilation? Sociological explorations of the foundations of theories of special education. *Educational Foundations, 11*(1) 55–71.

Slee, R. (2001). Driven to the margins: Disabled students, inclusive schooling and the politics of possibility. *Cambridge Journal of Education, 31*(3), 385–397.

Sullivan, A. L. (2011). Disproportionality in special education identification and placement of English language learners. *Exceptional Children, 77*(3), 317–334.

Taubman, P. M. (2009). *Teaching by numbers: Deconstructing the discourse of standards and accountability in education.* New York, NY: Routledge.

Thompson, J. B. (1990). *Ideology and modern culture: Critical social theory in the era of mass communication.* Stanford, CA: Stanford University Press.

Trent, S., Artiles, A., Firchett-Bazemore, K., McDaniel, L., & Coleman-Sorrell, A. (2002). Addressing theory, ethics, power, and privilege in inclusion research and practice. *Teacher Education and Special Education, 25*(1), 11–22.

Tyack, D. B. (1974). *The one best system: A history of American urban education.* Cambridge, MA: Harvard University Press.

Valencia, R. R. (1997). Conceptualizing the notion of deficit thinking. In R. Valencia (Ed.), *The evolution of deficit thinking: Educational thought and practice* (pp. 113–131). London: Routledge Falmer.

Voltz, D. L., & Fore III, C. (2006). Urban special education in the context of standards based reform. *Remedial and Special Education, 27*(6), 329–336.

Vygotsky, L. S. (1986). *Thought and language.* Cambridge, MA: MIT Press.

Wald, J., & Losen, D., (2003). *Defining and redirecting a school-to-prison pipeline.* Retrieved from http://www.woodsfund.org/community/Folder_1036081004377/File_1084877618748

Ware, L. P. (2002). A moral conversation on disability: Risking the personal in educational contexts. *Hypatia, 17*(3), 143–172.

Zinn, H. (1980). *A people's history of the United States: 1492 to present.* New York, NY: Harper Collins Publishers.

CHAPTER 6

Vulnerable to Exclusion: The Place for Segregated Education within Conceptions of Inclusion

Emily A. Nusbaum

Abstract

This research was undertaken to understand how general education teachers who work in inclusive classrooms conceptualise inclusive education and understand their individual commitments to this practice. This study intended to make explicit the social meaning that resides in and is constituted by teachers doing their everyday work in school (Erickson, 1977), and in doing so add depth to the body of work in the field of inclusive education that has largely approached research by trying to understand its technical implementation. Analysis of ethnographic data collected at an urban elementary school that had been inclusive for over a decade before adding a segregated classroom for some students with disabilities to the site, demonstrated that the meanings attached to inclusive education were quite variable and elastic for most of the teachers in the study. The study concludes that inclusive education needs to be discussed and taught as an ideological commitment.

Keywords

curriculum and instruction – politics of education – inclusive education

1 Introduction

Public Law 94–142, the Education for all Handicapped Children Act (EHA) of 1975, was later reauthorised by the USA Congress as the Individuals with Disabilities Education Act and, most recently, as the Individuals with Disabilities Education Improvement Act (2006). This landmark piece of legislation in the USA protected the rights of students with disabilities and gave them access to a 'free and appropriate public education' in the 'least restrictive environment.' For the first time, children with disabilities could not be excluded from US

© KONINKLIJKE BRILL NV, LEIDEN, 2020 | DOI:10.1163/9789004402690_007

VULNERABLE TO EXCLUSION

public schools on the basis of disability. Instead, they were given legal entitlement to be educated with non-disabled peers, and the right to receive individualised educational supports and services as outlined in an individualised education programme (IEP). Federal legislation in the USA also codified into law the identification of student disability based largely on medicalised and deficit-based indicators as well as a 'continuum of placement options' that legally required local districts to have a range of places where special education services could be delivered.

This continuum resulted in educational supports and services that were delivered in a range of locations. Students were matched to places that were associated with the amount and type of disability that they were identified to have; therefore, despite the intent of the EHA to guarantee access to general education environments for students with disabilities, integration into these environments was largely realised on a case-by-case basis. The process of integration, or mainstreaming, still required that students with disabilities be placed in separate classrooms and then be given access to general education classrooms and school contexts for various portions of the school day. The ability to be integrated often depended on an individual student's ability to do grade-level work, as well as on 'deal-making' between special and general educators (Ferguson, 1995). Ferguson also identified a critical flaw in the educational practice of integration: that is, in order for students to be integrated, they first had to be segregated.

Since the passage of federal legislation, a large body of practice-based research has emerged that supports the successful inclusion of students with disabilities as members of general education classrooms. Researchers in the field of inclusive education have focused on the development of those practices that can support teaching and learning for all students in the 'place' of the general education classrooms. A well-developed body of literature exists that describes the programmatic features of inclusive classrooms and schools, broader school reform efforts (Causton-Theoharis, 2009; Copeland & Cosbey, 2008–2009; Fisher & Frey, 2001; Halvorsen & Neary, 2009; Kugelmass, 1996; Sailor & Roger, 2005; Villa & Thousand, 2000), and research on the educational outcomes of students with and without disabilities in inclusive classrooms and schools (Hunt & Goetz, 1997; Hunt & McDonnell, 2007; Jackson, Ryndak, & Wehmeyer, 2008–2009; McGregor & Vogelsberg, 1998). Largely, this body of literature focuses on the 'how to' of inclusive education (e.g. students are members of chronologically age-appropriate classrooms; differentiated instruction and cooperative learning are effective practices for heterogeneous groups of students) and identifies the features of structural reform at both the school and district levels. Currently, some scholars view inclusive education as a model of whole-school reform (Causton-Theoharis & Theoharis, 2008; Causton-Theoharis et al., 2011; Sailor & Roger, 2005) aimed at providing an equitable education for all students.

1.1   *Critiques Unchallenged by Research in Inclusive Education*

With this rise in research in the field of inclusive education, some scholars identified the underlying assumptions about disability and student learning that remained unchallenged by federal legislation and subsequent research and reform efforts. These assumptions are largely rooted in reductionist thinking about disability and in the maintenance of educational mechanisms that exist to identify individual deficit in order to 'fix' it.

Early, critical special education scholars[1] such as Heshusius (1989) and Iano (1986), for example, advocated a shift away from rational-technical research methods that are used for the identification, intervention, remediation, and measurement of student 'problems.' Additionally, Skrtic (1991) critiqued the design and conceptualisation of the special education system because it was predicated on the following presuppositions about student disability: (a) disabilities are pathological conditions that students have; (b) differential diagnosis or identification of disability is objective and useful; (c) special education is a rationally conceived and coordinated system of services that benefits diagnosed students; and (d) progress in the field of special education results from rational/technological improvements in diagnostic and instructional practices (p. 152). Skrtic (1991, 2005) claimed that the structural mechanisms that bureaucracies must employ in order to 'screen out' students with unconventional needs from mainstream educational systems achieved two ends. First, it shifted the blame for school failure to students through medicalised discourses. Second, special education, however, it is delivered, has emerged as a legitimate and necessary educational practice. Other early, critical special education scholars have similarly responded to the normative beliefs, practices, and assumptions about disability that are the foundation of the special education system (see the early work of those such as Len Barton, Doug Biklen, Burton Blatt, Dianne Ferguson, Philip Ferguson, Roger Slee, and Steve Taylor).

1.2   *Assumptions about Student Learning That Were Not Challenged by the Development of Inclusive Education*

Unchallenged assumptions about student learning are the following: (a) students are responsible for their own learning, (b) when students do not learn, there is something wrong with them, and (c) the job of schools is to determine what is wrong with these students with as much precision as possible so that they can be appropriately remediated or 'fixed,' often through specialised curriculum, teachers, and classrooms that match their ability profile (Allan, 2012; Brantlinger, 2006; Ferguson, 1995; Skrtic, 1991). Although these scholars argue there has been a shift to providing specialised services in the context of natural environments and general education classrooms through the creation of inclusive classrooms and schools, the dominant, deficit-based discourse surrounding student learning and intelligence was not challenged. As such, children in publicly supported schools receive additional support only when they are unable to successfully negotiate the mandated curriculum and their failure to do so is attributed to a set of factors that resides within an individual student (Kugelmass, 2004). Additionally, some authors argue that both research and systemic reform need to deconstruct deep-rooted assumptions that sort and separate students according to presumptions about student ability, achievement, and eventual social contribution (Ainscow et al., 2003). It is this 'unmasking' of the ideology of special education that Brantlinger (2006) takes up across contexts such as history, teacher textbooks, multicultural curricula, and accountability demands. Challenging reductionist and normative perspectives of disability creates the opportunity for school professionals to understand student disability as being constructed by the social and learning contexts that an individual student is placed in, versus as an individual 'problem' to be solved (Brantlinger, 2006; Gallagher, 2001).

2 Background of the Study

The larger study from which this analysis comes attempted to understand how general education teachers who work in inclusive classrooms conceptualise inclusive education and understand their individual commitments to the inclusion of students with labelled disabilities. This study intended to make explicit the social meaning that resides in, and is constituted by, teachers doing their everyday work in schools (Erickson, 1977), and in doing so add depth to the body of research and scholarly work in the field of inclusive education that has largely attempted to understand its technical implementation. This research attempted to answer the following question: how do teachers articulate their conception of, and commitments to, inclusive education?

To answer this question, I used methods consistent with a focused ethnography (Erickson, 1977; Knoblauch, 2005), allowing me to describe and analyse the practices and beliefs of a community. Both data collection and analysis adhered to a constructivist and interpretative perspective in order to study the meanings, intentions, and actions of the participants in my study (Charmaz, 2001; Charmaz & Mitchell, 2001; Geertz, 2001). I targeted my research on a subset of teachers at an urban, elementary school. The data were collected over a 15-month period, and included extensive fieldwork, semi-structured interviews, and review of material artifacts, such as local websites.

2.1 *The Site*

East Elementary, the school site where data were collected, is located in the Bay Area School District (BASD), an urban school district in Northern California. Historically, East had been described as inclusive, meaning that all students, regardless of disability label, were members of age-appropriate, general education classrooms. In March 2006, East Elementary was informed that the following school year their site would add a seg-regated classroom for students with disabilities from a number of schools on the other side of the district.[2] This classroom, East was informed, would come with a special education teacher and students already assigned to it, and the school was granted one year to plan for the addition. The teacher for this classroom had been a long-term substitute at another school prior to the year of data collection. During the year that data were collected East continued to provide services to some students with a range of support needs and disability labels in the context of age-appropriate general education classrooms; however, East now provides educational services to some students with disability labels in the segregated classroom.

Because East had not provided services to students with IEPs in segregated classrooms for the previous 10 years, I assumed there would be a shared conception of, and commitment to, inclusive education by school professionals on the site. Therefore, I felt that East provided a rich and unique opportunity to study teachers' belief systems and value orientations about inclusive education, as enacted through their daily work in classrooms and around the school (Lightfoot, 1973). I hypothesised that the addition of a segregated, special education classroom to the school site would place teachers' conceptions about inclusive education in sharp relief, allowing me to understand how robust their conceptions were in light of the decision to segregate some students with disabilities on the site. I had not originally intended to focus my research on the exclusionary forces on the site as I anticipated that a school, which had had a public face of being inclusive for over a decade, would respond in certain ways to the mandate to segregate some students with disabilities. However, I found that uncovering the nature of cultural exclusion for some students with disabilities at East was central to my research and to understanding teachers' meanings about inclusion. What resulted was largely a critical investigation of oppressive and exclusive cultural practices that worked to reinforce and

VULNERABLE TO EXCLUSION

sustain ways of thinking that sorted, separated, and marginalised many students at the school site. As such, the analysis attempted to illuminate the ways schools are a significant force of ablement/disablement and inclusion/exclusion through deeply ingrained structural and cultural mechanisms (Brantlinger, 2004; Slee & Allan, 2001).

I make the argument that the variation in teachers' thinking about inclusive education at East was not known collectively and was perpetuated by a lack of dialogue among the staff. I also highlight the difference between those teachers who had very broad and elastic definitional boundaries for how they understood inclusive education and those teachers whose definitions were more tightly bound. The different degrees of elasticity in their conceptions of inclusive education, coupled with the lack of dialogue on the site about it, allowed some teachers to accommodate the addition of a segregated classroom to their school site into their definitional boundaries of being an inclusive school.

2.2   *Method and Data Sources*

This analysis relies on a review of material artifacts, including school district and school site websites at different points in time, as well as the schoolsite plan. Additionally, archival notes from a local, university professor who worked with East as a part of a federally funded, model demonstration grant were analysed. Also included is an analysis of interviews conducted with seven kindergarten-through-second-grade teachers that occurred prior to the start of the school year of data collection.

Analysis of interview data from June, prior to the addition of the segregated class, relied on an emically developed coding scheme after first developing coding categories based on the topic areas in the interview protocol. The initial coding categories included the following: (a) teachers' talk about 'my' or 'our' school, (b) teachers' stated definitions of inclusion, (c) teachers' descriptions about when the BASD mandated the addition of the segregated classroom, and (d) teachers' narratives about what they thought would happen in the fall when the segregated class was added to the school site. I identified every instance in which teachers used the words 'inclusion' or 'inclusive education' to understand if 'inclusion' was a salient category of meaning for the participants and if so, what individual meaning was made about 'inclusion.' Narratives about the addition of the segregated classroom that existed in addition to what I specifically asked participants about were also examined. I used visual displays, such as conceptual maps, to understand relationships between more fine-grained codes and concepts that emerged from analytic categories (Miles & Huberman, 1994).

3   The Historical Conception of an Inclusive School

The history of active support for inclusive education at the district level dates to the hiring of a new superintendent in 1993 and the subsequent creation of district-level positions and policies exclusively for the development of inclusive practices. In 1993 the BASD hired a new superintendent who supported the request of a group of four families to have their children receive special education services in general education classrooms. Subsequently, this superintendent hired a new director of special education, who was committed to the development of inclusive education in the district, and also created another quasi-administrative position committed specifically to the development of inclusive schools. At this time, the district also partnered with a Bay Area university professor who was the director of a grant-funded, northern California inclusive education project. Throughout the 1993–1994 school year, large numbers of district-wide in-services about inclusive education were conducted, and the superintendent continued his commitment to inclusive education by stating that all schools would eventually offer this option. Meeting minutes from 1994 indicated that the then principal of East was one of 10 in the BASD to volunteer for her school to close segregated classrooms for students with disabilities and support all students in the context of age-appropriate general education classrooms. A quote from a teacher at that time indicates the shift that occurred at East: 'When these students were in a separate room I only saw their deficits. Now I see their contributions' (Anonymous, personal communication, February 1, 2008).

Subsequently, in the period from 2001 to 2004, there was a turnover of the principal and approximately half of the school staff. During this time, East also participated in a federal grant project that focused on effective practices to support inclusive schools. Finally, in 2006, with the addition of a new principal, a proliferation of pullout programmes began at East. It was during this year that the BASD mandated that East add a segregated classroom for some students with disabilities at the site.

4   Planning for the Addition of the Segregated Classroom at East

In the year prior to the addition of the segregated class, a site-based committee wrote a proposal for the addition of the segregated classroom. The proposal focused largely on issues of space and the loss of one general education teacher from the school site. It also stated that the committee felt that adding a third-through-fifth-grade, segregated classroom for students with disabilities would be important to consider for the school year following the implementation of the first one so that the school community at East would 'have a chance to create a successful model of a school that meets the needs of all of its students' (East Elementary Proposal, 2007). The committee specifically felt that it would be beneficial to students in the segregated class to spend all six years of primary education on one school campus and that the site would successfully be able to incorporate all of these students into the broader school community, while maintaining their placement in a segregated classroom.

The proposal also identified both potential losses to East because of the classroom addition, as well as gains from having a smaller student population (there are fewer students in segregated classrooms than general education classroom; additionally, East proposed to the BASD that they be able drop enrolment in each grade by 20 students if they were to 'accept' the special education classroom). The losses that the committee included were the following: (a) fewer families to volunteer at the school; (b) loss of revenue from donations and fundraising; (c) loss of funding because of reduced headcount; and (d) and loss of one general education teacher (East Elementary Proposal 2007). The committee also identified potential gains from having a smaller student population on site. These were the following: (a) reduced class size for all grades; (b) less crowded playgrounds and cafeteria; (c) eventual removal of some of the portable classrooms, which would increase current playground space, and (d) the ability to house the entire student body in the community room for assemblies (East Elementary Proposal 2007). Significantly, East's history as an inclusive school did not emerge in the proposal that the school site presented to the BASD. Rather, wavering commitments to inclusive education were institutionalised and reified in documents like the proposal and school site plan, and were also evident in early interviews with a subset of teachers on the site.

5   The Local Interpretation of East as an Inclusive School

An analysis of interview data from seven kindergarten through second grade teachers prior to the addition of the segregated class, in June 2007 (Table 6.1), demonstrated that most of these teachers had elastic definitions of inclusive education that were broad enough to accommodate a range of educational options for students with disabilities on the site; therefore, these teachers did not position the addition of a segregated classroom for students with disabilities as contradictory to their view of East as an inclusive school. A few of the teachers interviewed had more tightly bound definitions of inclusive education. This group of teachers could not include the addition of the

TABLE 6.1   East Elementary teachers who participated in interviews
             prior to the addition of the segregated class

Teacher	Grade	Years at East
Sylvia	Kindergarten	2
Laura	Kindergarten	16
Amy	Kindergarten	2
Jamie	1st	2
Patty	2nd	11
Karessa	Inclusion support	8

segregated classroom within their definitional boundaries of inclusive education, although data analysis demonstrates a pervasive silence among teachers at East related to both being an inclusive school, as well as the educational segregation of some students. As importantly, the implications of pervasive silence about educational segregation and inclusion were evident. The varying degrees of elasticity in teachers' definitions of inclusive education, coupled with a lack of dialogue at East about inclusive education and the creation of a segregated classroom, allowed that individual teachers were never confronted with the variation in definitional boundaries and that seemingly contradictory conceptions of their school could sit comfortably side-by-side.

During these interviews, following a brief series of questions about their teaching history, all of the teachers were asked if East was an inclusive school, and if so, how they knew that East inclusive. All but one of the teachers gave responses that characterised inclusivity at East as something that 'is,' but is also not talked about. There were slight variations in how teachers characterised their knowledge of East as an inclusive school site, largely between those teachers who had a long history at East versus those who were newer to the school site and had little experience with inclusive education in their teaching background. For example, when asked what she thought about inclusive education, Laura responded: '… nobody really questions it, it's just, I believe that it's just expected. It's just the way it is and what we do.' Sheila, who also has a long history at East, first as a parent of a student during the 1990s and currently as a teacher, also indicated 'it's just a part of life.' Amy and Sylvia, however, who had arrived at East within the last two years, agreed that inclusion was 'how it is' at East, but hedged their statements slightly through the use of words like 'seems to be' and 'I think it's how it is' (my own emphasis). Amy also identified a difference between her own ideas and the belief of the rest of the staff about

East as inclusive when she stated, 'Everybody else is so used to it (inclusive education), and it's such the norm for most of the teachers here that there's not a big deal made about it' (my own emphasis).

Jamie and Karessa deviated slightly from this declared knowledge of East as inclusive. Each of these teachers had a slightly more bounded understanding of inclusive education than teachers like Sylvia, Laura, and Amy. In regard to collective thinking about East as an inclusive school, Jamie was the only teacher who negated the collective sense that inclusion just 'is how things are at East' and replied '... I'm not sure. I don't feel like we're all on the same page as a whole school.' Over the course of this interview and the next school year, Jamie continued to deviate slightly from her peers who had definitions of inclusive education that could accommodate the segregation of some students with disabilities. Karessa had a somewhat different perspective from the other teachers, perhaps due to the role she has had at East (Karessa had been the inclusion support teacher at East for eight school years). Karessa stated, 'It's that feeling that you get, it's that community feeling that it's not your kids. They're in this class, they (general educators) take ownership, they're part of everything.' The perspective that Karessa had about teachers taking ownership for students with disabilities in their classrooms was important because, as demonstrated over the course of the next school year, both the addition of the segregated classroom and the proliferation of pull-out programmes on the site seemed to show that general educators in this study who had very elastic understandings of inclusive education often chose to relinquish responsibility for the students with disabilities in their classrooms, as well as those students who deviated in a range of ways from established norms.

All of the teachers interviewed acknowledged that there was no public dialogue about inclusive education at East, despite what many of those teachers identified (some more strongly than others) as the historic public conception of East as an inclusive school. When specifically asked if inclusive education was ever discussed as a whole staff, teachers clearly stated that inclusive education was 'not talked about as a staff.' Some of the teachers, such as Sylvia and Jamie, reference conversations that they had had with Karessa, the inclusion support teacher about individual students as the only real communication on the site about inclusive education that they could identify. Most teachers did not seem to be troubled by the lack of dialogue about inclusive education at East, likely based in the sense that it did not need to be spoken about since it is how things 'just are.' Laura, for example, said, 'We don't have a lot of time to talk to other teachers about it, about their philosophies, but just the fact that it's been like this for so long nobody really questions it.' Teachers like Laura demonstrated that when things are taken for granted, they often do not come up for discussion unless something interrupts 'the way things are.' Therefore, it might have been expected that the arrival of the segregated classroom would have prompted discussions about inclusive education, as it would seem to be incompatible with this way of being at East. However this was not the case, and this silence almost necessitated that teachers' ideas about inclusive education needed to be elastic enough to incorporate the addition of the segregated class.

Again, Jamie emerged as having a slightly different perspective on the public dialogue (or lack thereof) about inclusion at East: 'We really don't talk about inclusion as a school ... I don't know, it seems more like it's kept quiet.' Her statement that 'it's kept quiet' seemed to imply something more than most other teachers' responses that inclusive education just is not talked about. Karessa also agreed that East 'is an inclusive school' but was very specific about the fact that it was something the staff at East did not talk about. After describing how she knew that East was inclusive (teachers taking ownership of students with disabilities in their classrooms and the 'feeling' in the school community), Karessa responded to the question 'Is it something that the staff ever talks about?' with the statement: 'No. I mean I don't recall. No. It's more like "this is how we do things here at East."'

The fact that only one of the seven teachers (Jaime) seemed to find the lack of dialogue about inclusive education disconcerting may or may not be important in and of itself. It does demonstrate the 'taken for granted-ness' that East's status had as an inclusive school by the teachers on the site. However, because of the silence that existed on the site about East's status as an inclusive school and the addition of a segregated class, there would have been opportunity for individuals to raise concerns or thoughts such as Jamie's. Because there was no dialogue at East about these issues beyond a discussion about the logistics of adding the segregated class and physically which classroom would house the class, Jamie would revert, over the course of this interview (and the entire next school year) to statements similar to those of the teachers who held very elastic definitions of inclusive education. Significantly, she represented the possibility for the addition of the segregated class to interrupt/disrupt the accepted, but not talked about, view of East as an inclusive school and, therefore, for things to have happened at East over the course of the next school year very differently than they did.

5.1   Teachers' Responses to the Addition of the Segregated Class

The public narrative about East as an inclusive school seemed to be a discursively based narrative, rooted in a retrospective view that teachers held about 'how things are' at their school (in contrast to the school's representation in public documents such as websites or school brochures). And while a certain response from staff at East to the externally imposed decision to add a segregated classroom for students with disabilities to the site might be expected, what proved unexpected was the expressed outrage over the loss of a teacher, but not about the addition of a segregated classroom to their inclusive school site. All of the teachers interviewed used highly emotional language to characterise their own, early response to the BASD mandate. What might seem to be an apparent contradiction to inclusion being 'how things are' and the creation of a segregated classroom for some students with identified disabilities on the site did not appear troubling at all. Laura, for example, remembered that 'the way it was done (the mandate from BASD) was horrifying ... everyone was just outraged.' Similarly, Sylvia describes it as being 'traumatic to the staff.' Amy and Sheila referenced the staff 'going in to shock' and that there was 'quite the uproar.' What is most interesting about the emotional language that many teachers used to describe the mandate, is what that language was used to describe. The most salient issue to these teachers was the required loss of one general education teacher and classroom. Segregation of students with disabilities versus inclusion of students with disabilities was not an issue, as might have been expected based on their own, previous statements about inclusion and the way things 'are' at East.

Jamie, however, was the only teacher who pointed out this seeming contradiction. While recalling her own reaction to the mandate of the addition of the segregated class she said, 'I mean, we kind of made a big deal out of the SDC[3] only because we had to let a teacher go and make space for that (classroom).' Jamie them wondered aloud: '... if we're an inclusion school, why do we need a differentiated classroom which is specifically SDC? I guess I don't understand why these students couldn't be mainstreamed.' Jamie was then asked what happened when she asked that question, and she replied that she never asked anyone about the issue. Instead, she reiterated her concerns about the displaced teacher. Again, during the course of the same transcript section, Jamie initially responded in a way that would indicate a more tightly bound definition of inclusive education at East than some of the other teachers; yet, she arrived at the same conclusion as those teachers whose ideas about inclusive education were much more elastic. It is important to recognise Jamie's initial question about why the staff at East would agree to segregate some students with disability labels.

If a space had existed in which she could bring up this issue, then the staff of East might have engaged in a dialogue about inclusive education from an ideological standpoint. The very absence of such a space to consider inclusion as ideology represents the circular and reciprocal relationship between institutions and ideology articulated by Brantlinger (1997). According to this discussion, ideology is embedded in the practices and structures of institutions such as schools. Thus, Brantlinger says, institutions evolve into hierarchical bureaucracies that generate ideologies that naturalise their existence. Because the space did not exist for discussion about inclusive ideology and the segregation of some students at East, most teachers were able to incorporate segregation into their conceptions of inclusion.

All of the teachers who focused on the issue of losing one general education classroom also emphasised that the school community was not 'against' a special education classroom, per se, but that they felt upset about the need to lose a general education classroom and teacher. It bears mention that these teachers insisted that they 'were not prejudiced against the SDC' and that the reason for their 'outrage.' Laura stated:

> I don't think anybody at this school had an issue with a (SDC) class coming in here. When I was first at East we had an SDC class in Room One. I mean it was just like part of the community and there was no big deal and who cares. We're already a full inclusion school. That is not the issue ... it's not the fact that there's going to be an SDC again. I don't think anyone has issues with that.

Laura went on to again point out that 'the issue' is that she and other staff members felt as if they were treated disrespectfully by the BASD and that East was 'inclusive enough' to 'include' a segregated classroom on the school site.

Some teachers, like Amy and Sylvia, whose teaching experiences prior to coming to East were in schools that had only segregated classes for students with disabilities, expressed their comfort with the SDC based on past experience: 'I never had an issue with that because I worked only in special ed classrooms, so it's like "oh, okay."' Amy reconciled the addition of an SDC by stating her understanding of inclusive education as one programmatic placement option for students with disabilities: '... well, we're inclusion and it works really well here, and yeah, that's true. But some children need a different setting.' She underscored 'the issue' as being one of space and having to lose one general education classroom. Amy also identified what she saw as a positive aspect of the addition of the segregated class, which was echoed by Laura, Sylvia, and Sheila: 'I'm personally kind of happy with the way it's working out, because this is a big school and downsizing a tad is not a bad idea.' This is significant as the size of East Elementary and the number of students using public spaces in the schools at certain times of the day were of concern to teachers on the site (e.g. Laura states that she is happy about the addition of the segregated class and the loss of a kindergarten class because it meant a reduction from 100 to 80 kindergarten students on the kindergarten yard at recess). In making

VULNERABLE TO EXCLUSION

this point, all of the teachers who responded this way shifted their concerns back to the school site. None of the four teachers who had the most elastic definitional boundaries of inclusive education returned to their earlier statements about East being an inclusive site. Rather, their definitional boundaries of inclusive education were elastic enough that they could incorporate the existence of the segregated classrooms within their understandings of being an inclusive school and were also able to identify school-wide positive aspects of it.

Patty and Karessa also acknowledged the concerns that most staff had about losing one general education classroom and teacher. Both of these teachers identified a sense of personal unhappiness about the addition of the segregated class, yet the conclusions that each of them made about the addition of the class were very different from one another. When asked what her reaction was to the mandate that East add a segregated classroom, Karessa first responded 'I was like, what?! You know, I didn't understand it ... this has been an inclusive school.' By the end of this section of the interview transcript, however, Karessa seemed to have moved away from the problem of adding a segregated classroom to an inclusive school, and made the following statement: 'If we're going to have a special day class, yeah, it is a special day class, but let's include them in the school community.' It could be assumed that Karessa, who was the inclusion support teacher at East, might have a tightly bound definition of inclusive education that was unable to include the existence of a segregated classroom. However, over the course of 10 transcript lines, Karessa made the transition from questioning the addition of a segregated class at an inclusive school site to acceptance of it.

Patty specifically made the point that she 'wasn't against' more students with 'identified disabilities' coming to East and that she felt the additional year to plan for the addition of the segregated classroom was a good thing:

> I thought, 'yeah, what's wrong with waiting a year?' And since it wasn't inclusion, and it was a special day class, and I had mixed feelings anyway, I thought 'you know, I think it's a really good idea to do that, so that we can include these students as much as possible.'

After Patty referenced 'including' the students in the segregated class, she continued on:

> I think it's a wonderful goal to turn a special day class into an inclusive classroom. So in that way I can see us learning a lot together, and learning how to make our school a real inclusive type of place no matter what student comes to learn at our school ... so it'll be a learning process.

It is notable that the notion of increasing the number of students with labelled disabilities, who were supported as members of age-appropriate general education classrooms, was not addressed by teachers other than Patty, or within documents revised during the year of planning (including websites, the proposal written by East staff, or the amended school site plan). Highlighting the different ways that Patty and Karessa initially responded to the addition of the class allows us to further understand the variation in individual teachers' understanding of inclusive education at East. Karessa seemed to indicate that the segregated class would remain segregated, but that she would like it to not be totally separate. Patty is the only teacher interviewed who specifically addressed the idea that it should be a goal to merge the segregated classroom into the inclusion support services that already existed on the site. For Patty, the existence of a segregated classroom at East exceeded her definitional boundaries of inclusive education, and so it would be expected that she would talk about merging this classroom into the inclusion programme on the site.

5.2   Teachers' Hopes and Expectations for the Addition of the Segregated Class

All of the teachers interviewed in June brought up the notion of inclusivity when talking about their hopes and/or expectations for the addition of the segregated class. All of them reported, to some degree, statements similar to Laura's: 'I hope that the classroom will not be like a separate entity.' Sylvia made a similar point: 'I don't want them to feel like they're excluded. I feel that there needs to be some kind of integration.' Amy used phrases like 'I'm real hopeful' and 'I hope it works out that way' to reinforce her statement: 'I can see that with the inclusion, the kids don't feel separated out. And I really hope that with this classroom they're going to feel like they're part of the community and really part of things.' The way in which all of the teachers expressed their hopes for the addition of the segregated classroom seemed to support their tacit knowledge of East as an inclusive school. All of these teachers, however, spoke about their hopes for experience of the segregated class at East in very general terms. None of these teachers operationalised their hopes, meaning they rooted their hopes in general statements about 'feeling included' without identifying any sort of personal action they might take to see their hopes realised.

Again Jamie emerged as having a slightly more articulated version of her hopes and expectations for the segregated classroom: 'I just want to make sure that they feel like they're part of our community too ... I'd like to feel like we're one school, not East and the special day class.' Jamie seemed troubled by the place of the SDC within East's school community, but like the other teachers, she did not attach any sense of specific personal action or what she might do

VULNERABLE TO EXCLUSION

in order to make her 'hopes' realised. Instead she reverted to a more elastic definition of inclusive education and thus was able to place the segregated classroom within her definitional boundaries.

Karessa had a 'plan' for the segregated class, which seemed to get lost in a notion of the segregated class teacher 'getting ready' to integrate her students into general education classrooms:

> I'm very positive about it (her plan for the segregated classroom) right now because I like the vibe of the teacher, and I kind of know where she's going. But because she's a brand new teacher, for her to get really settled with her class, over the fall—... I want to give her time. Time to get settled, time to get her routines down and get to know the kids and that kind of thing. And then by the spring I would work with her into mainstreaming those kids into different classrooms. And we would work out schedules and that kind of thing.

Karessa added weight to her statement that the segregated class teacher use the fall, in essence, to get ready to integrate some of her students into general education classrooms in the spring by stating a number of times that the fall semester is hard for herself, which means it will be 'especially hard' for the new teacher. By the end of the interview, Karessa spoke more generally about her 'hopes' for the addition of the segregated class. In a final reference to her plan for the addition of the segregated class she concluded, 'That's my hope, but who knows.' Karessa's final statement points to the lack of dialogue on the site and the lack of planning for the addition of the segregated classroom.

Patty emerged as having the strongest and most clearly defined 'hopes' for the segregated class students and teacher. Early in the interview she said: '... my goal was that it would start off as a special day class and then that teacher would eventually turn into an inclusion teacher, so that all those students would be included.' Patty does use the word 'hope,' although in a very different sense from other teachers. She specifically linked her 'hope' with the vision for the classroom and the actions she would like to take to achieve that vision:

> I just have all these goals for this classroom. It's (the segregated classroom) in my hall, so I thought the second graders could naturally be included in my classroom. And the teacher—she said she would like to start out with just mainstreaming. And I said 'Well, if that's the way you feel, and you're the teacher, it's an okay place to start.' So I really have high hopes for this classroom, and a lot of goals in my own mind, which I haven't voiced to everyone.

This transcript segment offers important insights. First, Patty emerged as the only teacher whose hopes for the segregated classroom remained action-oriented and focused specifically on her understanding of inclusive education. Her use of the word 'goal,' in reference to having the segregated classroom become 'inclusion' attaches more of a sense of purpose than most teachers' talk about being 'hopeful.' Finally, like other teachers, she also points to the issue that there is no ongoing dialogue on the site about the addition of the segregated class by stating that she has not shared her goals with the other teachers on the site.

6   Discussion

Analysis across all data sources indicated that a public narrative existed about East as an inclusive school, which seemed to be a discursively based narrative, rooted in retrospective ideas from the past that teachers had about 'how things are' at the school. Additionally, the meanings attached to inclusive education were quite variable and elastic for most of the teachers in the study. Further, the prevailing response of most teachers to the mandate to segregate some students with disabilities was unexpected, as many teachers expressed outrage, but not about the addition of a segregated classroom to their inclusive school site. Rather, most of them were upset at needing to lose a general education teacher and classroom on the site. The different degrees of elasticity in teachers' conceptions of inclusive education at East, coupled with the lack of dialogue on the site about it, allowed some teachers to accommodate the addition of a segregated classroom to their school site into their definitional boundaries of being an inclusive school. The lack of dialogue also allowed that individual teachers were never confronted with the variation in definitional boundaries and that seemingly contradictory conceptions of their school (being an inclusive school, while segregating some students with disabilities) could sit comfortably side-by-side. This culture of silence was evident in all data sources throughout the year of data collection and worked to reinforce the school's public status as 'inclusive' and thus legitimised the systematic exclusion of the students in the segregated classroom, as well as encouraged ways of thinking about some students that would lead to their eventual marginalisation and stigmatisation. Therefore, inclusive education at East was not self-evident, but rather, served as 'a Trojan horse for assimilation' (Slee & Allan, 2001), as students who challenged some teachers' expectations for student learning and performance, were deemed to require educational segregation. Further, the tacit acceptance of silence on the topic meant that normalising discourses, which affirmed or negated particular students, became the predominant way of understanding student disability and difference for some of the teachers in the study. My results point to the need to conceptualise and teach inclusive education as ideology embedded in policy and practice.

The role of ideology in disability-related research in education has been debated and critiqued by traditional and critical special educators (most recently, see Gallagher, 2006; Kauffman & Sasso, 2006). I use the word 'ideology' as it is addressed in the work of Brantlinger (1997) and Ware (2002, 2003, 2004, 2005) in order to convey the importance of understanding the social, cultural, and moral parameters surrounding the position of disability in school. Brantlinger (1997, 2004, citing Althusser, 1976) defines ideology as, '... systems of representations [images, myths, ideas, beliefs] that in profoundly unconscious ways mediate one's understanding of the world.' Therefore, she says, there is 'automaticity of ideological triggering' through which individuals act with little conscious understanding of the ideological grounding from which their actions stemmed (p. 20). Coupled with what Ware (2002) has identified as the lack of 'moral conversation' about the meaning of educational inclusion and the principles needed to guide implementation of the spirit of federal legislation, that the development of inclusive education was merely a 'shifting in geography' (Slee & Allan, 2001) is perhaps not so surprising. Shifting the nature of the conversation about disability with pre-service teachers and encouraging school leaders to engage staff in discussions about disability and learning 'problems' creates the potential to consciously identify the ideological grounding of school policies about student disability and difference and begin 'moral conversations' of the sort that Ware advocates (Ashby, 2012; Oyler, 2011). Brantlinger (2004) concluded that without an examination or attention to the 'value underpinnings of educational practice' the movement and advocacy towards inclusive schools will continue to replicate and perpetuate an exclusive and marginalising system (p. 11).

Brantlinger (1997) also argued that schools should resist their natural tendency to reproduce powerful members of society as advantaged and oppress those with little power (such as the practice of giving students with identified disabilities stigmatising labels and being placed in limiting environments) (also see Skrtic, 2005; Ware, 2004). According to these scholars, making conversations about inclusive education explicitly ideological could cause disruptions in these natural tendencies. These conversations represent the place from which our teaching about inclusive education can move away from the focus on technical implementation of practices, and work to broaden our conception of humanity. As described by Gallagher (1998), engaging in a collective and open discourse about inclusive education that is more fundamentally moral and ideological in nature holds the potential to return to 'the finest accomplishment of special education ... advocacy for the human dignity and civil rights of individuals with exceptionalities' (p. 500).

Notes

1 Ware (2001, 2005, 2010) described critical special education scholars as early 'alternative paradigm thinkers' (see Meyen & Skrtic, 1988) whose critique subsequently informed the foundation for disability studies in education. The critical gaze of these scholars, Ware explained, took on many meanings including (a) that which refers to special education's overreliance on the medial model of disability, (b) the impulse to 'fix' the unfit child, (c) the rush to equate human difference with limited capacity and individual pathology, and (d) the paradigmatic change that was urgently needed to coax the field away from its exclusively behaviourists and reductionist worldview (p. 254).

2 Research and scholarly work in the fields of both inclusive education and disability studies in education addresses the issues of race and disability—particularly the overrepresentation of students of colour in certain disability groups as well as in segregated educational settings (among others see Artiles & Trent, 1994; Artiles, 2011; Losen & Orfield, 2002). These students are also underrepresented in special education literature (see Ferri & Connor, 2005). The analysis here does not focus on the dynamics of race that existed at the school site where data were collected, as this research was focused on the category of disability and students who were labelled as such, and/or existed outside individual teachers' normative frameworks and expectations. The reader should realise, however, as I talk about the students and the segregated classroom throughout this article that all of these students were non-White; 10 out of 11 students in the segregated classroom were African-American or Latino. Students from general education classrooms at East who were moved or whose teachers were considering the move from general education into the segregated classroom were also Latino or African-American.

3 'SDC' is the acronym for 'special day class,' which was the label for segregated classrooms in the BASD. Across school districts in the USA these labels (and their corresponding acronyms and descriptors for the students who inhabit them) vary; in the school districts that the author has worked in these labels have ranged from 'SDC,' 'functional skills,' 'severe special needs,' 'significant support needs,' to 'affective needs' classrooms.

References

Ainscow, M., Howes, A., Farrell, P., & Frankham, J. (2003). Making sense of the development of inclusive practices. *European Journal of Special Needs Education, 18*(2), 227–242.

Allan, J. (2012). The sociology of disability and the struggle for inclusive education. In M. Arnot (Ed.), *The sociology of disability and inclusive education* (pp. 75–91). New York, NY: Routledge.

Artiles, A. J. (2011). Toward an interdisciplinary understanding of educational equity and difference: The case of the racialization of ability. *Educational Researcher, 40*(9), 431–445. doi:10.3102/0013189X11429391

Artiles, A. J., & Trent, S. C. (1994). Overrepresentation of minority students in special education: A continuing debate. *Journal of Special Education, 27*(4), 410–437. doi:10.1177/002246699402700404

Ashby, C. (2012). Disability studies and inclusive teacher preparation: A socially just path for teacher education. *Research & Practice for Persons with Severe Disabilities, 37*(2), 89–99.

Brantlinger, E. (1997). Using ideology: Cases of non-recognition of the politics of research and practice in special education. *Review of Educational Research, 67*(4), 425–459.

Brantlinger, E. (2004). Ideologies discerned, values determined: Getting past the hierarchies of special education. In L. Ware (Ed.), *Ideology and the politics of (in)exclusion* (pp. 11–29). New York, NY: Peter Lang.

Brantlinger, E. (2006). *Who benefits from special education? Remediating (fixing) other people's children.* Mahwah, NJ: L. Erlbaum Associates.

Causton-Theoharis, J. (2009). *The paraprofessional's handbook for effective support in inclusive classrooms.* Baltimore, MD: Paul H. Brookes.

Causton-Theoharis, J., & Theoharis, G. (2008). Creating inclusive schools for all students. *The School Administrator, 65*(8), 24–31.

Causton-Theoharis, J., Theoharis, G., Bull, T., Cosier, M., & Dempf-Aldrich, K. (2011). Schools of promise: A school district-university partnership centered on inclusive school reform. *Remedial and Special Education, 32*(3), 192–205.

Charmaz, K. (2001). Grounded theory. In R. M. Emerson (Ed.), *Contemporary field research: Perspectives and formulations* (2nd ed., pp. 335–353). Prospect Heights, IL: Waveland Press.

Charmaz, K., & Mitchell, R. G. (2001). Grounded theory in ethnography. In P. Atkinson, A. Coffey, S. Delamont, J. Lofland, & L. Lofland (Eds.), *Handbook of ethnography* (pp. 160–176). London: Sage Publications.

Copeland, S. R., & Cosbey, J. (2008–2009). Making progress in the general curriculum: Rethinking effective instructional practices. *Research and Practice for Persons with Severe Disabilities, 33*(4), 214 – 227.

East Elementary. (2007). *Proposal to the BASD*. San Francisco, CA.

Erickson, F. (1977). Some approaches to inquiry in school-community ethnography. *Anthropology and Education Quarterly, 8*(2), 58–69. Retrieved April 17, 2007, from http://www.jstor.org

Ferguson, D. (1995). The real challenge of inclusion: Confessions of a 'rabid inclusionist.' *Phi Delta Kappan, 77*(4), 281–287.

Ferri, B., & Connor, D. J. (2005). Tools of exclusion: Race, disability, and (re)segregated education. *Teachers College Record, 107*(3), 453–474.

Fisher, D., & Frey, N. (2001). Access to the core curriculum: Critical ingredients for student success. *Remedial and Special Education, 22*(3), 148–57.

Gallagher, D. J. (1998). The scientific knowledge base of special education: Do we know what we think we know? *Exceptional Children, 64*(4), 493–502.

Gallagher, D. J. (2001). Neutrality as a moral standpoint, conceptual confusion, and the full inclusion debate. *Disability & Society, 16*(5), 637–653.

Gallagher, D. J. (2006). If not absolute objectivity, then what? A reply to Kauffman and Sasso. *Exceptionality, 14*(2), 91–107.

Geertz, C. (2001). Thick description: Toward an interpretive theory of culture. In R. M. Emerson (Ed.), *Contemporary field research: Perspectives and formulations* (2nd ed., pp. 55–75). Prospect Heights, IL: Waveland Press. (Originally published in C. Geertz, *The interpretation of cultures: Selected essays*, New York, NY: Basic Books, 1973)

Halvorsen, A., & Neary, T. (2009). *Building inclusive schools: Tools and strategies for success* (2nd ed.). Boston, MA: Allyn & Bacon.

Heshusius, L. (1989). The Newtonian mechanistic paradigm, special education and contours of alternatives: An overview. *Journal of Learning Disabilities, 22*(7), 403–415.

Hunt, P., & Goetz, L. (1997). Research on inclusive education programs, practices and outcomes for students with severe disabilities. *Journal of Special Education, 31*(1), 3–29.

Hunt, P., & McDonnell, J. (2007). Inclusive education. In S. L. Odom, R. H. Horner, M. E. Snell, & J. Blacher (Eds.), *Handbook of developmental disabilities* (pp. 269–291). New York, NY: Guilford Press.

Iano, R. (1986). The study and development of teaching: With implications for the advancement of special education. *Remedial and Special Education, 7*(5), 50–61.

Individuals with Disabilities Education Improvement Act of 2006, USC, 34CFR §300.114–120.

Jackson, L. M., Ryndak, D. L., & Wehmeyer, M. L. (2008–2009). Context, curriculum, and student learning: A case for inclusive education as a research-based practice. *Research and Practice for Persons with Severe Disabilities, 33*(4), 175–195.

Kauffman, J. M., & Sasso, G. (2006). Rejoinder: Certainty, doubt and the reduction of uncertainty. *Exceptionality, 14*(2), 109–120.

VULNERABLE TO EXCLUSION

Knoblauch, H. (2005). Focused ethnography. *Forum: Qualitative Research, 6*(3). Retrieved from http://www.qualitativeresearch.net/index.php/fqs/article/view/20/43

Kugelmass, J. W. (1996). Reconstructing curriculum for systemic inclusion. In M. S. Berres, D. Ferguson, P. Knoblock, & C. Woods (Eds.), *Creating tomorrow's schools today: Stories of inclusion, change, and renewal* (pp. 38–65). New York, NY: Teachers College Press.

Kugelmass, J. W. (2004). *The inclusive school: Sustaining equity and standards.* New York, NY: Teachers College Press.

Lightfoot, S. L. (1973). Politics and reasoning: Through the eyes of teachers and children. *Educational Review, 43*(2), 197–244.

Losen, D., & Orfield, G. (Eds.). (2002). *Racial inequity in special education.* Cambridge, MA: The Civil Rights Project, Harvard Education Press.

McGregor, G., & Vogelsberg, R. T. (1998). *Inclusive schooling practices: Pedagogical and research foundations. A synthesis of the literature that informs best practices about inclusive schooling.* Philadelphia, PA: Allegheny University of the Health Sciences.

Meyen, E., & Skrtic, T. (1988). *Exceptional children and youth: An introduction.* Denver: Love Publishing.

Miles, M. B., & Huberman, A. M. (1994). *Qualitative data analysis* (2nd ed.). Thousand Oaks, CA: Sage.

Oyler, C. (2011). Teacher preparation for inclusive and critical (special) education. *Teacher Education and Special Education, 34*(3), 201–218.

Sailor, W., & Roger, B. (2005). Rethinking inclusion: School-wide applications. *Phi Delta Kappan, 86*(7), 503–509.

Skrtic, T. (1991). The special education paradox: Equity as the way to excellence. *Harvard Educational Review, 61*(2), 148–206.

Skrtic, T. (2005). A political economy of learning disabilities. *Learning Disability Quarterly, 28*(2), 149–155. Retrieved August 25, 2006, from http://ldq.sagepub.com/content/28/2.toc

Slee, R., & Allan, J. (2001). Excluding the included: A reconsideration of inclusive education. *International Studies in Sociology of Education, 11*(2), 173–191.

Villa, R. A., & Thousand, J. S. (2000). *Restructuring for caring and effective education: Piecing the puzzle together.* Baltimore, MD: Paul H. Brookes.

Ware, L. P. (2001). Writing, identity, and the other: Dare we do disability studies? *Journal of Teacher Education, 52*(2), 107–123.

Ware, L. P. (2002). A moral conversation on disability: Risking the personal in educational context. *Hypatia: A Journal of Feminist Philosophy, 17*(3), 143–171.

Ware, L. (2003). Working past pity: What we make of disability in schools. In J. Allan (Ed.), *Inclusion, participation and democracy: What is the purpose?* (pp. 117–137). Dordrecht: Kluwer Academic Publishers.

Ware, L. P. (2004). *Ideology and the politics of (in)exclusion*. New York, NY: Peter Lang.

Ware, L. P. (2005). Many possible futures, many different directions: Merging critical special education and disability studies. In S. L. Gabel (Ed.), *Disability studies in education: Readings in theory and method* (pp. 103–124). New York, NY: Peter Lang.

Ware, L. P. (2010). Disability studies in education. In S. Tozer, A. Henry, B. Gallegos, M. B. Greiner, & P. G. Price (Eds.), *The handbook of research in the social foundations of education* (pp. 244–260). New York, NY: Routledge.

CHAPTER 7

The Impact of Standards-Based Reform: Applying Brantlinger's Critique of "Hierarchical Ideologies"

Jessica Bacon and Beth Ferri

Abstract

Brantlinger's (2004b) critique of hierarchical ideologies lay bare the logics embedded in standards-based reform. Drawing on Brantlinger's insightful analysis, the authors trace how hierarchical ideologies impacted inclusive practice at one urban elementary school, deemed "failing" under the No Child Left Behind Act. Drawing on qualitative analysis of data from interviews, public forums, and documents, the authors chart some of the negative effects of hierarchical ideologies on inclusive practice. Among these, they note a variety of segregated programmes aimed at increasing test scores; the emphasis on grade-level expectations; the need for content modification to justify exclusion and graduation requirements that negatively impact students with disabilities.

Keywords

special education – special education needs – inclusive education

> Hierarchies are not purposeless, passive rankings, but represent important interdependent relations among people of different ranks. Indeed, the role, and perhaps even raison d'etre of dominant groups hinge on the existence of Others who can be designated as inferior and less worthy ... For some students to pass and excel, Others must do poorly and fail. Routines of the accountability and standards movement rely on the dynamic of some teachers and schools judged as excellent models of best practice, while others are declared incompetent and failing.
>
> BRANTLINGER, (2006, p. 201)

•••

© TAYLOR & FRANCIS, 2013 | DOI:10.1163/9789004402690_008

When we look at development's ebb and flow over a lifetime, the fine distinctions in rates of human learning that were observed tend to dissipate and disappear. Oh, that we could reach that wisdom at an earlier age.

BRANTLINGER (2005, p. 136)

∴

1 Standards-Based Reform and Special Education in the USA

The origins of standards-based reform (SBR) in the USA can be traced to the first systemic push for national curriculum linked to high-stakes examinations in the 1950s Cold War era. After the launch of Sputnik in the 1960s, the USA increasingly linked educational reform to global competition (Kreitzer, Madaus, & Haney, 1989). In subsequent decades, reforms continued to evolve; however, formal legislation did not require high-stakes tests, accountability systems, and sanctions for 'failing schools' until the No Child Left Behind Act (NCLB) in 2001. Additionally, Race to the Top (US Department of Education, 2009) federal grants provide hundreds of millions of dollars to states that institute a national set of common core standards, teacher and leader evaluation systems, and proscribed steps to improve low-achieving schools. Both NCLB and Race to the Top reflected a neoliberal agenda (Apple, 2004) by greatly expanding charter schools.

SBR has transformed education for all students in the USA, with specific consequences for students with disabilities. After the implementation of NCLB, all but 1–2% of students with disabilities were required to participate in high-stakes examinations and be included in accountability data. Research documenting the impact on students with disabilities has been mixed. Because they are now included in assessment and accountability systems, students with disabilities have gained more access to general education curriculum (Defur, 2002; Thompson & Thurlow, 2003; Ysseldyke et al., 2004) and are held to higher expectations (Flowers, Ahlgrim-Delzell, Browder, & Spooner, 2005; Nelson, 2002; Thompson & Thurlow, 2001). Less positive outcomes include increased tracking and segregation (Sandholtz, Ogawa, & Scribner, 2004; Smyth, 2008) and higher dropout rates (Cole, 2006; Lillard & DeCicca, 2001). In this paper, we draw on Brantlinger's work to offer insights into how SBR reflects and reinforces hierarchical ideologies.

THE IMPACT OF STANDARDS-BASED REFORM

2 Brantlinger's Critique of SBR

Brantlinger (1997) argued that ideology preserves "existing social structures and power relations" (p. 437). While accusing pro-inclusionists of allowing ideology to guide practice, traditionalists in the field, have often denied the existence of ideology in their own work. Brantlinger (1997), however, revealed that ideology permeates all aspects of social life, although ideologies that serve as dominant groups are often uncritically viewed as neutral. Brantlinger (2004b) distinguished between two types of ideology: "hierarchical" and "communal." Hierarchical ideologies establish "social hierarchies through interpersonal competition and stratifying practices" (p. 20). Communal ideologies are based on "human dignity, commonality, equality, and reciprocity" (p. 20). Examples of stratifying practices, grounded in hierarchical ideologies, include ability grouping, tracking, and pullout instruction. SBR reflects hierarchical ideology, whilst inclusion is grounded in a communal ideology.

Emerging as a key element of educational policy, Brantlinger (2001, 2004a, 2004b, 2006) considered how privilege would be perpetuated by practices, such as SBR. In reasking Gramsci's essential question, "Who benefits?" Brantlinger (2006) revealed how school structures, such as SBR, served existing hierarchies. Because dominate groups "set, get consensus for, and enforce normative standards ... to designate themselves as competent and Others as inadequate" (p. 200). Brantlinger argued that SBR policies define the subordinate Other, while reinforcing existing hierarchy.

Brantlinger (2004a) was particularly interested in how accountability, standardized curriculum, and mandatory exit exams perpetuated social class inequities in schools and diminished ideologies more supportive of inclusion. Acknowledging that states used "gateway tests" tied to graduation requirements to signify a certain standard of knowledge, Brantlinger (2001) demonstrated how a disproportionate number of students with disabilities, students of color, and poor students failed to graduate as a result. Thus high-stakes exams, according to Brantlinger (2001), ultimately served more privileged groups and cut off social mobility for less privileged groups.

By considering who benefits and who loses under SBR, Brantlinger (2006) illustrated that in addition to reproducing hegemony and serving the interests of dominant groups, SBR served neoliberal ends benefiting test producers, transglobal capitalists, media outlets, politicians, and members of the educated middle class. In this paper, we draw on Brantlinger's work to uncover how hierarchal ideologies undergirding SBR diminished inclusive practice and communal ideologies in one urban school context.

3 Method

The focal point of this research was an urban elementary school labelled 'failing' under the NCLB. Westvale, a K-5 urban elementary school in New York State (NYS), was a particularly apt example of resegregation and overrepresentation of students of color. The approximate demographics of the school were: 95% free and reduced lunch, 40% limited English proficiency, and 20% students with disabilities. The racial makeup of the school was: 50% Hispanic or Latino, 35% Black or African-American, and 10% white. The urban school district (Springertown) had roughly 20,000 students.

Data were drawn from 19 semi-structured interviews with 22 educators, school- and district-level administrators, and state-level policy-makers. All participants had intimate knowledge of Westvale and the district or had a position in which they provided oversight to the district. Table 7.1 provides a description of the participants included in this study. All participant, school, and district names are pseudonyms and job titles are kept purposely vague in order to protect the confidentiality of participants.

Data were also drawn from observations of 15 public meetings, including presentations, district-level community and parent meetings, and state-level policy meetings. Public documents were also analysed for themes that connected to primary data sources. Examples of documents included national, state, and local policy statements, media documents, websites, and research briefs.

TABLE 7.1   Participant demographics

Name	Job title	Years of work experience	Gender	Race/ ethnicity
Mr. Johnson	School-level educator	5–10	M	White
Ms. Songer	School-level educator	20+	F	White
Ms. Clark	School-level educator	5–10	F	White
Mr. Kroger	School-level administrator	20+	M	White
Ms. Allan	School-level administrator	15–20	F	White
Ms. Slater	School-level administrator	20+	F	White
Mr. Copper	District-level administrator	30+	M	White
Mr. Klosher	District-level administrator	30+	M	White
Ms. Garcia	District-level administrator	15–20	F	Latina
Ms. Hoffman	State-level administrator, NYSED	30+	F	White
Ms. Davern	State-level administrator, NYSED	30+	F	White

THE IMPACT OF STANDARDS-BASED REFORM   129

Although we incorporated grounded theory (Corbin & Strauss, 1990) for our data analysis, Brantlinger's concept of hierarchical knowledge was also useful in highlighting power structures embedded in the data. As we analysed our data, we tacked back and forth between themes that emerged from data sources and Brantlinger's (2004b) critical work, which helped to reveal the workings of hierarchical ideologies.

4   Findings

Findings from the study extend Brantlinger's criticisms by showing how SBR policies led to the resegregation of students with disabilities in one urban school. Westvale Elementary School, for instance, instituted segregated educational programmes as a direct result of SBR. Similarly, Springertown School District adopted practices in which students were increasingly tracked into remedial classes at the secondary level. As Brantlinger (2005) noted, "the most troubling aspects of special education (i.e. segregation, watered down curriculum, and tracking) are a part of the "same phenomenon" and common to all low status arrangements in schools" (p. 131).

4.1   *From a School in Good Standing to Persistently Low Achieving*
During the 2008–2009 school year, Westvale was designated by the state of New York, in compliance with NCLB requirements, as a "School in Need of Improvement." This designation was shared with many urban school districts across the USA that had high numbers of English Language Learners (ELLS), who consistently underperformed on state exams, but were suddenly included in accountability measures. At this stage, schools receive federal funds and are required to take action to improve test scores, while families can opt to transfer students to other district schools. The following school year (2009–2010), Westvale continued to miss accountability targets and was labelled a "School Under Registration Review" (SURR). Before Westvale could implement the sanctions tied to holding a SURR status, the next year (2010–2011), NYS required the "bottom five percent of Title I schools' previously identified as SURR be identified as 'Persistently Lowest Achieving'" (PLA) (NYSED, 2012, p. 1). Thus, in the span of just three years, Westvale was recast from a school in 'good standing' to a PLA school.

Because of PLA requirements, Westvale was required to select one of four intervention strategies authorised by the state in an effort to improve test scores and meet accountability targets. Administrators at Springertown School District chose a "transformation model," which required that a redesign team

be convened, school-level administration be replaced, and teachers be rein-
terviewed for their jobs (NYSED, 2011)—a practice Darling-Hammond (2010)
argued often exacerbates rather than diminishes achievement gaps. A new
instructional programme called "Expeditionary Learning" (EL) was also implemented. The school day was extended by one hour and Response to Intervention and Positive Behaviour and Intervention Supports were instituted, also by
administrative fiat. The school was allotted in excess of seven million dollars
over three years to implement the school transformation plan.

Unfortunately, during this process, Westvale also 'transformed' from a school
that had been moving towards a fully inclusive model, to one that reverted to
a variety of segregated, tracked, and pullout classes. Ms. Allan, an administrator, spearheaded Westvale's evolution towards full inclusion two years prior
to the "transformation process." Unfortunately, because of the mandated stip-
ulations of adopting a "transformation model," Ms. Allan was forced to leave
Westvale Elementary School, even though the district had previously rated her
as a "highly effective" administrator. During her tenure, Ms. Allan successfully
adopted a communal ideology (Brantlinger, 2004b), which led her to fight for
inclusion at Westvale, even though, as she explained, "people thought I was
crazy."

Unfortunately, in conformance to the mandated reform at Westvale,
Ms. Allan's successor did not commit to building on a communal ideology. The
implications for special education would be particularly impacted, though in
the long run, all students would be denied the experience of inclusive community building at Westvale. When the redesign team was organised it included
a parent, a NYS Department of Education employee, a Westvale teacher, and a
district-level administer. The "transformation" plan they outlined failed to consider the model of service delivery for special education students. Ms. Slater,
the administrator appointed to deal with special education after the transformation was completed, explained that special education initially fell outside
the redesign team's focus on "general ed. kids getting 3's and 4's and passing
[the state exam and] us getting off of the state list" (PLA). This failure to consider special education was not attributed to oversight, but rather to the belief
that special education did not figure into the "transformation" of the school.

Because special education was not considered during the planning process,
Ms. Slater led the way in implementing a service delivery model, which was
comprised of a combination of "inclusive" or co-taught classrooms, resource
rooms, self-contained classrooms, and a range of pullout services. Ms. Slater
justified these settings by arguing that students who were behind academically
were not "getting their needs met" in inclusive settings, particularly because
they were not learning skills necessary for success on state examinations.

THE IMPACT OF STANDARDS-BASED REFORM   131

Similarly, Mr. Kroger, a school-level administrator, explained that because students with disabilities were not meeting NCLB accountability requirements, he hoped that increased pullout instruction would help to "fine tune and pinpoint … their weaknesses."

Ms. Slater's and Mr. Kroger's reasoning was embedded in hierarchical ideologies (Brantlinger, 2004b), in which service delivery is aligned with grade-level norms. Moreover, the ease in which the school shifted from inclusive to traditional service delivery points to the "danger" that Brantlinger (2004b) identified in adopting policy or practices without explicitly connecting those practices to an underlying ideology. In other words, because the ideology grounding inclusive practice at Westvale was not explicit or fully internalised at the time of its launch, segregated special education (like inclusion previously) could be seen as simply one more value-neutral option for service delivery in a school that was accustomed to cycling through a range of service delivery options mandated by the district or the state. The professionals, did not feel it necessary to consult with families assuming that, "because of their specialized training, they know what is best for other people's children" (Brantlinger, 2006, vii).

4.2   Grade-Level Instruction

From the outset, SBR expanded pullout instruction and homogenous ability grouping at Westvale. Moreover, the threat of sanctions reinforced hierarchical ideology (Brantlinger, 2004b), where more restrictive placements were seen as necessary for those students who could not 'keep up' with grade-level norms. Many of those we interviewed stated that it was difficult to include students with disabilities because of pressures stemming from SBR. Educators at Westvale assumed that students with disabilities, who presumably could not keep up with the fast pace of content standards, had to be pulled out of class to remediate *their* deficits and to allow regular education classrooms to move more rapidly through content. As Brantlinger (2005) noted, because "narrow skills-based curriculum" and individualised pullout instruction represent the "*modus operandi* for special education," their validity, efficacy, and appropriateness are taken for granted (p. 133) and seen as "beyond criticism" (p. 126). Thus, the inclusion of the special education students into the general education curriculum was not even a consideration in the early stages of planning.

The implementation of EL (Expeditionary Learning, 2012) at Westvale highlighted how hierarchical ideology (Brantlinger, 2004b) influenced educators' perceptions. Many educators, for instance, praised EL's focus on meaningful and culturally relevant instruction. Semester-long interdisciplinary projects proved to be engaging, creative, and authentic ways to capture student learning. Teachers drew on the content standards and worked in grade-level teams to develop curriculum that related to the topic of the semester. Student work was shared in weekly school wide assemblies. In brief, the school invested tremendous time and resources to successfully implement the EL curriculum. Unfortunately, this initiative failed to shift the instruction for many students identified with disabilities, despite the fact that some administrators and faculty believed it would be a good fit for all students. District-level administrator, Mr. Copper, for instance, suggested that EL was an approach that fit the instructional needs of students with disabilities. He clarified that the hands-on, interactive aspects of EL were particularly effective for students with disabilities. Ms Songer, a special education teacher assigned to a co-taught inclusive classroom, stated that EL was working well for students with disabilities because her "team has been great about differentiating ...We're trying to do a lot of technology with it ... The kids are so into it." Both Mr. Copper and Ms. Songer believed that the EL model held great promise for students with disabilities; unfortunately, however, they represented a minority view.

Mr. Johnson taught a self-contained classroom of nine boys who were primarily Hispanic and labelled as Emotionally Disturbed. Because the class was multi-aged, his students participated in the fifth grade EL group, rather than with their grade-level peers. Mr. Johnson rationalised that because his students were not on grade level, it was common sense that they were excluded from grade-level projects. He reasoned that many of his self-contained students would find grade-level EL work "overwhelming" and that it might "lead to a meltdown or just acting out." Instead, he modified the content of EL so that his students would be successful. Mr. Johnson perceived regular education classes as spaces that could not adequately differentiate or modify EL instruction even though the students in his class were fully included in regular education the previous year.

Brantlinger (2004b) argued that although educators (such as Mr. Johnson) were benevolent in believing in the efficacy of special education, they were less inclined to consider that special education is not a neutral or "natural response to [supposed] flaws in affected children" (p. 11). In fact, the seeming benevolence of special education and special educators, according to Brantlinger, only serves to "silence criticisms and depoliticize" (p. 4) the negative impact of special education practice on children. Families and students also begin to believe that low-tracked and segregated classrooms are in their own best interest, perpetuating hierarchical ideologies. As a result, students come to "internalize messages about their own inferiority" (p. 4).

Ms. Clark, a speech and language pathologist likewise argued that EL was not appropriate for students in self-contained classrooms. She justified their exclusion, by saying that their teachers,

THE IMPACT OF STANDARDS-BASED REFORM 133

need to be teaching ABCs ... [and] more of these basic skills ... In the eight to 10 year-old self-contained classroom, she [the teacher] has one student that pushes in with the other fourth graders, but she can read and write, so it's more appropriate [for her].

School-level administrator, Ms. Slater, also suggested that students with disabilities should not be included in general education EL instruction and, instead, should get a "double dose of reading—because reading is a skill that they will truly use in their life." In each of these instances, the curricular expectations for students with disabilities reflect low expectations of students with disabilities and of general education teachers, who are not expected to differentiate instruction for diverse learners.

Ms. Songer, who taught in an inclusive setting, was able to adopt a more communal ideology, viewing EL as beneficial for all students. In contrast, Ms. Clark, Mr. Johnson and Ms. Slater (who all taught in segregated settings) adopted a hierarchical ideology in suggesting that EL was an approach that was not appropriate for students in special education. Instead, they felt students in these settings needed instruction that was entirely different from what general education students needed. In fact, hierarchical thinking led to circular logic: the more students were segregated because of their perceived deficits, the more it was assumed that they were in need of remediation and the less they were perceived as benefiting from grade-level instruction.

A similar logic of basic skills and remediation strategies prompted Ms. Garcia, a district-level administrator, to question whether EL was a good approach for Westvale as a whole. In her view, the entire school should be focusing on functional skills in order to rectify their status as a failing school.

> You have to focus on one thing and that is good instruction ... I don't think it's [EL] a good model for the school. I think that they need to focus on early literacy right now and ... foundation skills if they're going to be successful.

Thus, Ms Garcia believed that Westvale students needed to spend time focusing on what they were lacking. From her perception, the entire school lacked early literacy skills and was not ready to use an approach like EL. This deficit perception was likely tied to the "failing" label of the school and compounded by the demographics of a typical urban school in the USA. This view also signifies the ways that deficit thinking becomes a "slippery" construct (Brantlinger, 2005)—cutting across race, class, and disability status.

Brantlinger (1997, 2005) critiqued the view that students who perform below the norm will improve through intensive individualised instruction. Similarly,

Gentry (2006) explained that focusing on remediating deficits "is counterintuitive, as children learn best when they have elements of interest, challenge, choice, and enjoyment in their learning experiences" (p. 24)—in other words, in ways that were reflected in the EL curriculum. Yet deficit-driven, skill and drill approaches continue to be seen as necessary and appropriate for poor and minority students as well as students with disabilities (Brantlinger, 2005; Darling-Hammond, 2010; Gentry, 2006).

4.3 Modified and Prioritised Curriculum Classes

The pressure to segregate students can increase as students get closer to graduation. By high school, schools often assume that students with disabilities cannot be included because they lack basic skills and content knowledge (that they likely did not have access to in the first place). Issues of segregation of students are elided in such discussions of 'needs' and so too, in the example of Springertown which relied upon stratifying practices as students moved into high school. As Brantlinger (2004b) argued, however, "ranked relations [i.e. ability tracks] are based on the assumption that two groups are fundamentally different with an irreversible dissymmetry between them" (p. 20). She also noted how "administrators segregated [students] by "ability" not as a result of convictions about "best practice," but because of pressures for examination success rates" (p. 134). These assumptions fuelled the response to reform tracking structures across Springertown.

District-level administrator, Mr. Copper, suggested that inclusion was increasingly difficult in high school, because of increased curricular demands. Yet, according to NYS policy, a student cannot "be removed from education in age-appropriate general education classes solely because of needed modifications in the general curriculum" (NYSED, 2010a, p. 58). However, because more accountability and sanctions are linked to SBR than the Individuals with Disabilities Education Improvement Act of 2004 (IDEIA, 2004), SBR often takes precedence. Thus, many schools uncritically assume that if a student's work needs to be modified, it justifies his/her exclusion. Tracking at Springertown was characterised as a natural response to deficits within the student (Brantlinger, 2004b) rather than the result of classroom practices that failed to provide access to the curriculum.

District-level administrator, Mr. Klosher, lamented that teachers often questioned the 'fairness' of allotting students who receive modifications the same grades as other students. As Mr. Klosher aptly pointed out, standardised curriculum linked to exit examinations reinforced the idea that if a student cannot meet grade-level expectations, then s/he should not be able to pass the class. In terms of inclusive practice, "fair isn't always equal" (Wormeli, 2006, p. 1).

Unfortunately, the hierarchical ideology (Brantlinger, 2004b) of SBR intensifies the assumption that grades must be dispersed fairly and that course grades must accurately represent a child's ability to perform not simply on course related material, but on state examinations.

District-level administrator, Mr Copper noted the contradiction between scores on state-level tests and grades in high school courses. He explained that a student "might have an 80% pass rate in algebra one ... [and is] passing the course, but [he/she also] got a 25% pass on the Regent's [state examination]." When this occurs too often, the school will get labelled PLA. Mr Copper, thus, laid out the dilemma created when a student's performance in high school courses are expected to match his or her performance on the state exit examinations. Moreover, many students who attend schools that are deemed low-achieving do not perform adequately on the state-level tests and are, thus, assumed not to benefit from regular education courses.

Although the NYSED (2010a) guidance document states that the need for a modification in curriculum is not a valid justification for exclusion, state-level policy-makers admit that in practice it is likely to be used as a justification. State-level employee, Ms. Davern, for instance, stated:

> I think most students with disabilities need to be able to master the content in the Regents exams. And I think ... principals in schools need to be paying special attention to places where students are passing Regent's level courses and failing Regents exams ... Given that passing the Regent's course is supposed to represent proficiency in the learning standards that are required within that course, we shouldn't be seeing a big discrepancy between success in the course and success [on the state exit exam].

Thus, according to Ms. Davern, if a student cannot pass a state-level exit exam, they should not be able to pass a regular education course. Ms Davern's statement uncritically assumes that state-level tests are valid measures of achievement for students with and without disabilities, which may not necessarily the case (Ravitch, 2010).

This dilemma leads schools to segregate students and emphasise teaching to the test, a ramification of SBR that Brantlinger (2004a) lamented. Students with disabilities are more likely to excel when given meaningful, engaging, universally designed curriculum and assessments (Valle & Connor, 2010). Thus, it is quite possible that a student would be successful in well-designed inclusive classes, even though they may falter on a high-stakes exam. In fact, it is not uncommon for students without disabilities to score below their class average on high-stakes tests. Yet, if there is a discrepancy between a course grade and a state exam score, the exam is unquestionably positioned as more valid. However, as Brantlinger (2005) argued, "statistically normed, objective seeming measures" reflect particular ideologies that are uncritically assumed to be "fair and legitimate" (p. 132). Conversely, a tenant of an inclusive ideology is that "learning is enhanced by contact and interaction" in settings where students are expected to have diverse learning needs and learn at different rates (Brantlinger, 1997, p. 435). Unfortunately, Springertown responded to this modification dilemma with increased tracking for high school students.

The only official guidance that NYSED offers on graduation requirements linked to modified courses is that students with disabilities are eligible to receive a Regents (or regular education) diploma when they are "enrolled in coursework that leads to a diploma" (NYSED, 2010b 'Opportunity to Earn,' p. 3). There is no guidance, however, about whether a student can or cannot receive course credit if the course content is modified as per a child's Individualised Education Plan (IEP). Thus, to assume that a student cannot receive course credit because content is modified goes against the IDEIA as well as direction from NYS.

Yet, Springertown school district responded by creating a new track of self-contained courses available for students with disabilities at the high school level. According to Mr/Copper, a district-level administrator, students with disabilities in these courses could receive an "80% modification" rate and still receive credit for the course. The classes were called as prioritised curriculum (PC) classes and were designed exclusively for students with disabilities. The administrator said that although it might be tempting to put general education students who fall behind in these slower paced rooms, they would be restricted to students with disabilities because, "it has to be pure ... We only have a certain number of slots and, obviously, I want them going to my [special education] kids because we're facing ... graduation rates in the 30s."

When developing the content for these PC courses, Mr. Copper explained how groups of general and special education teachers met and "literally black lined parts of [the] curriculum." The fact that the PC courses are comprised of less content and are only available for students with disabilities raises many questions about how these courses influence teacher expectations of students with disabilities and whether these classes violate Least Restrictive Environment provisions of the IDEIA. As Kintz (2011) warned, "once placed in a certain tracking ability level' students rarely move from that track" (p. 57). Informed by hierarchical ideology, Springertown administrators responded to SBR by increasing traditional special education sorting and stratifying practices (Brantlinger, 1997, 2004b).

THE IMPACT OF STANDARDS-BASED REFORM   137

Districts and schools across the USA have responded to SBR and high-stakes exams with increasing stratification of curriculum and viewing achievement in ever more narrow ways. Schools and districts have been forced to make choices that undermine the inclusion of students with disabilities in regular education classes. Self-contained programmes, such as the PC classroom, result in segregating many students who would otherwise have been included in regular education courses. Brantlinger (2006) explained that, all children "benefit from ... access to advanced curriculum and programs ... [but] unfortunately, these conditions rarely exist for' students in under-resourced schools and low-tracked classrooms" (p. 197). Low-tracked classrooms linked to exit exams illustrate Brantlinger's (2006) predictions about how SBR would perpetuate hierarchical ideologies and magnify the inequitable education for students with disabilities, particularly for those who attend under-resourced schools and districts.

4.4   *Diploma Options*

Brantlinger (2001, 2004a, 2006) was particularly disheartened that an increasing number of states were instituting high-stakes exams as graduation requirements a practice that has led to increased drop out rates rather than increased achievement. Brantlinger (2004a) argued that exit exams benefit dominant groups, who create the norms that others are held accountable for meeting. As a result, exit examinations are often "one more instance of failure for students who already fail" (Brantlinger, 2006, p. 206). NYS has recently aligned its diploma options with exit examinations. These more stringent requirements both ostracise and stigmatise students with disabilities.

NYS legislation now requires that students pass state examinations in order to graduate from high school with a regular education diploma. These new diploma requirements would mean that many students could literally get left behind (Brantlinger, 2004a). Interview participants, however, explained that NYS wanted to eliminate alternative (or IEP) diploma options for students with disabilities but, at the same time, they wanted to link Regents (exit) examinations with diploma requirements. According to a state-level employee, the IEP diploma was only a certificate of attendance and was basically a "ticket to nowhere." Thus, in 2012, a new diploma, called the "Skills and Achievement Commencement Credential," was approved by NYS. This new credential functions similarly to the IEP diploma, but would only be available for the 1–2% of students who qualify to take the alternate assessments under NCLB. According to district-level administrator, Mr. Copper, the new credential reflects "a CTE [career and technical education] and is based on the CDOS [Career Development and Occupational Studies] standards." In other words, the new credential is not a diploma, but is linked to a set of non-academic standards and is only available for a small number of students with disabilities. This new credential reinforces both physical and curricular stratifications based on who is likely to pass the state-level exit examination.

Because the new credential is available to only a small portion of students with dis-abilities and because NYS acknowledges that some students with disabilities who do not qualify for the alternate assessment will not likely pass the Regents examination, NYS has also adopted a third diploma option, called a "local diploma." Several interview participants explained that NYS was concerned that many students with disabilities would fall through the cracks and earn neither a "Skills and Achievement Commencement Credential" nor a Regents diploma; these students were described by interview participants as "gap area" or "grey area" kids. In order to provide a graduation option for these students, the NYS Board of Regents voted that the local diploma requirements be altered and be made available only for students with disabilities (Hildebray, 2012; NYSED, 2013). This local diploma was previously available for all students.

As documented in an observation of the NYS Commissioner Advisory Panel for Special Education meeting, a member of the group who worked for an organisation that advocates for youth questioned the decision to only have the diploma available for students with disabilities. She commented that, "in the big picture, we are still giving a diploma that is just for a student with a disability. We have a different expectation level ... because you have a disability." A NYS representative responded that, "The decision is, at this point ... to keep it available [only] for students with disabilities." Special education advocates fought to keep the local diploma an option—at least for students with disabilities. However, it is likely that as the local diploma becomes associated as a diploma only for students with disabilities, it will become stigmatised and equated with low expectations similar to the IEP diploma in previous years.

As Brantlinger (2004a) pointed out, SBR policies tend to harm those who are already disenfranchised. Thus, eliminating the local diploma option for regular education students would disproportionally harm students who are black, Latino, and ELLs. In fact, Advocates for Children of New York (2010) released a document responding to inequities that would be likely if the local diploma option was limited to students with disabilities. The group explained that a disproportionate number of black, Latino, and ELL students relied on the local diploma as a pathway to graduation. For instance, the group noted that in 2009, only 21.7% of ELLs received a Regents diploma, whereas 43.7% ... received a local diploma.

We wonder what might have happened to the 20% of students who graduated with a local diploma, had that not been an option. Are there additional

THE IMPACT OF STANDARDS-BASED REFORM   139

supports for them to meet the increased graduation requirements? Furthermore, many students with disabilities will not be held to high expectations, originally touted as a rationale for including them in the accountability system in the first place, because the local diploma allowed for a significantly different set of expectations. Brantlinger (2006) suggested that the relative lack of resistance against these measures is due to the fact that those most affected are "students already on the losing end of the school evaluative and status continua and bottom rung of hierarchies" (p. 206).

State-level employee, Ms Hoffman, further warned of the limitations faced by students with disabilities who do not obtain a regular education diploma as they exit high school:

> If you have a Regents [regular education] diploma, you can go to any kind of college you want to. If you have a local diploma, especially in the last few years, it means you are a student with a disability ... so the anonymity is gone. I don't think most colleges, most four-year colleges, will take you.

Thus, the type of diploma students receive largely determines their prospects as they transition out of high school. Narrow and stringent diploma options preclude many students with and without disabilities from having the option to enter into meaningful post-school lives. Thus, students segregated into self-contained classrooms or low-tracked classes because they are unable to meet grade-level standards, will not likely be able to receive a Regents diploma. This is indeed a high-stakes exam, because it threatens to not only limit the inclusion of students in school, but also in society.

5   Conclusion

Brantlinger's corpus of work continues to provide an important framework for understanding contemporary educational reform. Like Brantlinger, we have found that SBR serves hegemony and benefits already dominant groups. Brantlinger's prescient work leads us to call for continued vigilance about how school reform disproportionately disadvantages students of colour, ELLs and students with disabilities.

Brantlinger's work highlights how hierarchical ideologies are deeply embedded within schools as students are sorted and tracked in ways that mirror racial, class, and disability divisions. Hierarchical ideologies are likewise evident between highly resourced suburban schools and underfunded urban and rural schools, whose students are subject to inequitable funding based on property tax, yet held to the same accountability measures (Darling-Hammond, 2010). Thus, whether operating at the inter-school or intra-school level, hierarchical ideologies become further entrenched under SBR. Of particular importance to our continued commitment to inclusive practice is how SBR perpetuated what Brantlinger (2004b) called as "hierarchical" knowledges, thereby weakening "communal" ideologies that reflect a more inclusive orientation. We found that even as some students with disabilities were receiving increased access to regular education curriculum as a result of SBR, these same students were more likely to receive this instruction in segregated classrooms. Many participants reported that it was preferable for students with disabilities (particularly those who were behind in grade-level literacy and math skills) to spend more time in segregated classes so that they could pass state-level tests. It was as if inclusion never happened in Springertown as special education students were increasingly siphoned away and relegated to restrictive environments where the focus of instruction tended to be on remediation and basic skills.

Although the segregation of students with disabilities persists at the middle and high school levels, we were surprised at the extent that the school district responded to the demands of high-stakes tests by creating new self-contained tracks for students with disabilities. "Prioritised Curriculum" classes, designed for students with disabilities, were based on a modified set of content standards. Administrators and teachers operated on the uninterrogated belief that these classes were necessary, because they considered modifying content in regular education classes unfair or untenable. Moreover, participants supported the belief that if a child could not pass the state-level exit exam, then they should not be able to do well in the class. We also found it striking that few attempts were made to keep students in regular classrooms by using the inclusive practices that Brantlinger (1997) and others have promoted as best practices. As Brantlinger feared, SBR appears to be revalidating the taken for granted hierarchical ideologies of special education traditionalists.

SBR tied to stringent diploma requirements represents a threat to the inclusion of students with disabilities in both school and society. Brantlinger (2006) warned that 'gateway' exams linked to diploma requirements would disproportionately impact students who are already disenfranchised in schools. Although students with disabilities are still able to access alternate diplomas, these credentials (because they are quickly associated with special education) do little to help secure a student's future. Furthermore, students who do not have disabilities and who do not succeed on state tests are likewise left with no viable option to graduate high school—significantly contributing to high dropout rates (Brantlinger, 2001; Lillard & DeCicca, 2001).

Brantlinger's work continues to inform the ways that school structures and practices shape the lives of all students. As a result of NCLB legislation and Race to the Top funding grants, the stakes have never been higher. Education is increasingly prescriptive and schools and teachers are evaluated (either directly or indirectly) based on how well their students' do on high-stakes exams. When students are unable to develop knowledge in a linear way, as prescribed by content standards, and when they cannot demonstrate their knowledge through standardised exams, they are viewed as unworthy of being included in classrooms and in society at large. Educators, too, are embedded within the same hierarchical logic. Brantlinger's (2006) call for "a counter-movement to oppose stratifying measures and work to overcome hierarchical and excluding relations in school and society" (p. 224) issued a clarion plea to the inclusion movement and to those of us who attempt to extend her work through disability studies in education. We would do well to heed her call in promoting policies and practices that support the inclusion of all students.

Acknowledgement

This chapter originally appeared in *International Journal of Inclusive Education, 17*(12), 2013, 1312–1325. Reprinted here with permission from the publisher.

References

Apple, M. W. (2004). Creating difference: Neo-liberalism, neo-conservatism and the politics of educational reform. *Educational Policy, 18*(1), 12–44.

Brantlinger, E. A. (1997). Using ideology: Cases of nonrecognition of the politics of research and practice in special education. *Review of Educational Research, 67*(4), 425–459.

Brantlinger, E. A. (2001). Poverty, class, and disability: A historical, social, and political perspective. *Focus on Exceptional Children, 33*(7), 1–19.

Brantlinger, E. (2004a). An application of Gramsci's 'who benefits?' to high-stakes testing. *Workplace, 6*(1). Retrieved from http://www.cust.educ.ubc.ca/workplace/issue6p1/brantlinger.html

Brantlinger, E. A. (2004b). Ideologies discerned, values determined: Getting past the hierarchies of special education. In L. Ware (Ed.), *Ideology and the politics of (in) exclusion*. New York, NY: Peter Lang.

Brantlinger, E. A. (2005). Slippery shibboleths: The shady side of truisms in special education. In L. Ware (Ed.), *Disability studies in education: Readings in theory and method*. New York, NY: Peter Lang.

Brantlinger, E. A. (2006). Winners need losers: The basis for school competition and hierarchies. In A. Brantlinger (Ed.), *Who benefits from special education? Remediating [fixing] other people's children.* Mahwah, NJ: Lawrence Erlbaum Associates.

Cole, C. (2006). Closing the achievement gap series, part III: What is the impact of NCLB on the inclusion of students with disabilities? *Center for Evaluation and Education Policy Brief, 4*(11), 1–12.

Corbin, J., & Strauss, A. (1990). Grounded theory research: Procedures, canons, and evaluative criteria. *Qualitative Sociology, 13*(1), 418–427.

Darling-Hammond, L. (2010). *The flat world and education: How America's commitment to equity will determine our future.* New York, NY: Teachers College Press.

Defur, S. (2002). Education reform, high stakes assessment, and students with disabilities: One state's approach. *Remedial and Special Education, 23*(4), 203–211.

Expeditionary Learning. (2012). Retrieved from http://elschools.org/

Flowers, C., Ahlgrim-Delzell, L., Browder, D., & Spooner, F. (2005). Teachers' perceptions of alternate assessment. *Research and Practice for Persons with Severe Disabilities, 30*, 81–92.

Gentry, M. (2006). No child left behind: Neglecting excellence. *Roeper Review, 29*(1), 24–27.

Hildebray, J. (2012, October 9). Regents rule change aids special education. *Long Island Newsday* (Long Island Section). Retrieved from http://www.newsday.com/long-island/regents-rule-change-aids-special-education-1.4095211

Individuals with Disabilities Education Improvement Act (IDEIA). (2004). Public Law 108–446.

Kintz, M. (2011). Ability grouping and how it is affecting American classrooms. *ESSAI, 9*(20), 55–58.

Kreitzer, A. E., Madaus, G. F., & Haney, W. (1989). Competency testing and dropouts. In E. Farrar Weise & H. G. Petrie (Eds.), *Dropouts from school: Issues, Dilemmas, and Solutions.* Albany, NY: State University of New York Press.

Lillard, D. R., & DeCicca, P. P. (2001). Higher standards, more dropouts? Evidence within and across time. *Economics of Education Review, 20*(5), 459–473.

Nelson, J. R. (2002). *Closing or widening the gap of inequality: The intended and unintended consequences of minnesota's basic standards tests for students with disabilities* (PhD dissertation). University of Minnesota, Minneapolis, MN.

NYSED (New York State Education Department). (2010a). *Special education: Guide to quality Individualized Education Program development and implementation.* Retrieved from http://www.p12.nysed.gov/specialed/publications/iepguidance.htm

NYSED. (2010b). *Special education: Individualized Education Program (IEP) diploma.* Retrieved from http://www.p12.nysed.gov/specialed/publications/iepdiploma.htm

NYSED. (2011). *Questions and answers about schools identified as persistently lowest-achieving and concurrently as schools under registration review.* Retrieved from http://www.p12.nysed.gov/pla/FAQ.html

NYSED. (2012). *Persistently lowest-achieving schools*. Retrieved from
http://www.p12.nysed.gov/pla/

NYSED. (2013). *Diploma/credential requirements*. Retrieved from
http://www.p12.nysed.gov/ciai/gradreq/diploma-credential-summary.pdf

Ravitch, D. (2010). *The death and life of the great American school system: How testing and choice are undermining education*. New York, NY: Basic Books.

Sandholtz, J. H., Ogawa, R. T., & Scribner, S. P. (2004). Standards gaps: Unintended consequences of local standards-based reform. *Teachers College Record, 106*(6), 1177–1202.

Smyth, T. S. (2008). Who is no child left behind leaving behind? *The Clearinghouse: A Journal of Educational Strategies, Issues and Ideas, 81*(13), 133–137.

Thompson, S., & Thurlow, M. L. (2001). *2001 State special education outcomes: A report on state activities at the beginning of a new decade*. Minneapolis, MN: University of Minnesota, National Center on Educational Outcomes.

Thompson, S., & Thurlow, M. L. (2003). *2003 State special education outcomes: Marching forward*. Minneapolis, MN: University of Minnesota, National Center on Educational Outcomes.

US Department of Education. (2009). *Race to the top program: Executive summary*. Washington, DC: US Department of Education. Retrieved from
http://www2.ed.gov/programs/racetothetop/executive-summary.pdf

Valle, J. W., & Conner, D. J. (2010). *Rethinking disability: A disability studies approach to inclusive practices*. New York, NY: McGraw Hill.

Wormeli, R. (2006). *Fair isn't always equal: Assessing and grading in the differentiated classroom*. Portland, ME: Stenhouse Publishers.

Ysseldyke, J., Nelson, J., Christenson, S., Johnson, D., Dennison, A., Trizenberg, H., Sharpe, M., & Howes, M. (2004). What we know and need to know about the consequences of high-stakes testing for students with disabilities. *Exceptional Children, 71*(1), 75–95.

CHAPTER 8

Family Portraits: Past and Present Representations of Parents in Special Education Text Books

Dianne L. Ferguson, Philip M. Ferguson, Joanne Kim and Corrine Li

Abstract

This chapter analyzes the descriptions of families of children with disabilities as contained in introductory special education texts over the last 50 years. These textbooks are typically used in pre-service teacher education courses as surveys of the education of 'exceptional children.' The textbooks reflect the mainstream professional assumptions of the era about topics such as disability, special education, inclusion, and family/school linkages. However, they also shape the assumptions of the next generation of educators about the same topics. The chapter summarizes the results of a qualitative document analysis of a sample of these textbooks from two different eras. The authors compare and contrast how the representation of families, by leading scholars in special education have changed over time.

Keywords

disability – special education – curriculum and instruction

1 Introduction

As Ellen Brantlinger (1997) so usefully explained in her analysis of the "traditionalist" critiques of inclusion, ideology is most dependably present when it is being denounced in others. In a neutral sense, ideologies are simply "systems of representations (images, myths, ideas) which, in profoundly unconscious ways, mediate one's understanding of the world (Brantlinger, 1997, p. 438). In short, ideology is everywhere. It is the standpoint from which we perceive the world; the discursive assumptions from which we interpret what we see. What makes the analysis of ideology important, then, is not to discover its presence; it is always present. What is useful (and this is the power of much

© TAYLOR & FRANCIS, 2013 | DOI:10.1163/9789004402690_009

of Brantlinger's work) is to reveal its influence on those who disavow any ideological component to their work. This study follows Brantlinger's lead by analyzing the underlying ideological frames that can be found in one of the most ubiquitous but under-analyzed settings for the representation of special education knowledge: the large, introductory texts used in almost every teacher education program in the United States (and elsewhere).

Not only is ideology everywhere; so are the "big glossies." To borrow Ellen Brantlinger's (2006) wonderful term, the "big glossies" are the introductory textbooks churned out by the handful of publishing conglomerates that increasingly dominate the market. Almost everyone connected to teacher education is familiar with them. As students in teacher education programs, almost all of us took at least one course that was organized around one of these texts. As instructors, many of us have felt immense pressure to use one of these texts in a course. Others of us have contributed chapters to edited collections that seem to require revision for a new edition every other year. Of course, those new editions arrive free of charge in our mailboxes. Now they come packaged with their own websites, testing resources, and links to online instructor assistance. In the near future, the expectation is that these books will become almost entirely web-based. They are, truly, an omnipresent feature of teacher education and have been for over 50 years.

Within special education teacher preparation programs in the United States, the most common place to find a "big glossy" in use is as the main required textbook for the introductory course. That course goes by many names, but it is usually some variant of "Introduction to Exceptional Learners." Coincidentally, that description also applies to the titles of the books seeking adoption for use in those courses. In traditional teacher preparation programs, this course may be the only one required for pre-service general educators where disability issues are discussed at length. For those preparing for careers in special education, it is the initial framework for their gradual induction into the professional context of teaching children with disabilities. In short, these books have played what would seem to be an immensely important role in shaping the underlying assumptions, beliefs, and expectations of generations of general and special education teachers about how we should support children with disabilities and their families.

Despite this prominence, the special education textbooks have received relatively little critical analysis from what might be called a disability studies perspective. As already mentioned, an important exception to this is Ellen Brantlinger's careful analysis of "The big glossies: How textbooks structure (special) education" (2006). Brantlinger's work focused on how the books she examined construct disability itself. Within a powerful review of how corporations work to control the discourse of teacher preparation, she asked whether and how the books discuss structural issues of systemic inequity; how they frame issues of race and class; and whether inclusive instructional approaches are discussed. She tied her analysis to the work of more familiar critics within a general education context (e.g. Apple, 1989; Apple & Christian-Smith, 1991; Kohn, 2003).

In many ways, we see these textbooks as "lagging indicators" of the paradigm shift in disability studies and special education. They will be the last to change because of an institutional conservatism built into the process of teacher preparation and course book design. As Brantlinger persuasively argues, the content of these texts is, to a great extent, governed by the economics of book publishing (Brantlinger, 2006, p. 51). The books must be adopted for use in courses or they will not stay in print. The market forces, then, push textbook authors to "pitch" their textbooks to appeal to the largest possible audience, which means changed content in texts can be expected to change only after those changes have made their way into the policies and practices of teachers and students. The introductory courses at which they are aimed are, in turn, designed to address the official standards of knowledge and skill presented by both professional organizations such as the Council for Exceptional Children and by the teacher credentialing agencies of the various states. While improvement in these official standards of professional "expertise" should be noted, they nonetheless continue to be imbued with the assumptions of individual deficits, behavioral assessment and instruction, and placement continuums. Given this, then a review of how much (or how little) the content of these textbooks has changed over time can serve as a rough measure of how thorough-going has been the shift to more social models of disability with the corollaries of family partnerships and community inclusion.

One important area of content that Brantlinger did not focus on is how the introductory textbooks frame and discuss the families of the children with disabilities. This is where our study picks up.[1] In addition, we were interested in whether and how the discussion of families within these textbooks had changed over time. This study is also part of a larger analysis that we are doing that explores more generally the personal and professional portrayal of families as it has evolved over the last century or so (Ferguson & Ferguson, 2010; Ferguson, 2008; Ferguson & Ferguson, 2006). Specifically, we asked the following questions:

1. How do textbooks designed for introductory courses in pre-service special education programs portray parents/families of children with disabilities?

2. How do the textbooks describe and discuss family/school linkages?

FAMILY PORTRAITS

3.   How have the portrayals and descriptions contained in these textbooks changed over time?

2   Methodological Approach

To answer these questions, we used conventional methods of qualitative document analysis located within an interpretivist research tradition (Bogdan & Biklen, 2007; Ferguson, Ferguson, & Taylor, 1992; Rossman & Rallis, 2003). We used a purposefully chosen sample of 14 textbooks as the source documents for analysis. The list of selected books is included in Table 1. The books are also starred (*) in the reference list at the end of the paper. We chose the textbooks according to criteria designed to produce a representative cross-section of the most-used texts of their respective eras. These criteria included:

-   Date of publication: The study included books published between roughly 1960 and 2012 with seven of the books coming from before 2000 and seven coming after 2000.
-   Publisher: We emphasized books published by the larger, more influential publishers in the United States of education texts (e.g., Houghton-Mifflin, Little/Brown, Pearson/Merrill/Prentice Hall, Cengage/Wadsworth, McGraw-Hill).
-   Longevity: The study also emphasized books that have had multiple editions, with longevity inferred to be a marker of popularity in courses. For example, the text by Samuel Kirk (1962)—and the additional authors added in later editions—has gone through 13 editions and has been a standard, introductory text for some 50 years.
-   Focus: While most of the textbooks that we selected cover the full range of "exceptionality," we also included a few texts that focus on specific categories of disability. Partly, this reflects the emphasis of the eras. In the 1960s and 1970s, some of the most influential textbooks (e.g., Chinn, Drew, & Logan, 1975) focused on "mental retardation," although this label included many children who would have different (or perhaps no) labels in today's schools. This also allows some additional comparisons between descriptions of families across specific categories of disability (e.g., are families of children identified as learning disabled portrayed differently than families of children identified and intellectually disabled?).

For our analysis, we used a process of systematic but flexible document analysis. All passages containing more than passing references to parents and other family members of children with disabilities were identified for coding. We used both a more analytic approach associated with grounded theory as well as a comparative process that used themes of discourse that we had already identified in some of our earlier work. We coded the individual passages and then used a more wholistic comparison to the earlier themes for family linkage discourse. After one of us had identified and coded passages from one of the books, the others would review those passages in a version of peer debriefing (Marshall & Rossman, 2006). Finally, we did an additional analysis of all the "call outs" that first began appearing in 1989. These are the passages that are "boxed off" from the regular text, and often include photos and other information, some focused on family or personal narratives. We analyzed the content that included mention or focus on families first and then completed a second more wholistic look at the messages of all the call outs and photos. The final stages of wholistic comparison and thematic summary and interpretation were done together.

3   Discourses of Family Involvement

Following the coding of individual passages, we added a second stage of analysis where we compared our findings to our earlier research that has described three broad categories of rhetoric and policy in educational approaches to family/school linkages (Ferguson, Hanreddy, & Ferguson, in press). This earlier analysis emerged from our analysis of both scholarly work on family/school linkages and the language used by teachers and administrators with whom we have worked over the years. We have labeled the three approaches or rhetorics of family involvement as (1) rights-based, (2) educational benefits, and (3) social justice/equity. One outcome of this new study has been to evaluate how well these previous themes work in summarizing the content of both past and present textbooks. Obviously, in using this two-stage approach to the analysis of our data, we needed to critically reflect on how our earlier findings might unduly influence our analysis in the current study. However, we feel that the traditional techniques of surfacing and bracketing assumptions allowed us to benefit from this previous research while remaining open to revision and contrast. The three family discourses, then, served as a frame on which we can build our current analysis rather than imprison it.

Before turning to our results, it may be useful to review the three discourses used by scholars and special education professionals to talk about families of children with disabilities. Each of these has its strengths, but each, as well, can definitely be problematic. Our argument about these discourses has two basic points. First, the very existence of the different discourses and how they explain and justify family involvement is important to notice. Otherwise, the hidden assumptions or alternative interpretations may be overlooked. Second,

FAMILY PORTRAITS

once we start paying attention to the various discourses, it quickly becomes clear that the social justice/social relations approach remains largely on the fringes of the dominant views in special education.

The *rights-based approach*, in an American context, is best exemplified by a focus on the requirements of *Individuals with Disabilities Education Act* (IDEA). Within that federal legislation governing special education, there is a range of legal requirements that schools "*have to*" do in order to be in compliance with the law. This approach will often describe the rise of parent activism and disability advocacy as keys to the current status of family involvement. Yet within this approach the desired outcome of genuine partnership between school personnel and families in providing educational support to students with special educational needs all too often proceeds with only minimal (or even no) contribution from families, or deteriorates into a series of formalistic procedures or even adversarial relationships. The current "sign off" practices in many American schools of "parent compacts" in order to meet the requirements for family involvement or the practice of having an IEP already prepared by the professionals for the IEP meeting (with the expectation that family members will simply sign off) are examples of the perfunctory type of family involvement. In many ways, this discourse about families is what Brantlinger refers to as a "legalistic" model of disability (Brantlinger, 2006, p. 52). Perhaps the most familiar example of the adversarial style occurs when the legalistic elements of due process hearings overtake the IEP procedures.

A second type of family-involvement discourse might be called an *educational benefits approach*. This approach is one that most schools use to decide how to engage families whether or not the child has a disability. This approach is less dominated by an emphasis on procedural requirements and, instead, uses a type of cost-benefit analysis. That is, will the activity—whatever it is—result in some amount of educational benefit that is "worth" the cost of engaging in the activity in the first place? Will it result in families assisting the school to teach the students in some way? By bringing in additional resources, by directly helping teachers prepare and deliver instruction, or by extending learning activities past the school day, into the evenings and weekends. These activities or offerings are often things that schools *can* do without too much cost in terms of energy, time, or resources while still obtaining the benefit to the school, teacher, or the student in terms of improved learning achievement. There are both positive and negative versions of this discourse. On the positive side, the approach tends to see at least some families as *resources* who can help the school and extend the school agenda. But only some families are seen as resources by school personnel. On the negative side, then, certain families are seen as needing "work" in the form of instruction and training on how to parent and how to support the school agenda (Harry, Kalyanpur, & Day, 1999; Lareau, 2005; Lightfoot, 2004). Unfortunately, this last group can sometimes seem to "cost" more than schools receive in benefit. In the end family activities in this approach can end up being either haphazard or ritualistic. The occasional efforts to reach out to families or the occasional family training event are examples of the first, while parent/teacher conferences and "family nights" can all too often be stale examples of the second.

There is a third approach, although it is only addressed by a relatively small number of schools and scholars in special education (Brantlinger, 1993, 2003; Harry, Kalyanpur, & Day, 1999; Lopez, Scribner, & Mahitivanichcha, 2001). This *social relations/social justice approach* is one that requires school personnel to first understand the issues embedded in our cultural, socioeconomic and other forms of human diversity and then to use this understanding to "filter" all efforts toward families in order to better reach and engage *all* of those families. As Brantlinger put it in her powerful analysis of how schools embody and perpetuate the same hierarchical inequities found in the larger society,

> Unless the desires and intentionality behind advantage and the negotiations of the winners in stratified schools are examined and confronted, school reform that is (purportedly) aimed at increasing equity will never succeed. ... As long as the lay public, policy makers, school managers, and educational scholars locate the problem in school losers and direct their efforts at changing them, a dent will not be put in the ubiquitous class-biased practices in school. (Brantlinger, 2003, p. 192)

Despite their scarcity, specific examples can be found of efforts to overcome the inequities faced by students and their families within both general and special education contexts, from large policy commitments to small acts of daily practice. Making sure that all school communication (not just those documents required by law) is translated into a family's first language is one obvious, but often very difficult, example of this kind of outreach and honoring of students' families (Ferguson & Galindo, 2008). Building teachers' capacity to understand, appreciate, and take into account issues of differing social/cultural capital, family lifestyles, socioeconomic advantages and needs, as well as families "funds of knowledge" (Gonzalez, Moll, & Amanti, 2005; Moll & Greenberg, 1990) is required to fully employ a social relations/social justice approach in such a way that truly inclusive and democratic school communities that successfully engage *all* families in students' learning and achievement. This approach, however, is often too hard and time consuming, especially in

FAMILY PORTRAITS   151

terms of the capacity building required of school personnel to be more than
rhetoric in most schools, if it even rises to that level of awareness. Even schools
that make good faith efforts in this area find it difficult to maintain such efforts
over time or expand to accommodate new populations of families as student
demographics change.

4   Results

Certainly these textbooks reveal that the attention afforded families has both
grown and changed over the last 50 years. However, as is often the case, the
devil is in the details. In this section, we will provide both a summative and
interpretive analysis of what we found in our readings of the 'big glossies'.
A list of books reviewed is provided in Table 1. The books are organized first by
publication date with the exception that multiple editions of two of the most
prominent textbooks (six editions of the "Kirk" textbook and three editions
of the "Hallahan and Kauffman" textbook) are grouped together for easier
comparison.

In addition to the publication dates, Table 1 summarizes several types of
information. Although our primary focus when analyzing these texts was what
was said about families more than what was said about disabilities, there is an
obvious overlap. So, following Brantlinger's example (Brantlinger, 2006), we
have identified the "disability discourse" used by each book. By this, we are
primarily describing whether the text employed a categorical approach or not,
organizing its contents around chapters separately devoted to specific categories of disability. As Brantlinger described in her analysis of the big glossies,
the politics of publishing make it difficult for textbook authors to use anything
but the traditionalist, categorical approach where "each disability category or
disabling condition was outlined as including students who were clearly dis-
tinctive from students with other types of disabilities and students without
disabilities" (Brantlinger, 2006, p. 52). As can be seen by Table 1, at least for our
sample of books, the categorical approach remains the dominant one. (There
are a few introductory texts that have tried to buck this categorical approach,
for example Sands, Kozleski, & French, 2000, but they remain the exception
rather than the rule.)

The table also presents a summary of whether the text has a separate chapter explicitly addressing family or family/school issues. Of course, this information by itself is little more than suggestive. It provides no information about
the content of that separate chapter, should it exist. It says nothing about
how much discussion of families is provided in other parts of the text. Still,

it seemed to provide a rough indication of one of the basic changes that we noticed in comparing older versus newer textbooks. The attention given to family issues has undeniably increased.

Finally, Table 1 also summarizes our overall assessment of whether and how prominent the three family discourses that we have already discussed were in each of the texts. For each book in our sample we assigned a level of prominence for each of the family discourses: primary (P), secondary (S), incidental (I). If we found no evidence of a particular discourse, we used a "not found" label (NF). Our basis for these summative characterizations for what could be—especially in a few of the most recent textbooks—a complicated variety of comments about families, was obviously impressionistic. However, the characterizations emerged from joint discussions following our independent review and coding of each text. We did develop one "bright line" test for the assessment of "social justice" discourse. After much discussion, we decided that it was essentially contradictory to say that a textbook organized around a categorical approach to disability used social justice as its "primary" discursive approach. At best, such books used social justice in a significant but secondary manner.

A final important distinction used in the table involves the two strands of educational benefits discourse that emerged as one of the clearest distinctions between the older textbooks and the more recent ones. As we will discuss at more length later, what little attention the earliest texts gave to families was largely negative in tone and emphasis. The "benefit" that children received from educational involvement with parents was of a preventive nature: it could minimize or reverse the negative influences that neurotic, grief-stricken, over-protective or rejecting parents inflicted on their children. This version of the educational benefits discourse contrasts with the more recent rhetoric that is—at least on the surface—predominantly positive in tone and emphasis. Families (no longer just parents) in these texts are seen as resources for the school to draw upon. Families are important team-members, partners, and collaborators who can further the work of educators to the positive educational benefit of the children. Finally, some texts had roughly equal amounts of both positive and negative benefits language. So, in Table 8.1, when Educational Benefits language was found, we added a further description as "Negative" (NEG), "Positive" (POS) or "Mixed" (Mixed).

5   "Simple" Quantity

Certainly, over time, the amount that has been said about families in these introductory textbooks has noticeably grown. There is a progress from fewer than 10 instances where parents were mentioned in the earlier texts to a fairly consistent pattern of a single chapter devoted to families, their experiences and their role in the education of their child with disabilities beginning about 1990. In between mere mentions of parents or families grew gradually to a couple of pages, then 15 pages until the separate chapters began which range in length from 25–30 pages. Usually these pages took the form of a short section on families or parents in some, but not all chapters. Only one of our more recent texts (Friend, 2011) departed from the chapter approach in favor of a section in every chapter with the heading "Parent and Family Perspectives." But the choice of a single chapter in the other examples explored here– with a few important exceptions (Turnbull, Turnbull, & Wehmeyer, 2010)—usually meant that few other mentions of families were included in other chapters. A few of the later texts offer vignettes written by family members or persons with disabilities, but in the case of family/parent narratives the focus typically emphasizes the "educational benefits" discourse.

Over time then these authors of introductory textbooks have paid more attention to families and that attention has become more positive overall. However, the attention afforded families and their role in the education of their children still only represents a tiny proportion of the material in these texts. Most of the texts run a little over 400 pages. A few run closer to 500, and one nearly 600, but when all mention of families whether in a separate chapter or in sections scattered throughout the book is taken together it only amounts to 3–5% of the material in the text.

One could argue, of course, that families are not the focus of such introductory texts and that there are certainly separate texts devoted to the experiences and roles of families in the lives of children and adults with disabilities (e.g., Turnbull, Turnbull, Erwin, Soodak, & Shogren, 2010). Yet in education more broadly there is a growing conversation about the critical importance of family/school linkages to not only improve learning and achievement outcomes for children and youth (e.g., Ferguson, Ramos, Rudo, & Wood, 2008; Henderson & Mapp, 2002) but also an increasing focus on the need to shift the discourse from "family involvement" [in schools] characterized by the dominant "educational benefits" discourse to a discourse of family/school linkages that is meant to benefit not only student learning outcomes and assist educators in better "do their jobs," but also to benefit the family and the community in ways that strengthen family and community ties, foster social justice, and contribute to socially just communities (e.g., Kalyanpur, Harry, & Skrtic, 2000; Rao, 2000). As other parts of education pursue this discussion, it seems the special education community could benefit from joining the conversation as well—at least in terms of attention paid in introductory textbooks (Brantlinger, 2003, 2010).

TABLE 8.1   Textbooks reviewed by publication date and content analysis

PUB (ed.)	PUB date	Disability approach	Separate family chap	Family discourse approach		
				Educ. benefits	Parent rights	Social justice
Kirk (1st)	1962	Categorical	No	I (Neg)	NF	NF
Kirk (2nd)	1972	Categorical	No	I (Neg)	NF	NF
Kirk/Gallagher (3rd)	1979	Categorical	No	I(Mixed)	S	I
Kirk/Gallagher (6th)	1989	Categorical	No	P(Mixed)	S	I
Kirk/Gallagher/Anastasiow (8th)	1997	Categorical	No	P (Mixed)	S	I
Kirk/Gallagher Coleman/Anastasiow (13th)	2012	Categorical	Yes	P (Pos)	S	I
Smith/Neisworth	1975	Functional	Yes (Family Probs)	P		
Hallahan/Kauffman	1978	Categorical	No	I (Neg)		
Hallahan/Kauffman (9th)	2003	Categorical	Yes	P	S	NA
Hallahan/Kauffman/Pullen (12th)	2012	Categorical	Yes	P (Pos)	S	I
Friend (3rd)	2011	Categorical	No (but section in each chap)	P (Pos)	I	S
Heward (9th)	2009	Categorical	Yes	P (Pos)	S	I
Turnbull/Turnbull/Wehmeyer (6th)	2010	Categorical	Yes	P (Pos)	S	I
Rosenberg/Westling/McLeskey (2nd)	2011	Categorical	No	P (Pos)	I	NA

P = Primary   S = Secondary   I = Incidental   NA = Missing/Absent
POS = Positive Educational Benefits   NEG = Negative Educational Benefits

In a similar way, while the use of various types of "call-outs" began modestly with just a few different examples (e.g., focusing questions for the chapter, chapter summaries). Soon this feature was commonly used to present brief vignettes or narratives, some of which focused on families. However, the use of call outs expanded rapidly so that by late 1990s in addition to vignettes, they reference, for example, Council for Exceptional Children (CES) standards, resources of various types, educational strategies, websites, resources, key concepts, misconceptions and moral dilemmas. With the most recent examples in our sample, the use of call outs continues to expand with more content-directed items including practice tips, technology outcomes, partnership tips in addition to "My Voice" narratives. So even here family focused call-outs or narratives of youth or adults with disabilities only represent a small proportion of the content offered in this "boxed off" or "set apart" way.

6   Not-So-Simple Quality

Our analysis tried to move beyond a simple quantitative content analysis of the texts. Our overall purpose was to see whether the discursive approaches had evolved as well. Certainly, much has changed over the last 50 years in the how leading scholars portray the families of children with disabilities in books aimed at training the next generation of special educators. As we have mentioned, in the earlier textbooks, families were largely absent. However, even more striking is that when families were mentioned, it was usually to describe the problems they presented to professionals. In the first edition of his classic introductory textbook, *Educating Exceptional Children,* Samuel Kirk (1962), describes the goal of parent volunteers for special education classrooms as misguided: "Parents of severely retarded children do not generally succeed [as helpers] in classes in which their own child is enrolled" (p. 141). Indeed, for Kirk, the main goal of teachers in terms of parents is to respond to and control the problems they create. Parents of blind children tend to "overprotect"—governed as they are by "guilt, hostility, anxiety, or simply lack of knowledge" (p. 223). The attitudes of parents of "crippled children ... whether rejecting or overprotecting, tend to be more extreme than their attitudes toward normal children" (p. 287). Even by 1975, a similar introductory volume (from a major publisher of education texts) was still explaining why mothers were often more problematic than fathers: "It is the mother who 'produces' the infant, it is she who 'gives' it birth. If the 'product' turns out to be defective, the mother is likely to perceive this as a defect in something she has labored to produce" (Smith & Neisworth, 1975, p. 181). Fortunately, this type of psychoanalytic "mother-blaming" is much less common today—at least in such blatant terms.

In response to the supposed symptoms and neuroses presented by parents, prospective teachers are told to notice and compensate for the mistakes made at home. In both the first and second editions of his text, Kirk recommends that teachers practice something he calls the "scientific neglect" of children who have been overprotected and attended to by parents (Kirk, 1962, p. 290; Kirk, 1972, p. 377). Another early text (Smith & Neisworth, 1975) recommends "periodic" conferences with parents. However, the purpose of the conferences seems primarily to diagnose the specific problems they present. "As a result of the conference, and any information you have available, estimate the parents' competence in working with you. Are they naïve, misinformed, pushy, prone to compare the child with siblings, apparently incapable of following a supplementary program of any complexity, or too demanding of the child" (p. 215).

7 Evolution of the Discourse

In the years immediately following 1975 and the passage of *Education of All Handicapped Children Act*, there is some noticeable change in both the tone and the content of the textbooks. It is interesting to follow these changes as they occur through various editions of a single textbook. For the Third Edition of his successful book, Samuel Kirk had James Gallagher join him as a co-author. Gallagher's influence can be seen especially in the discussion of parents. An entirely new section of a chapter on future directions in special education focuses on the "Changing Role of Parents." The section is organized around four proposed stages through which parents have struggled to gain their proper place.

> The parents have gone through a number of phases and roles which may be referred to as: (1) parents as scapegoats, (2) parents as program organizers, (3) parents as political activists, and (4) parents as program participants and partners. (Kirk & Gallagher, 1979, p. 467)

The authors go on to claim that general progress has been made in overcoming the past tendencies to blame parents unfairly. They approvingly quote another text as a sign of the changed perspective:

> Have we as professionals working in a field that traditionally has been child-centered unwittingly cast parents into the role of adversary, object

FAMILY PORTRAITS

of pity, inhibitor of growth, or automatic misfit, while expecting them
to perform in a way expected of no other parents? Have we been too
quick to focus on weakness and too slow to recognize the normality of
the behaviors we see? (Cansler, Martin, & Valand, 1975, as cited in Kirk &
Gallagher, 1979, p. 468)

With the publication of the sixth edition of the book in 1989, this earlier section was gone. Replacing it, however, is a total of 12 pages at the beginning
of the book that continues to assert that the "tendency to set parents up as
scapegoats has changed" (Kirk & Gallagher, 1979, p. 20). The new section covers
an impressive range of issues, including in the influence of family life cycles,
influences on stress and coping, and even a few paragraphs on siblings. A long
story about Ed Roberts and the emergence of the independent living movement is integrated within the family material, capturing the sense of advocacy
and political activism that had emerged over the past two decades. By the 8th
edition in 1997, there is language added about "parent empowerment," and parents as "team members" (Kirk, Gallagher, & Anastasiow, 1997, p. 30). The shift
is also beginning here to talk about families more than parents. The changing demographics of family structure are discussed in fairly neutral terms:
more single-parent households, more dual-career families, more recognition
of fathers as part of thecare-giving equation. A chart in the book details how
instead of training mothers to become essentially home-based paraprofession-
als, the "current approach" asserts that

> Families need encouragement and ways to ensure that the child has a
> functional education taught in natural environments by natural help-
> ers in those environments (e.g, family friends, store clerks, busdrivers,
> scout leaders). (Gartner, Lipsky, & Turnbull, as cited in Kirk, Gallagher, &
> Anastasiow, 1997, p. 31)

Over the same period of these striking changes in tone and content, the Kirk
et al., books continued to use the traditional list of psycho-analytic categories to characterize the response of "most parents" to the birth of a child with
disabilities. Parent of children with disabilities are still seen as dramatically
different from other families, "reifying" (Brantlinger, 1997, p. 440) the difference and "naturalizing" the response in the same way that segregated special
education is traditionally justified. The parent is still described as having to
overcome the "symbolic death of the child who was to be" (p. 17). Upon hearing
their child's diagnosis, "most parents feel shock, then denial, guilt, anger, and
sadness, before they finally adjust .... Many move through the grieving process,
as though their child had died" (p. 20). In another major textbook that was first

158   FERGUSON ET AL.

published in 1978 (Hallahan & Kauffman, 1978), there is a similar assessment of parental emotions. Having a retarded (*sic*) child is said to evoke feelings of "honest agony, hatred, sorrow, and frustration" (p. 60).

8   Rights-Based Discourse

We were somewhat surprised with the relatively small amount of what we would clearly identify as "rights-based" language in the discussion of families in the more recent textbooks. The textbooks published in the late 1970s showed an understandable emphasis in this area. However, in textbooks from the last 5 years, we found very little about legal process laying out the requirements for parent involvement. Instead, we found most of the conversation in recent texts using language and concepts that we associate with the "educational benefits" approach. The Heward text (2009) provides a typical example of this:

> *Extensive evidence shows that the effectiveness of educational* programs for children with disabilities is increased when parents and families are actively involved .... At the very least, teachers and students benefit when parents provide information about their children's use of specific skills outside the classroom. But parents can do much more than just report on behavior change. They can provide extra skill practice and teach their children new skills in the home and community. When parents are involved in identifying what skills their children need to learn ... the hard work expended by teachers is more likely to produce outcomes with real significance in the lives of children and their families. (Heward, 2009, p. 92)

Heward does go on to spend several paragraphs on the "mandating parent and family involvement" steps that Congress placed in the earliest version of IDEA (rights-based). However, the overall tone of the book is that teachers and schools should encourage parents to be involved in because it produces improved outcomes for children.

Another example of this approach can be found in the recent text by Rosenberg, Westling, and McLeskey (2011). While the book breaks the pattern of most recent texts and does not include a self-contained chapter on families, it does have short discussions of specific issues that may arise in family/school interactions. The discussions emphasize the cost-benefit calculation that many schools implicitly employ when considering family involvement: how should teachers respond to families that "want more than you can offer" (p. 394)? The recommendation in such situations is to evaluate and respond

FAMILY PORTRAITS

cautiously after adding up costs and benefits. When parents request something that is "uncalled for":

> It is always important to listen and support them in their quest to find what is best. You can do this without committing yourself, and then you can learn more about what it is they want. When you have attained a level of knowledge about what they are asking for, then you can have an honest conversation with them about its merits and limitations. (Rosenberg, Westling, & McLeskey, 2011, p. 395)

8.1   *Social Relations/Social Justice Discourse*

With the most recent books, the signs of progress are easily found. The portraits of families drawn by recent introductory text books in special education are generally much more focused on ways to increase and improve family involvement in schools. The most recent edition of one such popular text (Turnbull, Turnbull, & Wehmeyer, 2010) draws a picture of parents of children with disabilities as more like than unlike parents of children in general education.

> Like the parents of children who are developing typically, parents of children who have various exceptionalities face challenges of family life: job changes and loss, the deaths of family members, financial problems, physical or mental illnesses, substance abuse, child abuse or community violence, and uncertainty about the future. They also experience many of the joys of life: graduations, job promotions, vacations, birthday parties, weddings, and births. (p. 101)

In a perfect example of what we label a "positive" version of the educational benefits approach, recent books tend to identify families as a resource to be supported and shared rather than a problem to be avoided or controlled. Speaking directly to its audience of future special educators, the authors go on to conclude that, "Whether required by federal or state policy or not, it is sound educational practice to form partnerships with the families of all your students" (Turnbull, Turnbull, & Wehmeyer, 2010, p. 103).

However, even in the most recent texts, there is still only cautious and incomplete use of what we would label as a social justice approach. The work of Beth Harry, Maya Kalyanpur and a few others is now commonly cited in textbook discussions of issues such as disproportionality and class bias in schools. However, we found little if any discussion of social or cultural capital. Little attention is given to the difference elaborated by researchers such as Annette Lareau between family involvement in schools and family involvement with their children. While a surface acknowledgment of how the social construction of disability can influence family perceptions of how support must be provided, the "cult of expertise" that has long dominated special education culture is still allowed to bolster a deficit model where the keys are accurate assessment and ""evidence-based" intervention. As we have already mentioned, none of the most recent books sampled here navigated away from the categorical approach to disability. As such there is in these books—at their very organizational heart—an implicit endorsement in all of these texts of the status quo in special education.

9   Some Further Findings: Disability Variations, Messages and Marginalization

Brantlinger was an early and persistent advocate of listening to the voice of the marginalized and devalued in society (Brantlinger, 1993, 2003; Brantlinger, Klein, & Guskin, 1994). Her book length ethnographies provided that balance of personal detail and narrative voice along side her interpretive insight and theoretical summary. In that sense, one could argue that the vignettes and personal stories offered in the call-out sections common to more recent textbooks, is a genuine attempt to provide a more direct and personal voice of the student and the family.

However, we think that Brantlinger herself would note the mixed ideological messages that trouble us about this stylistic development. The very use of call-outs to provide information about families raises a positionality issue. Boxing off stories of the experiences of families and persons with disabilities positions them as less objective and—more personal and less important than the information in the text in the same way that students are too often boxed off in school either in separate environments or in separated spaces in typical classrooms. Still for many of these future educators reading these textbooks, this subtle message as well as the content of the call out is as much as they will be offered or learn about the experiences of families and their role in schools and they most often depict the themes presented in the text.

Similarly, the content included in the call-outs while it has changed over the years, has not shifted dramatically. In our sample, the earliest texts using call-outs date from 1997 (Kirk, Gallagher & Anastasiow) and while not framing the having of a child with disability as a "family disaster," there is a lot of discussion and messages about family stress and how unprepared families are to parent a child with disabilities. In many of the call outs that focus on strategies for teachers, but that also mention families, there is a strong message that it is the role of school professionals to teach families to parent differently and the role of family members to listen to the expert advice of school professionals. With regard to emotional and behavioral disorders, there is a strong message that poverty, family violence, drug use, and parental psychological disorders are responsible for the child's behavior. Even by 2012 (Kirk, Gallagher, Coleman & Anastasiow) not much changes. There is more emphasis on family systems and different kinds of families, but the emphasis on family stress remains and the grief/mourning motif about the loss the disabled child represents continues to be emphasized even when trying to describe how families cope and adjust. The allegorical story (Kingsley, 1987) of flying to Italy only to land in Holland gets repeated in several of even the more current texts. The "loss that will never, never go away because of the lost dreams" and that somehow the new life in Holland is "less" than the planned life and is only partly mitigated by the positive notions that one learns to appreciate and even love Holland, and presumably, the new child with a disability.

In some accounts, mothers are depicted as heroines. In other accounts, professionals are said to play the role of "bridging the gap" between family beliefs and preferences and what experts know is "best" for the child. There are also noticeable exceptions to these patterns. In Heward (2009), for example, there is a shift to emphasize partnerships and diminish the persistent power differential that often exists between school professionals and family members.

The Hallahan et al. (2003, 2012) texts present a unique emphasis on special education as essential—it is intensive, relentless and specific and without this approach many children would be lost to their disabilities. There is also a strong anti-inclusion message including the call out that lists 5 reasons parents offer for including their child in general education and 10 reasons parents list against such placements. This orientation is played out even in the stories about families such as Nolan, who has Down Syndrome and gets "intensive, relentless, and specific" early intervention services and in elementary school can spend only half his day in a third grade class and the rest in pull out for "intensive" instruction coordinated through "relentless collaboration among educators and Nolan's parents.

The most recent texts (e.g., Rosenburg, Westling, & McLeskey, 2011; Turnbull, Turnbull, & Wehmeyer, 2010) do reveal some more progressive depictions. Certainly there is more diversity in visual images and narratives which cover a range of situations: single parent families, families that distrust schools because of their own experiences, parents using due process to obtain adequate services, effective partnerships that benefit student learning, and so on. These more recent texts also tend to have more first person narratives from both families and youth with disabilities rather than presenting information about families and people with disabilities in a third person voice.

162   FERGUSON ET AL.

10   A Concluding Summary

It would be surprising if no substantive changes were found between works published in the 1960s and 70s and works published in the last decade. In many cases, the changes we found have little to do with disability as such. For example, the cultural diversity of families was dealt with poorly or not at all in the early books, with issues of economic class and racial difference often troublingly conflated. For the most part, the traditional nuclear family—both birth parents living together with children in school, father working, mother at home—was at least implicitly assumed as the norm. Many of the recent textbooks acknowledged the diversity of family structure and composition. Indeed, as one recent textbook put it, the definition of what counts as a "family" should include any group of two or more people who both "regard themselves" as a family, and "carry out the functions" typically performed by families (Turnbull, Turnbull, & Wehmeyer, 2010, p. 100).

In many ways, we believe that the discussion of families in these textbooks has moved forward more quickly than we had anticipated, given the market forces that govern textbook publishing. Our impression is that the discussion of families in these textbooks has evolved more quickly than the discussion of disability in general. There is a lot of language to point to that seems to recognize the systemic inequities faced by families who differ from the dominant discourse of our schools. The conversation about families in these texts has seemingly learned more from general education about the importance of cultural diversity and social capital than it has from disability studies about the complicated interpretation of stigma and oppression. If the portraits of families drawn by the "big glossies" have become more lifelike and multi-layered on the one hand, they remain frustratingly incomplete on the other.

Acknowledgment

This chapter originally appeared in *International Journal of Inclusive Education*, *17*(12), 2013, 1326–1341. Reprinted here with permission from the publisher.

Note

1   The authors would like to thank the anonymous reviewers for suggesting that this specific focus on representation of families in textbooks could be usefully expanded

to family-school-community collaboration. That is the ultimate goal of our work, but exceeded the limits of space and focus for this special issue of IJIE.

References

Apple, M. W. (1989). *Teachers and texts: A political economy of class and gender relations in education.* New York, NY: Routledge.

Apple, M. W., & Christian-Smith, L. K. (Eds.). (1991). *The politics of the textbook.* New York, NY: Routledge.

Bogdan, R. C., & Biklen, S. K. (2007). *Qualitative research for education: An introduction to theories and methods* (5th ed.). Boston, MA: Allyn and Bacon.

Brantlinger, E. (1997). Using ideology: Cases of nonrecognition of the politics of research and practice in special education. *Review of Educational Research, 67,* 425–459.

Brantlinger, E. (2003). *Dividing classes: How the middle class negotiates and rationalizes school advantage.* New York, NY: Routledge.

Brantlinger, E. (2006). The big glossies: How textbooks structure (special) education. In E. Brantlinger (Ed.), *Who benefits from special education: Remediating [fixing] other people's children* (pp. 45–75). Mahwah, NJ: Lawrence Erlbaum.

Brantlinger, E. A., Klein, S. M., & Guskin, S. L. (1994). *Fighting for Darla: Challenges for family care and professional responsibility.* New York, NY: Teachers College Press.

Chinn, P. C., Drew, C. J., & Logan, D. R. (1975). *Mental retardation: A life cycle approach.* St. Louis, MO: C. V. Mosby.

Drew, C. J., Hardman, M. L., & Logan, D. R. (1996). *Intellectual disabilities across the life span* (9th ed.). Englewood Cliffs, NJ: Merrill-Prentice Hall.

Ferguson, C., Ramos, M., Rudo, Z., & Wood, L. (2008). *The school-family connection: Looking at the larger picture: A review of current literature.* Austin, TX: Southwest Educational Development Lab. Retrieved from www.sedl.org/connections/resources/sfclitrev.pdf

Ferguson, D. L., & Ferguson, P. M. (2010, May). *Family planning: Using a social justice approach to improving family/school linkages.* Paper presented at the annual conference of the American Educational Research Association, Denver, CO.

Ferguson, D. L., & Galindo, R. (2008). Improving family/school linkages through inquiry and action: Reports from sixteen schools in two states. *New Hampshire of Education, XI,* 66–75.

Ferguson, D. L., & Galindo, R. (2008). Improving family/school linkages through inquiry and action: Reports from 16 schools in two states. *The New Hampshire Journal of Education, 11,* 66–75.

Ferguson, D. L., Hanreddy, A., & Ferguson, P. M. (in press). Finding a voice: Families roles in schools. In L. Florian (Ed.), *Handbook on special education* (2nd ed.). Thousand Oaks, CA: Sage Publications.

Ferguson, P. M. (2008). The doubting dance: Contributions to a history of parent/professional interactions in early 20th century America. *Research and Practice for Persons with Severe Disabilities, 33*, 48–58.

Ferguson, P. M., & Ferguson, D. L. (2006). Finding the "proper attitude": The potential of disability studies to reframe family/school linkages. In S. Danforth & S. L. Gabel (Eds.), *Vital questions facing disability studies in education* (pp. 217–235). New York, NY: Peter Lang.

Ferguson, P. M., Ferguson, D. L., & Taylor, S. J. (1992). Introduction: Interpretivism and disability studies. In P. M. Ferguson, D. L. Ferguson, & S. J. Taylor (Eds.), *Interpreting disability: A qualitative reader* (pp. 1–11). New York, NY: Teachers College Press.

Friend, M. (2011). *Special education: Contemporary perspectives for school professionals.* Upper Saddle River, NJ: Pearson.

Gartner, A., Lipsky, D. K., & Turnbull, A. P. (1991). *Supporting families with a child with a disability: An international outlook.* Baltimore, MD: Paul Brookes.

Gonzalez, N., Moll, L. C., & Amanti, C. (2005). *Funds of knowledge: Theorizing practice in households, communities, and classrooms.* Mahwah, NJ: L. Erlbaum and Associates.

Hallahan, D. P., & Kauffman, J. M. (1978). *Exceptional children: Introduction to special education.* Englewood Cliffs, NJ: Prentice-Hall.

Harry, B., Kalyanpur, M., & Day, M. (1999). *Building cultural reciprocity with families: Case studies in special education.* Baltimore, MD: Paul H. Brookes Publishing Co.

Henderson, A. T., & Mapp, K. L. (2002). *A new wave of evidence: The impact of school, family and community connections on student achievement.* Austin, TX: Southwest Educational Development Lab. Retrieved from www.sedl.org/connections/resources/evidence.pdf

Heward, W. L. (2009). *Exceptional children: An introduction to special education* (9th ed.). Upper Saddle River, NJ: Merrill Pearson.

Kalayanpur, M., Harry, B., & Skrtic, T. (2000). Equity and advocacy expectations of culturally diverse families' participation in special education. *International Journal of Disability, Development and Education, 47*(2), 119–136.

Kingsley, E. P. (1987). *Welcome to Holland.* Retrieved from http://www.our-kids.org/Archives/Holland.html

Kirk, S. A. (1962). *Educating exceptional children.* Boston, MA: Houghton Mifflin.

Kirk, S. A. (1972). *Educating exceptional children* (2nd ed.). Boston, MA: Houghton Mifflin.

Kirk, S. A., & Gallagher, J. J. (1979). *Educating exceptional children* (3rd ed.). Boston, MA: Houghton Mifflin.

FAMILY PORTRAITS 165

Kirk, S. A., & Gallagher, J. J. (1989). *Educating exceptional children* (6th ed.). Boston, MA: Houghton Mifflin.

Kirk, S. A., Gallagher, J. J., & Anastasiow, N. J. (1997). *Educating exceptional children* (8th ed.). Boston, MA: Houghton Mifflin.

Kirk, S. A., Gallagher, J. J., & Coleman, M. R., & Anastasiow, N. J. (2009). *Educating exceptional children* (12th ed.). Florence, KY: Wadsworth.

Kohn, A., & Shannon, P. (Eds.). (2003). *Education, Inc.: Turning learning into a business.* Portsmouth, NH: Heinemann.

Lareau, A. (2005). *Home advantage: Social class and parental intervention in elementary education.* Mahwah, NJ: Lawrence Erlbaum Associates.

Lightfoot, S. L. (2004). "Some parents just don't care": Decoding the meanings of parental involvement in Urban schools. *Urban Education, 39*(1), 91–107.

Lopez, G. R., Scribner, J. D., & Mahitivanichcha, K. (2001). Redefining parental involvement: Lessons from high-performing migrant-impacted schools. *American Educational Research Journal, 38*(2), 253–288.

Marshall, C., & Rossman, G. B. (2006). *Designing qualitative research* (4th ed.). Thousand Oaks, CA: Sage.

Moll, L., & Greenberg, J. (1990). Creating zones of possibility: Combining social contexts for instruction. In L. Moll (Ed.), *Vygotsky and education* (pp. 319–348). Cambridge: Cambridge University Press.

Rao, S. S. (2000). Perspectives of an African-American mother on parent-professional relationships in special education. *Mental Retardation, 38*, 473–488.

Rosenberg, M., Westling, D., & McLeskey, J. (2011). *Special education for today's teachers: An introduction* (2nd ed.). Boston, MA: Pearson.

Rossman, G. B., & Rallis, S. F. (2003). *Learning in the field: An introduction to qualitative research* (2nd ed.). Thousand Oaks, CA: Sage.

Sands, D. J., Kozleski, E., & French, N. (2000). *Inclusive education for the 21st century: A new introduction to special education.* Belmont, CA: Wadsworth.

Smith, R. M., & Neisworth, J. T. (1975). *The exceptional child: A functional approach.* New York, NY: McGraw-Hill.

Turnbull, A., Turnbull, R., Erwin, E. J., Soodak, L. C., & Shogren, K. A. (2010). *Families, professionals, and exceptionality: Positive outcomes through partnerships and trust* (6th ed). New York, NY: Pearson.

Turnbull, A., Turnbull, R., & Wehmeyer, M. L. (2010). *Exceptional lives: Special education in today's schools* (6th ed.). Columbus, OH: Merrill.

Index

ableism 82, 83, 91

abuse 13, 58, 159

access 4, 15, 49, 53, 89, 90, 92, 102, 103, 126, 134, 137, 140

accessible 15, 39, 41, 53, 54, 57

activism 1, 24

administrator 128, 130–137

advocacy 9, 20, 51, 56, 119, 120, 157

agency 6, 47–55, 57–59

Allan, J. 2, 3, 5–7, 29–34, 36, 38, 39, 105, 107, 118, 119, 128, 130

American Education Research Association (AERA) 17, 21

Apple, M. 126, 146

Artiles, A. 84, 87, 88, 120

assumptions 4, 47, 48, 54, 55, 81, 85, 95, 104, 134, 144–146

autism 33, 47, 50, 53, 57

Bacon, J. 5, 7, 8

Baglieri, S. 6, 23, 81

Ballard, K. 2, 3, 29, 41

Barton, L. 2, 31, 90, 104

Baynton, D. 85

behaviour/behavior 39, 42, 53, 81, 91, 158, 161

Bernstein, B. 35

Blatt, B. 55, 104

Bogdan, R. 49, 147

career 1, 4, 5, 11, 12, 23, 24, 137, 157

category 20, 36, 107, 120

Cazden, C. B. 57

Collins, K. M. 3, 5–7, 23

community 4, 5, 16, 19, 21, 38, 42, 47, 54, 55, 58, 93, 95, 105, 109, 111, 112, 114–116, 128, 130, 146, 153, 158, 159, 163

Connor, D. J. 2, 3, 5, 6, 15, 23, 34, 52, 86, 87, 91, 120, 135

Critical Race Theory (CRT) 82, 83, 86, 93, 94

Cultural/Historical Theory (C/HAT) 82–84, 93, 94

culture 13, 82, 84, 86, 118, 160

Danforth, S. 21, 23, 83, 84

Davis, L. J. 52, 53, 81, 85, 87

Delpit, L. 22

deviance 81, 85, 87

difference 34, 38, 40, 81, 82, 85, 87, 94, 107, 110, 119, 120, 157, 159, 162

Disability Studies in Education (DSE) 3, 5, 11, 14, 15, 19, 21, 23, 24, 82, 83, 85, 93, 94

Eagleton, T. 29, 30, 41

Edgerton, R. B. 55, 58

Erevelles, N. 41, 85, 90

ethical 29, 56, 57

exclusion 3, 7, 8, 32, 40, 41, 106, 118, 132, 134, 135

Ferguson, D. 8, 18, 21, 23, 49, 103–105, 146, 147, 153

Ferguson, P. 8, 18, 21, 23, 49, 103,–105, 146, 147, 153

Ferri, B. 5, 7, 8, 14, 15, 23, 86, 88, 91, 120

Foucault, M. 5, 35, 37, 39, 92

Free and Appropriate Education (FAPE) 85

Gabel, S. 21, 23, 82

Gallagher, D. 21– 23, 33, 46, 89, 105, 119, 120, 154, 156, 157, 160

Geertz, C. 29, 105

Giroux, H. 48, 49, 53

Glesne, C. 58

Goffman, E. G. 55, 58

Gramsci, A. 13, 22, 92, 127

Hale, C. 20, 23

Heshusius, L. 2, 23, 104

ideology 3–5, 7, 28–33, 35–37, 39–42, 81–84, 87, 88, 91–95, 105, 113, 119, 127, 130, 131, 133, 135, 136, 144, 145

inclusion 1–5, 7, 8, 12, 13, 22, 30, 31, 33, 41, 42, 56, 85, 102, 103, 105–107, 110–119, 127, 130, 131, 134, 137, 139, 140, 141, 144, 146, 161

independence 51

individualized education plan 103, 136–138

inquiry 5, 50, 51, 55

institutionalization/
de-institutionalization 85
institutions 6, 29, 84, 92, 94, 113
International Journal of Inclusive Education
(IJIE) 2, 18, 25, 42, 55, 95, 141, 162, 163
intersectionality 24, 82

Kalyanpur, M. 153, 159
Klingner, J. 54, 80, 84, 88, 90

labels 85, 106, 113, 119, 120
Ladson-Billings, G. 82, 89, 92
Lawrence-Lightfoot, S. 48, 51, 53

neglect 156
New York State Education Department
(NYSED) 128–130, 134–136, 138
No Child Left Behind (NCLB) 7, 8, 88, 93,
126, 128, 129, 131, 137, 141

Oliver, M. 31, 36
oppression 14, 50, 86, 91, 92, 162
Oyler, C. 119

paradigm 28, 31, 120, 146
parents 9, 18–20, 34, 36, 39, 47, 54, 56, 57,
146, 153, 155–159, 161, 162
philosophy 30, 55, 85
positionality 5, 8, 37, 42, 160
possibility 5, 112
poverty 48, 89, 90, 161
power 8, 13, 14, 19, 20, 23, 24, 29, 31, 35, 36, 41,
42, 48, 50–52, 54, 57, 84, 87, 91–94, 119,
127, 129, 144, 161

principles 51, 85, 119
privilege 19, 20, 47, 88, 92, 127

race 7, 9, 13, 15, 17, 22, 24, 33, 34, 40, 52, 55,
58, 81, 83, 84, 86, 89, 91, 92, 95, 96, 120,
133, 146
Reid, K. 12, 15, 33, 50, 89

Sauer, J. 5, 6, 23, 47, 52, 53, 55
Skrtic, T. M. 2, 23, 104, 105, 119, 120, 153
Slee, R. 3, 18, 23, 29, 31–34, 36, 38, 39, 41, 82,
93, 104, 107, 118, 119
Sleeter, C. 34
Snelgrove, S. 56
stigma 82, 90, 95, 162
stories 4, 11, 54, 160, 161

Taylor, S. 21, 23, 49, 104, 147
Thompson, J. K. 29, 30, 31, 35, 39, 42, 126
Tomlinson, S. 2
tracking 19, 126, 127, 129, 134, 136
traditionalists 8, 13, 30, 127, 140
traditional special educators/
educationists 30–32
transformation 7, 8, 22, 51, 129, 130
Trent, J. 84, 120

uncertainty 37, 159

vigilance 139

Ware, L. 2, 3, 6, 21, 23, 33, 82, 119, 120

Printed in the United States
By Bookmasters